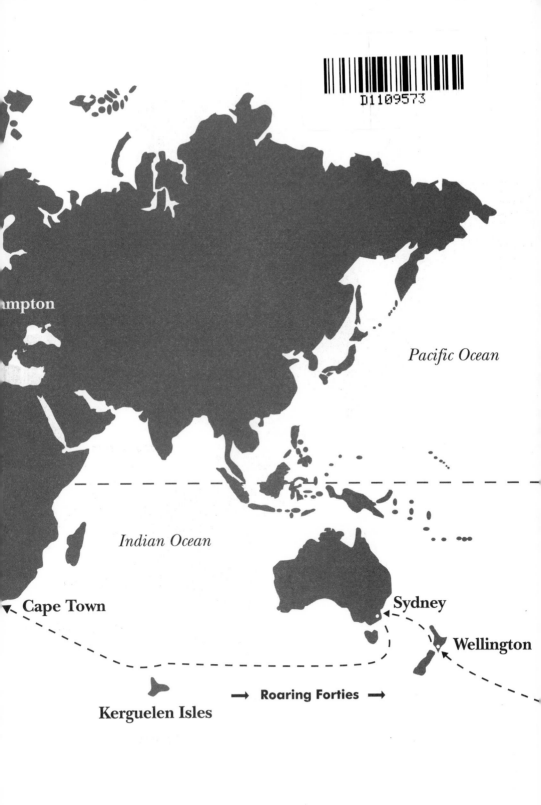

ampton

Pacific Ocean

Indian Ocean

Cape Town

Sydney

Wellington

Kerguelen Isles

→ Roaring Forties →

Global Challenge

BT

Centre *for*
High Performance
Development

MaST

Global Challenge

Leadership Lessons from
'The World's Toughest Yacht Race'

Humphrey Walters
Peter Mackie
Rosie Mackie
Andrea Bacon

The Book Guild Ltd
Sussex, England

The Book Guild Ltd.
25 High Street,
Lewes, Sussex

First published 1997
Second printing 1998
Third printing 1998
Fourth printing 1999
© British Telecommunications plc 1997
© Centre for High Performance Development 1997

Set in Baskerville

Designed and Typeset by
Elite Typesetting Techniques, Eastleigh, Hampshire, UK

Printed in Great Britain by
Bookcraft (Bath) Ltd, Avon

A catalogue record for this book is
available from the British Library

ISBN 1 85776 385 8

Dedicated to the skippers and crew of the
BT Global Challenge 1996/7

A special family of people.

CONTENTS

AUTHORS' BIOGRAPHIES

Humphrey Walters is the Group Chief Executive of MaST International, an international management training organisation. He is also a Director of the Centre *for* High Performance Development. He participated in the BT Global Challenge 1996/7 on board the yacht *Ocean Rover*, furthering his studies in leadership and team building with first-hand experience.

Peter Mackie MBE is the Managing Director of the Centre *for* High Performance Development, a division of MaST International. He was involved in the leadership training of the race skippers and team development of the disabled crew of the yacht *Time & Tide*.

Rosie Mackie is a senior consultant of the Centre *for* High Performance Development. She joined MaST International in 1994 and worked for the Leadership Development Team before joining the Centre *for* High Performance Development. She was involved in the team development of the disabled crew of the yacht *Time & Tide*.

Andrea Bacon is a freelance communications consultant. She participated in the BT Global Challenge 1996/7 on board the yacht *Group 4*. As communications officer she filed daily reports to both the BT press office and the Group 4 Internet site.

FOREWORD

I went and saw the BT Global Challenge yachts as they set off at the start in Southampton in September 1996 and remember thinking what an admirable thing it was to race round the world the wrong way. But it was for other people – people who had time, were younger, had already put any number of hours sailing behind them, gained qualifications and so on. It was only when I saw them again in Rio de Janeiro and someone from *Ocean Rover* said, "Why don't you join us for one of the legs?" that I began to think seriously about it. I said "No". Then it dawned on me that this was an opportunity of a lifetime. Provided I could get myself reasonably fit and clear my diary, here was the chance for me to dabble in something way beyond my normal experience and pit myself against the sea, the weather, the other yachts – and against myself. So the next time I was asked I said "Yes".

Sir Chay Blyth's BT Global Challenge became a way of life. As a proud legger on *Ocean Rover*, I covered only 1,200 miles in reasonable conditions, out of a total of 30,000 miles – much of it in the Southern Ocean. But what the rest of the crews achieved set them way above ordinary mortals. They had completed one of the greatest challenges that anybody could think of. This book describes the conditions that the yachts faced and the elements the crew had to cope with.

It is a tribute to them all. I thoroughly recommend it.

Michael

HRH Prince Michael of Kent

ACKNOWLEDGMENTS

This book would never have happened without Sir Chay Blyth, The Challenge Business, BT, sponsors, skippers, crew members and all others who have so willingly co-operated, and with such good humour. To all, we offer our sincere thanks.

As you can imagine, collating all the material and writing this book has been a massive undertaking. It is almost impossible to mention everyone but we would particularly like to acknowledge the tremendous efforts made by our colleagues at the Centre *for* High Performance Development, Peter Fairgrieve and Keith Liddiard. They have made a tremendous contribution, fitting writing into an already heavily committed schedule. They have our admiration and thanks.

The whole project has been great fun and a huge team effort. Perhaps a good example of what we have tried to portray in the book.

PHOTOGRAPHIC CREDITS

Our sincere thanks go to the following individuals whose photographs are reproduced within this book.

Robert Bruce	Stephen Munday
Andrew Dare	Mark Pepper/MPP
Andrew Fernandez	Henry Pritchard
Chris Kapetanllis	James Walker
Richard Langdon	Simon Walker
Clive Mason	Joanne Watson

INTRODUCTION

Sir Chay Blyth, CBE BEM has spent almost his entire life accepting challenges and pushing himself to achieve that which many people feel is impossible. In 1966, he successfully rowed across the North Atlantic with John Ridgway, and in 1970/1 he sailed single-handedly round the world, the wrong way.

His concept for The Challenge, a 30,000 mile yacht race round the world against prevailing winds and currents, gives ordinary people the opportunity to achieve the extraordinary. The Challenge dubbed 'The World's Toughest Yacht Race' is an inspirational event. In 1996/7 the race was sponsored by BT and entitled the BT Global Challenge.

This book is an account of the race, largely by those who took part. It is also a case study of human endeavour and of leadership and teamwork in a competitive and arduous environment, over a lengthy period of time.

It is not a book about the technicalities of sailing but on the fascinating lessons learned about personal, leadership and team behaviours. Not all are new. The most valuable lessons highlight the positive and negative effect of behaviour on the performance of the yachts and the atmosphere on board.

For the crew members, it was 'The Challenge of a Lifetime'. Looking back, some would not wish to repeat the experience, but if asked by potential crew volunteers, would reply :

"Do not hesitate, do not be dissuaded, do not fear for your incompetence and, above all, do not miss the opportunity to take part. You will never regret it."

HOW TO READ
THIS BOOK

We intended to produce a book which illustrated essential personal, leadership and team building lessons in an interesting, memorable and vivid way.

There are very few case studies, if any, that combine so many factors of personal and team endeavour, competition and duration - all the elements so critical to the performance of an organisation.

This book tracks the BT Global Challenge 1996/7 Round The World Yacht Race and highlights the personal, managerial and high performance behaviours that were vital to individual and team success.

The chapters describing each leg of the race are written in two halves. The first sets the scene, attempting to describe the conditions which the teams faced; the second, is an analysis of the behaviours that were demonstrated during each leg.

There is also reference to some unique research on High Performance Behaviours, necessary for individuals and teams who wish to perform at an outstanding level. This is probably the most interesting work to have been researched and validated in the field of management training.

A further chapter examines BT's management of the race sponsorship and the lessons learned in the planning and organisation of their massive global relationship marketing programme.

We hope that we touch a few raw nerves, as well as confirm the value of some of the behaviours that you use and experience.

This book should be read from the perspective of transferring the behaviours into the working environment. For the crew members who took part, sailing the yacht long distances over extended periods of time was considered a 'job of work', not a 'sailing jolly'.

We have been able to relate the lessons to our own company. We hope that you will be able to do the same and that it will contribute to improving your own performance, as well as that of your organisation.

MaST INTERNATIONAL & THE CENTRE *for* HIGH PERFORMANCE DEVELOPMENT

The BT Global Challenge 1996/7 has been a unique case study for the MaST International Organisation.

MaST International is a management training organisation which has been involved in improving the performance of people through a variety of management and skills training programmes. Over the last 25 years, MaST International has built up a large number of national and international clients and now operates in seven countries worldwide.

MaST International is well known for its innovative and practical approach to training and development. Its involvement with the BT Global Challenge is an example of the lengths it is prepared to go, to produce solutions that work in practice, and are based on actual case studies and research.

Through the Centre *for* High Performance Development (CHPD), it has utilised extensive research on High Performance Behaviours which is described in Chapter 2 and is unique to CHPD.

With the range of expertise available, MaST International is able to help a wide range of organisations and provide development solutions for newly appointed supervisors or managers through to Board Directors.

MaST International and CHPD have developed a range of leadership and team building programmes associated with the research from the BT Global Challenge. These ensure that the lessons learned are illustrated with vivid examples from the case study described in this book.

MaST International
Organisation plc
Hermitage House
Bath Road
Taplow
Maidenhead
Berkshire SL6 0AR

Centre *for* High
Performance Development
Elvetham Hall
Hartley Wintney
Basingstoke
Hampshire RG27 8AS

CHAPTER ONE

*"Our doubts are traitors and make us lose the good
we oft might win by fearing to attempt."*
Iroha, a Japanese proverb

"I had to scale the deck like climbing a cliff," said
Chay Blyth when thrown against a stanchion by a huge
wave which tried to throw him off the deck. He was in the
process of making history by being the first man to
circumnavigate the globe, the wrong way. In October
1970, he set sail from The Hamble on his 59ft ketch,
British Steel, against the advice of many senior
yachtsmen. They believed that no-one could sail single-
handed, non-stop round the world against the prevailing
winds and currents. His trip was to prove them wrong
and take him deep into the Southern Ocean, turning
north only after rounding the Cape of Good Hope. He
returned to The Hamble some 292 days later.

BACKGROUND TO THE CHALLENGE

The Beginning Of A Concept

In 1971, Chay Blyth became the first person to sail single-
handedly non-stop round the world against prevailing
winds and currents. The project was sponsored by the then
British Steel Corporation and his 59ft ketch was
consequently named *British Steel.*

This was the first major sponsorship that Chay had
initiated in his sailing career. It was, however, just the
beginning of a sailing, then business career that was to
flourish under the banner of sponsorship.

1

In the summer of 1972, Chay started up a charter holiday business called Supersail. This was not only a way of making a little money but also of financing the upkeep of *British Steel.* Any yacht is a huge drain on finances and this was no exception. Chay's resources were meagre and he needed to address the problem of mooring and maintaining the yacht through the tough British winter months.

Chay considered the idea of taking the yacht away from the United Kingdom to participate in the French-run Atlantic Triangle Race, a race from St Malo to Cape Town, Cape Town to Rio and Rio back to St Malo. The big problem however was finding the finances to pay the crew. Chay approached the French equivalent of the UK's Royal Ocean Racing Club, with an innovative suggestion. Under the race rules, could he accept fee-paying crew on board his yacht? The race committee, keen for entries, did not object.

Shortly afterwards, Chay was interviewed by Paul Hughes of the *Daily Mirror* on the success of his charter holiday business. At the conclusion of the interview, Hughes asked whether Chay intended to do anything else within the sailing arena. Chay, never one to miss an opportunity, seized the moment to announce his intention to enter *British Steel* in the Atlantic Triangle Race, selling the berths to fee-paying crew.

The news hit the tabloids because of its novel and unusual angle in the sailing fraternity and, before Chay could draw breath, he had filled the yacht with paying crew.

Greg Bertram, a South African, was one of those who signed up for a berth. He travelled to the UK to join Chay for the race. This initial introduction led on to other yacht races, and an attempt to beat a 5,000 mile trimaran record from New York to The Lizard. Their friendship flourished and, in 1987, Greg joined Chay as Finance Director of The Challenge Business Limited, a role he continues today.

"Business is based on relationships."
Sir Chay Blyth

Chay's adventurous spirit soon led him on to his next project, to skipper a yacht in the first Whitbread Round the World Yacht Race held in 1973/4. On this occasion, Chay received financial backing from Jack Hayward, one of Britain's great benefactors.

Sir Jack, as he is now, bought Lundy Island for the nation and financed the return of the *SS Great Britain* which was brought back to Bristol from the Falkland Islands. Throughout his life, Jack has supported numerous charities and his sponsorship of Chay's yacht, subsequently named *Great Britain II*, is just one example of his generous and supportive nature.

Sponsorship in those days covered only the cost of the yacht. Chay still had to raise enough to finance all the other requirements such as charts, food and the crew's wages. As fate would have it, the British Army approached Chay to discuss the possibility of borrowing *British Steel* for the same Whitbread race. The British Navy already had an entry in the race but the Ministry of Defence was not prepared to fund another. The MoD thought one entry sufficient for the services and the Army was left to fund its own project. Chay was delighted when he was asked to meet the Chief of the General Staff in order to give some assistance!

A deal was struck and Chay agreed on the basis that the Army would allow him to take crew volunteers from his old regiment, the Parachute Regiment, to crew *Great Britain II*. Not only did Chay see those young paratroopers as fit, healthy and determined young men, but he believed he could mould them into a team and teach them how to sail.

Any round the world yacht race involves a huge number of logistical and administrative issues, such as the transportation of stores, gear and equipment; insurance cover for every eventuality and methods of transferring crew back and forth between ports of call, should illness or injury prevent them from continuing the race.

This arrangement with the Army had a great many

advantages. With the crew volunteers from the Parachute Regiment came the solution to a whole set of logistical problems. Firstly, the food, medical equipment, charts and transport could be provided by the Army and a contingency plan already existed to cover any need for repatriation. The Army would also provide a Captain as the team's shore manager.

Over 300 applications were received *and* that was that. Chay had his crew and the concept for The Challenge.

The Challenge Concept

Sixteen years later, on 3 January 1989, Chay Blyth launched the British Steel Challenge, 'The World's Toughest Yacht Race'; a race round the world against the prevailing winds and currents, open to ordinary people who wanted the chance to sail round the globe and take part in an adventure of a lifetime.

Chay and The Challenge Business could provide both the opportunity and the necessary training for the recruits undertaking such a Challenge.

The concept for The Challenge was based on three basic principles already proven by Chay.

It was possible to
  a) sail round the world the wrong way single-handedly, and therefore feasible for a well-built yacht and a trained crew;
  b) find people to pay to crew a yacht; and
  c) train a group of people who had no previous sailing experience.

There was, then, no reason to question the validity of sending 13 amateurs with a professional skipper round the world, asking those 13 people to finance their own berth and being able to train and mould them into a team.

The British Steel Corporation was wholeheartedly

4

behind the idea of sponsoring a round the world yacht race. It had been during discussions with Dr David Grieves, the then Vice Chairman of British Steel and Ron Melvin, the then Communications Director of British Steel that the idea for making it a race round the world in the *wrong direction* – against prevailing winds and currents – came about.

Chay had proved it could be done and remained the only person in the world to have attempted and completed it in that direction. The element of adventure was even greater than to go the way of professional yacht races. This sponsorship, of course, also had strong links with British Steel and Chay's original single-handed round the world voyage.

The British Steel Corporation remained sceptical that people would actually pay for a berth. They introduced a clause in the contract which gave them the option to withdraw from the project should Chay be unable to recruit 25 people in the first nine months.

A press conference was called to announce the race. The television and press coverage was enormous and the level of interest generated among ordinary people was beyond belief. Within a day, Chay had signed up 30 recruits and the project was underway.

The Challenge

What Attracts Crew Volunteers? – In today's society, where so much has already been achieved and many more opportunities are open to people than ever before, the unusual is hard to find. What many people are looking for is a chance to do something different, something out of the ordinary, to undertake a *real* adventure and embrace a *real* challenge.

What Chay offers in 'The World's Toughest Yacht Race' *is* a real challenge for ordinary people, an adventure of a lifetime and an opportunity to race round the world.

It is something that would otherwise remain unavailable

in a sport that is not only difficult to get involved in, but also expensive and considered to be elitist.

The Challenge caught the imagination of the British public back in 1989 when over 2,000 people applied for the 110 places available and it recaptured people's imagination in 1993 when over 5,000 entries were received for 154 berths in the BT Global Challenge.

What Are The Benefits To Crew Volunteers? –
Some 536 crew volunteers have taken part in the two Challenges. Of those, 235 have circumnavigated the globe, while over 300 others have taken sponsor berths and joined a yacht for just one or two legs of the race.

Whatever part of the race the crew volunteers completed, they will have returned with a sense of achievement – self satisfaction that they have participated in 'The World's Toughest Yacht Race'. They have learnt how to sail, overcome their own limitations and survived the hostilities of the oceans. They have undertaken and experienced the adventure of a lifetime.

Every one of the crew volunteers will have changed in one way or another. For some, the experience will have totally altered their lives. Many have not returned to their former jobs or way of life. They have taken a fresh look at the world and moved on to new challenges with different ideas.

Those who have gone back to their former employment or way of life will have been touched in some other way. For The Challenge is not something that can be undertaken without having some effect. Levels of enthusiasm and determination are greater on return. There is a feeling among crew members that once they have competed in this adventure they can take on almost anything.

The experience is unique.

What Attracts Skippers? – While the opportunity to become a crew volunteer is open to anyone from any walk of life, with little or no experience of sailing, the opportunity to become a skipper is restricted to those looking for a springboard into the upper echelon of professional sailing. Chay is not interested in those who have already made it in the professional racing arena. He wants to help those coming up through the ranks.

The criteria for recruiting the skippers is that firstly they must have an Oceanmaster qualification – the highest standard of yachting qualification in the UK. Secondly, they must have crossed an ocean and, thirdly, they must have some racing experience. The final element, the most critical of all, is that they must have proven leadership qualities.

Skipper recruitment is carried out by Chay who personally interviews all the applicants, as he does the crew volunteers. He has not put in place any method of testing leadership skills, believing it to be unnecessary, providing the applicants have some leadership experience. If someone has run a large project team involved in the design and construction of a complicated and expensive system, that is good enough for him. Why should they not be able to handle a team of 13 people sailing round the world?

What Are The Benefits To Skippers? – One of the first pieces of advice that Chay gives to the newly recruited Challenge skippers is that they should have an agenda and a vision, which extends beyond the race and is maintained throughout. For many of the skippers, that vision often is to move into professional racing or to become a respected and well-known yachtsman. For others, it is to further their sailing careers, not in the racing arena but in a corporate environment. The second piece of advice Chay gives is to develop a relationship with the sponsor to whom each skipper has been assigned.

In the British Steel Challenge, the skippers were allocated to yacht sponsors, wherever possible, using a common denominator or linkage. Richard Tudor, for example, is a Welshman. He was assigned to *British Steel II*, the race sponsor's own yacht as British Steel had two large steel plants in Wales.

Paul Jeffes was Managing Director of a boatyard in Scotland which specialised in international paint treatment. He was therefore assigned to Interspray, an international paint company.

Pete Goss, a West Country man, was allocated to Hall & Woodhouse, the West Country brewers and skippered *Hofbräu Lager* in the British Steel Challenge. He developed a number of relationships with both individuals and businesses associated with the race and was subsequently supported by many of these in financing *Aqua Quorum*, the yacht he entered in the 1996 Vendée Globe Non-Stop Single-Handed Round the World Yacht Race.

Mike Golding was allocated to Group 4 Securitas. An ex-fireman, he was used to the disciplined approach synonymous with the security business. His relationship with Chairman Philip Sørensen flourished and Mike was later supported by Group 4 in his attempt to break Chay's record of non-stop single-handed circumnavigation of the globe, the wrong way. Mike broke the record and has continued his relationship with Group 4, skippering its yacht to victory in the BT Global Challenge 1996/7.

After winning the race, Mike announced plans to undertake Around Alone in 1998, a single-handed round the world race, and the Vendée Globe in 1999 in a newly designed and built Group 4 sponsored yacht. His relationship with his sponsor appears to be going from strength to strength.

What Attracts Sponsors? – One of the main attractions of The Challenge sponsorship package is that it offers companies a truly international exposure. With the yacht race visiting five cities on three continents, there are opportunities for global promotion of a corporate brand as well as marketing on a world-wide scale.

The sponsorship packages are tiered to provide differing benefits to the race title holder, the yacht sponsors and the Business Club Members. All include corporate hospitality sailing days in the UK and each port of call as well as branding opportunities on the yachts.

The race itself attracts publicity worldwide from national newspapers, television and radio. Individual companies can take advantage of this to raise their own media profile.

Fax polling of race information proved hugely successful during the British Steel Challenge, while the Internet was the preferred medium for followers of the BT Global Challenge. With over three million hits per month during the course of the race, the BT Global Challenge Web Site gave sponsors a new medium for corporate branding, while providing race followers with up-to-date race information.

As well as the hospitality and publicity opportunities, companies can also get involved in education, business to business networking, relationship marketing and employee participation. Yacht sponsors are allocated two employee berths for each leg of the race.

Each yacht sponsor has a different set of marketing and business objectives and this is reflected in their contract. Commercial Union, for example, during its four year sponsorship and prior to the race, opted to have a Round Britain Tour with its yacht hosting client events.

What Are The Benefits To Sponsors? – A typical Business Club Member was Pittards Plc, a well-known supplier of shoe and glove leather.

Pittards Plc became a Challenge Business Club Member in 1995, having identified a unique opportunity to utilise the BT Global Challenge Round the World Yacht Race for testing and developing its leather in one of the toughest and most rigorous environments known.

As leather supplier to some of the top names in leather

9

goods, Pittards was used to working in partnership with its customers round the world. It approached three of its footwear clients - Clarks, Church's and Dubarry of Ireland – who were already utilising Pittards' leather in the manufacture of their boat shoes. Pittards presented them with the opportunity to put these boat shoes to the test in the 'World's Toughest Yacht Race' and the three companies provided boat shoes, at cost, to the crew volunteers on specific yachts across the fleet.

The glove division of Pittards chose to work with Vaughan Tapscott, a UK glove manufacturer, introducing the firm to the sailing market. Vaughan Tapscott was keen to be involved and set about designing two gloves. One was a part-fingered leather glove specifically for rope handling and spinnaker trimming; the other, a mitt for protection against the extreme conditions to be faced in the Southern Ocean.

Being a Challenge Business Club Member not only provided Pittards with the opportunity to develop its leather and advance it technologically, in both the shoe and glove markets, but also gave it the chance to involve its key clients – witnessing the performance of its leather in action and the effects of the elements. In addition, it provided its shoe clients with over 300 potential boat shoe buyers - the crews.

"From the outset, the challenge for Pittards was not only to supply boat shoes and gloves to meet the demanding needs of crew aboard the race, but also to use the race to find out exactly how our leathers perform in extremes of weather conditions," stated Alan Wilkinson, Pittards' Technical Director.

Before the race started, Pittards tested its first boat shoe leather, *Atlantis*, and introduced its first version of a leather sailing glove and a Goretex and leather all-weather mitt. The company worked closely with the training skippers and crews who were more than willing to trial the products and provide essential feedback for their improvement. They were, after all, the people who would benefit from the

10

advancement of the leathering used for both the shoes and the gloves.

After two years of development, a second generation of Pittards' leather for boat shoes was introduced, together with a leather rope handling glove that would provide protection, resist abrasion and remain soft, despite wear and tear and, a leather-reinforced, Goretex over-mitt.

The race started and the key testing began.

In Wellington, the crews exchanged their original boat shoes. They had now sailed over 12,000 miles, much of this in Southern Ocean conditions. Pittards wanted to start the testing and move on to the next generation of leather. Meanwhile, comments and feedback on both the glove and the mitt were being collated.

Back in the UK, wear test analysis of the old shoes started and, by the time the fleet reached Boston, a third generation of leather had been introduced. The crews were issued with their last pair of boat shoes for the final sprint across the Atlantic.

The extensive feedback from the BT Global Challenge crews has moved Pittards even closer to its goal of producing the ultimate performance leather for the boat shoe market. As a direct result of the feedback, Pittards has won two new clients in the boat shoe sector – Timberland and Rockport – and will launch a new *Challenge* boat shoe leather at an Italian trade show in November 1997.

The successful development of leather for the glove sector has brought the company into discussions with a number of interested parties, while the knowledge assimilated in connection with the mitt will be taken to the glove industry for further development.

Utilising its Business Club Membership to the full, Pittards used The Challenge theme for one of its trade show stands in Hong Kong in 1996. The stand featured a plethora of sails and posters depicting breathtaking shots of the Southern Ocean. So committed was the firm to authenticity, it even freighted in an original Challenge yacht mast.

Pittards capitalised on its association with the yacht *Global Teamwork*, utilising it for corporate hospitality in ports of call. In Boston, the business centre of American footwear, the firm entertained 70 clients and even made Channel 7 news.

While sponsorship provided the company with direct commercial returns, it also enhanced Pittards' relationship with its clients, prompting Church's to become a Business Club Member itself. It also provided the firm with the opportunity to involve its employees giving them the chance to see the products in use.

Pittards employees adopted the crew of *Global Teamwork* and followed them avidly throughout the race. Huge poster boards were erected on the factory floors, daily race bulletins were posted on staff noticeboards and internal competitions were run.

During the course of the race, Pittards also introduced its own Internet worldwide web site, providing instant access to the latest race updates, as well as information on its products and manufacturing.

"Our involvement with the race has been a tremendous success. It has brought real commercial benefit, enabled us to demonstrate the product's performance in action and has helped us towards our goal to become the leading supplier of the ultimate performance leather for top name brands round the world," commented Amanda Beard, Marketing Manager.

The Development Of The Challenge

Lessons Learned From The British Steel Challenge – The leadership skills of the skippers in the British Steel Challenge race needed to be developed. This need was clearly demonstrated with crew problems occurring on board several of the yachts. In one instance, this led to a change of skipper after just one leg of the race and, on another yacht, an agreement was made with the first mate to hold the team together, following the appointment of a third skipper.

It was not easy for the skippers. They were given 13 amateurs sailors, from disparate backgrounds, each with a different agenda. Some were bright, some gregarious, some introvert. Often their personalities changed under stress and through fear. All were highly motivated, used to exercising their own initiative and used to challenging decisions within their own workplace.

The skippers found the situation difficult. Most were not used to working in teams or having others question their decisions. They were more familiar with single or double-handed racing.

The Challenge Business had not previously recognised just how difficult it was going to be for the skippers and the level of information and training they received was insufficient to cope with the diversity and complexity of the problems they were to face.

Lessons Learned From The BT Global Challenge – Five of the ten yacht sponsors from the British Steel Challenge signed up for the second race, the BT Global Challenge. Many of them had formed good relationships with their skippers and it was inevitable that they wanted to develop these further. Several requested the same skipper for the next race.

This could have been seen as a disadvantage to those sponsors and skippers coming into the race for the first time. Some skippers now knew their sponsors, others did not, and the second-time sponsors were already totally committed to the project. They had the benefit of experience and the skipper had the benefit of knowing the sponsor's business and its senior management team. If the skipper needed assistance, he knew who to approach to try to obtain what was needed.

Training for the BT Global Challenge skippers was more in-depth than before. While the British Steel

Challenge skippers had received just three days induction training, the BT Global Challenge skippers undertook a three week induction programme and, in addition, one week of leadership training at the MaST Leadership Training Centre in Oxfordshire.

At the end of the race, this level of training was still deemed insufficient.

The skippers lacked management skills. They had undertaken a leadership course but not enough time had been devoted to the management element.

The fundamental weakness of the majority of skippers lay in their inability to develop the full potential of their teams. They were uncomfortable drawing on the skills of others when they felt that they should know everything themselves. They were extremely good yachtsmen and competent in managing the yacht, but the race was more about the management of *people*.

> *"Knowledge dispels fear."*
> **Sir Chay Blyth**

Moving On To Challenge 2000 – In the year 2000, a new fleet of one-design yachts will set sail. The new yacht will be 72ft in length, 5ft longer than the current Challenge yacht, and four tonnes lighter. A different keel shape will make it faster and the design and layout down below will also be altered to accommodate 18 people, four more than previously.

The route of the race will also differ and crew volunteers will get their initial introduction to ocean racing as they set off on the first leg, across the Atlantic, to the USA.

The changes take account of a number of factors and lessons learned during the previous two races. Feedback from skippers, crews and sponsors has been invaluable in ensuring that the new yacht design, together with a revised race route, will improve the racing. While the design principles of safety, strength and seaworthiness remain the same, the Challenge 2000 yachts will be aesthetically and technologically more advanced.

There is no doubt that the yachts competing in Challenge 2000 will be more competitive and even more closely placed within the race. Using lasers to cut the steel will ensure the new yachts are more exactly alike than any other one-design vessel in existence. The steel pieces will come in a flat-pack kit that can be assembled anywhere in the world.

The Challenge 2000 crew volunteers have already been selected and from the autumn of 1997, will commence a training programme with training skipper, Martin Ley.

Skipper recruitment will begin in 1998 and an in-depth leadership and management course will be included in the induction training. Each skipper will be assessed and their management and leadership skills tested. The outcome of these assessments will be thoroughly reviewed before the skipper is allocated a yacht.

For the skippers, seamanship skills will be essential to ensure they are able to take their crews safely round the world. However, the two previous races have highlighted the fact that the leadership and management elements of the skipper's role are critical.

This book identifies the essential management elements to produce a happy crew and a successful yacht.

CHAPTER TWO

"The most important part of every business is to know what ought to be done."
Lucius Columell

Twenty-five years ago, the United States Navy realised the world was changing fast. The two superpowers were calling the shots. The world was becoming increasingly unstable and unpredictable and the US Navy believed the methods used to train their leaders and teams were totally unsuited to these environments. With the advent of global competition, rapid technological development and widespread political change, businesses were also facing the same challenges and were reaching similar conclusions about leadership. One of the most extensive international research projects ever undertaken, and now championed by the Centre *for* High Performance Development, was instigated. It challenged some of the basic assumptions about leadership and organisational development. The results have been ground-breaking. The following chapter charts the research and its relevance to all leaders and explains the skills which were tracked by Peter Mackie and his team during the BT Global Challenge 1996/7.

HIGH PERFORMANCE RESEARCH

The Changing Question

BANG! – The gun goes off. In under 10 seconds, six men cross the finish line. It is the 1992 Olympic final of the 100 metres and Linford Christie is victorious. The analysis

17

begins. What technique, strength and tactics propelled him to first place?

Such was the nature of competition, that sports scientists and psychologists had begun to ask different questions. "How can we predict who is likely to win?", "How can we coach an individual to maximise their high performance potential?" and "In what areas can an elite athlete be differentiated from the pack?" "Can mental as well as physical attributes determine who wins. If so what are these processes and how can they be measured and coached?"

BANG! – The mast snaps. A gale gusting force nine has hit from the west. It is the sixth consecutive day of mountainous seas in the Southern Ocean. It is the BT Global Challenge 1996/7. The unexpected has happened. The tired crew of *Concert* is now put to the test. Can they save the yacht and themselves? In the crisis, can they remain prepared for the unexpected? The crew are up to the task and the battered yacht survives. The analysis begins. Was the situation avoidable? Did the rehearsed systems and routines fall into place? How can we learn?

Necessary and valuable retrospection for improvement, but are other questions needed? How unexpected was this situation? How do we best train our leaders and teams to meet unpredictable events? How do we prepare and skill people, mentally and physically, to tackle a myriad of complex situations and confidently predict success.

BANG! – The Chief Executive Officer thumps his desk hard. "How could it happen?!" he exclaims angrily. His retail bank employing some 30,000 people has just been dramatically marked down on the stock market making it easy prey for take-over predators. It is May 1997. This has happened despite recent wholesale reorganisation. The timing could not be worse; a supermarket chain has opened up in direct competition; a powerful regulatory body is investigating

18

certain of his senior colleagues over allegations of fraud; management consultants have recommended a major investment in information technology across his whole business and a decision is overdue. On top of this, the CEO believes the company is missing opportunities in the emerging markets while the competition is forging new territories in the 'Tiger' economies of the Far East, Eastern Europe, South America and Africa.

In business, these questions often rain down on the managers below who have to react constantly to the shifting questions from above. But do we really have to be so reactive? Of course we need skills that will enable us to manage crises, but if change is so constant, what are successful leaders and outstanding organisations doing differently? Can we develop our people to meet these challenges and shape our organisations to become more pro-active in managing the complexity and dynamism of the environment?

The questions come thick and fast. "Why didn't we know about this?" The frustration of the CEO builds. "Who have we got that will manage this crisis?" "Who have we got that can take a lead in other areas?" The questions keep coming. Unfortunately, answers are in short supply. This CEO is not alone. On current rates of attrition, some 30% of 'Fortune 500' companies will not exist in six years' time. They will fall foul of external pressures and changes which buffet their organisations like a force nine gale in the Southern Ocean.

BANG! – The champagne cork explodes and ricochets off several pieces of office equipment, plopping out of sight among the reams of discarded paper around the room. It's the mid 1970's in Princeton University. Using a new methodology and changing the assumptions of the questions posed, the team has had its first positive results after three years and several million dollars investment. These show, for the first time, that certain leadership behaviours identified by the researchers, can not only be

19

measured accurately but, when used in competitive and dynamic situations lead to outstanding team performance.

The Necessary Beginning

This story started several years earlier. The United States Navy realised that the world was going to change dramatically. The decision makers knew that the superpower status they shared with the Soviet Union, which had produced an uneasy peace, was not going to last. They were not so concerned about the USSR, with whom they had a balance of firepower, and more importantly a fairly predictable relationship. What they *were* concerned about was that future attacks could come from directions least expected. The United States was having a torrid time in Vietnam and Cambodia, and its political and military leadership were clearly ill equipped to cope with such a dynamic and complex environment. Furthermore, they were getting their fingers burned without even realising it. "How can we fight a proper war when we are holed up here in bunkers, surrounded, and the enemy never comes out of the weeds?" So moaned the Commanding Officer of the US Marines during the siege of Khe Sanh in 1968. With the Tet offensive going on in Saigon at the same time, these two incidents were to become the major turning points in this sorry saga and perhaps highlighted to the US Military, more than anything, its inability to cope when conditions became unpredictable and complex.

Indeed, the US Forces was fighting an equally unpredictable battle at home. Its soldiers were expected to be heroic on the battlefield but were subsequently treated like mercenaries when they arrived home, due to a lack of domestic public support.

It was time to act and thus one of the most detailed and complex research projects of its kind ever, was undertaken. Its task was to identify the qualities necessary to develop the leaders and teams of tomorrow, so that they would be better equipped to cope with an environment which was going to become increasingly unpredictable, complex and fast changing.

The Princeton Experience

Professor Harry Schroder at Princeton University was approached by the Office for Naval Research – the US Navy's think tank – and asked if he would conduct a research programme to answer two fundamental questions. Firstly, is it possible to identify leadership and team skills that predict outstanding performance in complex, dynamic and hostile situations? And secondly, is it possible to coach and learn these skills? Funded by the Ford and Rockefeller Foundations, the research team started to look for the answers.

In the first instance, it seemed sensible to examine organisations that were already coping with a complex and ever-changing environment and find out what the leaders and teams did when the environment changed without warning. They concluded that most organisations in the early 1970's were operating in a relatively stable environment and were therefore unsuitable 'test beds' for studying the future.

The best organisations seemed technically very competent and this was where they differentiated themselves from the competition. The best banks were excellent money lenders; the best car manufacturers had the most efficient processes for building cars. Businesses seemed to survive and prosper almost despite their leadership. When a crisis happened it was the ability to fire-fight well which enabled them to cope. Most organisations knew who their competition was; knew the customers groups they delivered to and year-on-year produced similar products marketed through unchanging distribution channels. This was hardly an environment for predicting the future.

The task of the research team was to create environments in which they could increase the instability and complexity of the situations facing the leaders and teams. In this controlled way they could study who coped best; which teams were exceptional and ultimately who were the winners and losers.

In the laboratory the team created several simulated organisations. One was an inter-nation scenario, the second a business scenario and the third based on the stock exchange. Leaders and teams managed these simulations for extended periods of up to one year, wrestling with the problem of running a dynamic organisation in an ever-changing environment.

All the existing measures of ability, personality and leadership were used in order to identify the characteristics of people and teams that led to outstanding performance in dynamic environments.

But, after some three years of research and an expenditure of several million dollars, the research team had come up with no tangible results whatsoever. This was a slightly embarrassing situation for one of the greatest research universities in the world! In spite of this they continued to go 'cap in hand' to their sponsors who fortunately remained benevolent.

Like so often in our lives, the 'eureka' moment happens when we challenge the basic assumptions of what we are doing. In this instance, the major assumption of the research team was that the methodologies being used to measure people's capabilities were related to performance in dynamic environments. They were not.

Now the researchers changed their whole approach and decided that behaviourial observation was the most valuable method to identify the relevant behaviours. Slowly, patterns of behaviours emerged which correlated with superior performance in dynamic environments. They identified four different clusters of behaviour which we now call thinking, developmental, inspirational and achieving.

Once business began to get interested in this field and further research was conducted, a list of 11 behaviours emerged that appeared to predict superior performance if used by leaders and teams faced with complex, unpredictable environments.

High Performance Behaviours (HPB)

These behaviours were defined as follows:

Information Search – Gathers many different kinds of information and uses a wide variety of sources to build a rich informational environment in preparation for decision-making in the organisation.

Concept Formation – Builds frameworks or models or forms concepts, hypotheses or ideas on the basis of information. Becomes aware of patterns, trends and cause/effect relations by linking disparate information.

Conceptual Flexibility – Identifies feasible alternatives or multiple options in planning and decision-making. Holds different options in focus simultaneously and evaluates their pros and cons.

Empathy – Uses open and probing questions, summaries and paraphrasing to understand the ideas, concepts and feelings of another. Can comprehend events, issues, problems, opportunities from the viewpoint of others.

Teamwork – Involves others and is able to build co-operative teams in which group members feel valued and empowered and have shared goals.

Developing People – Creates a positive climate in which staff increase the accuracy of their own strengths and limitations. Provides coaching, training and developmental resources to improve performance.

Influence – Uses a variety of methods (eg persuasive arguments, modelling behaviour, inventing symbols, forming alliances and appealing to the interest of others) to gain support for ideas and strategies and values.

Building Confidence – States own "stand" or position on issues; unhesitatingly takes decisions when required and commits self and others accordingly. Expresses confidence in the future success of the actions to be taken.

Presentation – Presents ideas clearly, with ease and interest so that the other person (or audience) understands what is being communicated. Uses technical, symbolic, non-verbal and visual aids effectively.

Proactivity – Structures the task for the team. Implements plans and ideas. Takes responsibility for all aspects of the situation even beyond ordinary boundaries - and for the success and failure of the group.

Continuous Improvement – Possesses high internal work standards and sets ambitious, risky and yet attainable goals. Wants to do things better, to improve, to be more effective and efficient. Measures progress against targets.

Having distilled these behaviours, it was crucial to prove that they worked in the 'real world'. "These behaviours are great to know," an Operations Manager of a large car manufacturer points out, "but how do they improve the number of cars my unit turns out next week, the efficiency with which I do it and how do they ensure that I am better than the competition?"

It seemed that the first question – "Is it possible to identify leadership and team skills that predict outstanding performance in complex, dynamic and hostile situations?" had been answered. The question remained as to whether or not they worked in the long-term, sustaining a high level of performance, and whether they could be learned.

Theory Into Practice–The Crucial Bridge

Dr Tony Cockerill, a Director of the Centre *for* High Performance Development, was one of the researchers involved in the initial stages of the programme. His first task was to validate the 11 High Performance Behaviours to test if they did underpin superior performance in dynamic environments. His second task was to develop the methodology into a form that could be used in a variety of complex situations.

His research at the London Business School showed that these 11 High Performance Behaviours are indeed crucial for superior performance in dynamic environments. Furthermore, this research was the only work that had been properly validated by rigorous measures.

"We found, again and again, corporations investing in expensive systems, management development and training designed to perpetuate skills appropriate to the past," stated Dr Cockerill.

"This is what we have always been good at," was a common comment. That is fine if customers always want the same thing, staff are not more aspirational and competition is static and predictable.

"This is how you must behave around here to get promotion," was another familiar response. Again that is fine, but managers use certain skills to climb the corporate ladder and these often have a negative impact on performance. Their aim is to move on and up a rung before what they have implemented falls down. Others are left to pick up the pieces.

"What we did not find was leadership and management development focused sharply on organisational performance. Indeed many companies seemed to be finding it increasingly difficult to measure themselves," concluded Dr Cockerill.

Focusing On Performance

As the pace of change increased, traditional 'goal' measures such as sales growth, profitability and return on capital employed were not sufficiently sensitive to give a week by week indication of a company's performance. These measures only indicated a company's past performance and data usually arrived too late. Many companies today do not know how to measure their performance.

The research initially focused on the question of performance. Working with organisations and calling on some seminal work already done in this field, 'systems' measures were developed. These gave companies a continuous barometer for their business performance and predicted medium and long-term success against the 'goal' type measures of profitability.

In further field research conducted by the London Business School, the Department of Employment and the Florida Council for Education Management, it was shown that the increasing use of these behaviours by managers and leaders not only adds to the 'bottom line' but increases their ability to survive and prosper in the long-term, regardless of the area in which these teams and organisations operate. These behaviours were equally applicable to teams from business, sport, government, education and yachting.

Behavioural Sets

Dr Tony Cockerill found the 11 behaviours naturally clustered into four sets each having a definite impact on certain situations.

i) **Strategy** – For many years, management and leadership literature provided 'flavour of the month' theories about what individuals should do to become outstanding performers. Only a few studies actually considered cognitive behaviours and processes. It seemed that 'headless chickens' could run organisations as long as they were inspirational or empathetic or proactive. For the first time, this research distilled and measured the mental processes used in strategy formation, planning and understanding the seeming chaos around. Critical to this was the cluster of 'Thinking Behaviours'.

> ### *Thinking Behaviours - Information Search, Concept Formation, Conceptual Flexibility.*
> *These are crucial to forming winning strategies, to planning and seeing the 'bigger picture'. Interestingly they make the highest contribution to performance but, sadly, are the least developed and least valued in most organisations. When these skills are not well developed, organisations are continuously fire-fighting. Also you often find many unco-ordinated initiatives raining down on a confused workforce. A lack of information will often leave your strategy vulnerable to an Exocet missile appearing from over the horizon to blow it out of the water.*

ii) Teams And People – Often because the context of teams is not properly understood, behaviours in this cluster are often regarded by 'macho' managers as soft or woolly. Nothing could be further from the truth. In business, like in sports teams or round the world yacht crews, team functioning is critical to performance and even survival. As the business world becomes increasingly complex, it is critical that organisations work quickly with small teams across the organisation. The skills required to orchestrate this and create efficiency in the work place have a major impact on 'bottom line' performance.

> ### *Developmental Behaviours - Empathy, Teamwork, Developing People*
> *These are relevant to flat, flexible, team-based structures which have to integrate with other teams. They build the ownership, involvement and commitment of people and nurture their contribution. They improve the performance of people through development of their skills and creation of an atmosphere of learning.*

27

iii) Inspiration – People are fearful of change. As change becomes the norm, it is important for leaders to have the ability to provide clarity of purpose and gain acceptance of the goals and values of the team or organisation. When morale is low, leaders need skills to instil in others a sense of achievement and direction.

> ### *Inspirational Behaviours - Influence, Building Confidence, Presentation*
> *These relate particularly to building confidence and excitement throughout the team and are crucial to achieve 'buy in' to ideas. In a crisis where decisions are required quickly, these behaviours create an atmosphere of confidence within the team.*

iv) Achievement – As some of our more traditional structures and ways of working break down and change, it becomes important that vestiges of the past do not prevent us from getting on with what needs to be done. Old policies and bureaucracy can get in the way. Leaders need a sense of their own destiny and a need to take responsibility for their actions and get things done. Increasingly, all aspects of delivery must be measured in order that improvements can be made.

> ### *Achieving Behaviours - Proactivity, Continuous Improvement*
> *These behaviours make things happen and break through bureaucracy. They ensure that tasks are structured and that plans and ideas are implemented. They give people responsibility and encourage continuous attention to improving the performance of all aspects of the team.*

Another crucial element of the behavioural analysis was that for each of the 11 High Performance Behaviours there were different levels at which each skill was used. This followed a consistent pattern and a model was developed that described the five levels at which each behaviour could be exhibited.

High Performance Behaviours
Rating Scale

Level	Behaviour	Performance
5	Implements strategies, systems or processes to build value for and perpetuate the use of the HPB and the contribution it can make.	Associated with Superior Unit Performance
4	Uses higher order behaviour. This may use the HPB in a broader way which encompasses the work of other teams, units or organisations or it may be a higher level of behaviour which is built on the foundation provided by behaviour at adequacy level.	
3	Demonstrates the basic HPB behaviour which is directed towards and bounded by the specific task, problem, issue or situation being managed.	Adequate Performance
2	Does not demonstrate the minimum, basic behaviour required to cope adequately with the specific task, problem, issue or situation being managed.	Associated with Inadequate Workgroup Performance
1	Uses negative HPB behaviour and / or sets a climate which deters or devalues the use of the HPB by others.	

This model provided a robust measurable tool which was available to test and validate these findings in the real world.

The Question Of Unpredictability And Change

"I believe that in tackling the question of change, researchers in the 70's and 80's led many organisations down 'blind alleys'," reflects Dr Tony Cockerill. "The fundamental assumptions underpinning their methodologies were flawed. They believed that the behaviours which resulted in rapid promotion in stable hierarchies were the ones which produce high performance in dynamic environments. They are not.

Let's just continue sailing the yacht as if we were off Cowes on a languid Sunday afternoon – the way we always do. Let's just ignore the 90ft breakers, gale force winds, torrential rain and the ripped main sail. It is obviously nonsensical, but much of industry has ignored changes in the environment over the last 30 years.

"It's the business cycle," is a frequent excuse. "We just have to wait three to five years for the market to pick up," or "We just have to wait for the single currency issue to be resolved," or "We just have to wait for the exchange rates to shift."

The changes happening in the world around us are ignored by businesses at their peril. Time and again we hear of once great corporations falling foul to some supposedly unexpected 'hit'. Management text books are bursting with the analogies – the British Motor Cycle Industry decimated by the Japanese in the late 1960's; the American Car Market sent reeling or IBM in trouble.

For some, there is a cyclical aspect to business but change is more like an upward spiral. The cycle never returns you to where you were before but moves you up a phase. "The fact is, we do not want to train leaders to 'input' the future on some notional premise nor do we wish them to improve the current situation, maintain the status quo or just be better at what they have always done. We must give leaders the skills to manage change itself," said Dr Cockerill.

So the question of change is not a retrospective look at past success and building these 'outdated skills' into an organisation, nor is it a glimpse into the future followed by some guess work as to the types of leaders we may need, given some imaginative scenarios of what the world may look like. We must equip our leaders with the tools to manage change itself and, therefore, shape the future. It is to give them more than skills to fire-fight and cope when things go wrong. In the Centre *for* High Performance Development's research, the most dynamic leaders were equipped with an agenda to transform the way they developed themselves and their teams in order to produce superior performance.

Eureka! A major breakthrough in the development of tomorrow's leaders. And so it has proved.

Observing High Performance Behaviours During The BT Global Challenge

Clearly the BT Global Challenge provided one of the most complex, dynamic and unpredictable environments ever imagined. It contained all the elements so rigorously examined in both Princeton University and the London Business School research programmes. What better case study for proving these behaviours worked in action?

The key to the study conducted by MaST International and the Centre *for* High Performance Development during the race, was to track the use of both the essential management skills and the High Performance Behaviours that were being used by the skippers and crews of the various yachts and examine their relative degrees of success in terms of performance. What did each of the skippers and their teams do and what was the result?

Let us remember the elite athlete, the yacht skipper and the business leader. Can we train these individuals and the teams they work with to produce consistently outstanding performances no matter what the situation is now or in the future?

The proof of the pudding was going to be in the eating – or at least somewhere in the storms in the Southern Ocean.

CHAPTER THREE

*"Find a challenge in life so big it will challenge every
capacity to be at your best."*
David O McKay

RACE PREPARATION

Crew Volunteer Training

The race was first announced in July 1993 at a press
conference held at St Katherine's Haven, London. The
resulting press coverage brought in a flood of crew
volunteer applications from all across the UK and abroad.
Many of the berths had already been filled due to the
extensive waiting list that had been building since the
launch of the first Challenge race. Such was the extent of
the appeal that people had been signing up for the race
even before it was officially launched.

Crews were selected by Chay Blyth up to three years
before the start of the race. Crew volunteers were then
given a three year training schedule which would take them
from selection as a crew volunteer to selection as a crew
member of a specific yacht. The final crew selection was to
be announced at the London Boat Show at Earl's Court in
January 1996. For the two years of initial training, four
skippers were appointed to take the volunteers through
their paces. The training skippers were Pete Goss,
Mark Lodge, Andy Hindley and Martin Ley, three of whom
had competed in the previous race. These skippers would
be responsible for crew training, coaching, and assessments.
Their reports would assist in the allocation of crew

volunteers to yachts and ensure that the final crew distribution was as balanced and fair as possible. The criteria for the race was that 14 yachts, with one professional skipper and 13 amateur crew volunteers would race on as even a playing field as possible.

Each applicant had to pass an interview with Chay before being accepted for the race. The race was open to all people between the ages of 21 and 60, irrespective of sailing experience. What Chay was looking for was enthusiasm, determination and commitment. He wanted people who believed in themselves and were capable of being self sufficient. Sailing experience was not a requirement as the three year training programme would ensure everyone was competent before they set sail. All those provisionally accepted had to sail with a training skipper prior to final acceptance. This was purely to gauge potential and the ability to learn and to assess an individual's character. Each crew volunteer was asked to secure a minimum of an RYA Competent Crew Certificate, or equivalent, before commencing their training.

> *"It doesn't take great men to do great things, but it is doing things that makes men great."*
> **Arnold Glasgow**

The crew volunteers then underwent five periods of training (each four to five days in duration):

i) Induction – This was held on board the training yachts. There was an introduction to the yacht, including basic sailing, basic safety and general confidence building. Sailing was carried out during the day with a skipper and a mate.

ii) Continuation – As the name suggests, building from the induction sail, crews were introduced to night sailing and safety. Seamanship was tackled in more depth. The crews sailed with a skipper and a mate.

34

iii) Assessment – As well as furthering the volunteers' knowledge and skills, this session enabled the skipper and mate to monitor progress and record it formally. Each volunteer was asked to deliver a brief talk to his/her crew mates on a specific aspect of the yacht. A short written paper was also completed on terminology and knowledge of the yacht. Questions such as "How many fire extinguishers are there in the doghouse and what are their uses?" Sailing included night sailing and further safety training including 'Man Overboard' recovery with volunteers taking to the water in survival suits.

Just before the final phase of training, Chay distributed a training supplement letter to everyone, reminding them all that health and fitness were of the utmost importance to everyone taking part in the race. "You will feel out of it when the yachts start racing one another during training and you can't pull your weight."

He also warned them that they required a high level of professionalism. They were part of the BT Global Challenge and were going to be watched by thousands of people all round the world, some of whom would love to see them fail. Professionalism, he said, was a question of the right state of mind. It was all about attitude. Attitude was all about three words:-

Attitude

- *Anticipate* - are you ready for the next move?
- *Detail*   - pay attention to the small things
- *Speed*   - if you do it, do it quickly

Each has to be practised, practised, practised.

From *attitude* came

Style
- Be aware
- Look the part, feel the part

which led to

Professionalism
- Do it fast
- Do it now
- Do it right

iv) Placement – This part of the training was conducted without a skipper's mate. It was the start of identifying volunteers' roles. Potential watchleaders were given watches to lead and further analysis of potential crew distribution was undertaken.

v) Race Weekend – A crucial part of the training was to teach the crew the rudiments of racing as well as the rules. The crews were split into teams of six and assembled at Port Solent to sail in a series of races over a three day period. Each team was given a professional skipper and allocated to a 36ft racing yacht.

These races proved to be both extremely popular and extremely hazardous. This was the first opportunity for the crew volunteers to compete against each other. While they had all been trained in sailing a large Challenge yacht, once they switched to a light racing boat, with the added dimension of competition, there were the inevitable collisions and near misses.

It became apparent that the crews needed and wanted more training in the finer elements of yacht speed. Once the crews were formed into their race teams, some of the skippers subsequently spent time on teaching yacht racing and sail trimming as a crucial part of their crew induction.

"You learn by experience but mistakes teach you wisdom."
Sitting Bull

Crew Selection

On 6 January 1996 at the London Boat Show, Chay finally announced the crew lists for each yacht. For skippers and crew volunteers alike this was a tense time. Was it to be *Group 4* and a hard racing discipline for 10 months, or a more relaxed yacht where the odd drink and bar of chocolate were permitted, but winning was unlikely? The suite at Earl's Court to which all the crew volunteers had been invited was packed to capacity – standing room only. Crew members jostled with skippers and sponsor representatives as they stood nervously hopping from one foot to another waiting for the announcements to begin. The atmosphere was charged with tense emotion, so much so that the crew volunteers, who by now knew each other well, were unable even to make small talk. Their minds were elsewhere and their eyes were on the large screen where their name, skipper and sponsor would soon be flashed. As the teams were announced so their identities began to form. The crew of *Group 4* was taken immediately into a tiny room in the exhibition hall and given its crew kit and asked to change. Sporting it with pride, the crew members went out for dinner together. It was part of Mike Golding's belief in team building and his determination to show that he meant business. Theirs was to be a corporate mentality, a showpiece for their sponsor, Group 4. Other crews were not so quick to assume their new identity, but still went out to dinner together. For the four yachts still seeking a sponsor the crews suffered the disappointment of having no identity at all.

Crew Training

"Study the past if you would divine the future."
Confucius

From this moment on the clock was ticking for everyone. Only nine months to go before the start gun. Training was a huge challenge for each skipper. They questioned themselves, "Am I doing things right, or am I doing the right thing?"

Of the 14 crews, most came out of Earl's Court and 'turned left' and went off in search of as much sailing experience as possible, but a few 'turned right' and went in search of team building. They were to remain well up the fleet for most of the race.

Toshiba Wave Warrior, under Simon Walker, went off to a large holiday house in Wales. There Simon spent two days with his new crew talking about the race, their standards, their clothing, the last race etc. They sampled dried food and initiated their food programme. "It was a time of great team building," said Simon "and it allowed me time to assess my crew, to see who needed encouragement, who showed initiative and who was slow to pick up a tea towel!"

Simon followed this team building with on-board training on the former Whitbread racer, *Maiden.* This provided an early opportunity to sail as a team on a large yacht and to start race training.

On *Group 4* the pattern was similar. A culture of team building before sailing paid off. They worked as a team and played as a team. They began at the Group 4 training centre with a team build that was to stand them in good stead for the rest of the race. Mike insisted that those who were joining him on this voyage were racing and that they were there for the duration of the race – no getting off. Ultimately no one did and *Group 4* finished with the same crew as they started. Mike had a very structured approach, worked each crew member hard but worked every bit as hard himself and earned total respect. During training he felt that it was important that everyone knew what was being

38

done by everyone else. Mutual respect was essential. Everyone gave of their best as a result of the intense training and their reward was in the success they achieved. As part of their training they studied the work of Meredith Belbin and discovered their individual team roles and the best way they could contribute towards a cohesive and successful team.

Meredith Belbin began his research at Henley Management College. There, middle managers with board potential were taken through a course which culminated in a business simulation. For this simulation, the participants were divided into syndicates which were assessed on a profit and loss basis. The variations in the success or failure of these syndicates so intrigued the Henley Management College that it asked Belbin to research it. After many years of working with the data – testing it, discarding it and retrying – his findings were so accurate that he was able to predict the success of the syndicates by the results of his questionnaires. His work rapidly became accepted as one of the most influential pieces of research on teams ever undertaken. It has been constantly updated by the data received from those who work with it, and is now a highly sophisticated computer driven system used by many organisations worldwide to determine roles within existing teams and for the successful appointment of new team members.

Belbin discovered that individuals naturally took on particular roles and that the correct balance of these roles within a team was crucial to the team's success. A poor balance produced a poor outcome. A group of like-minded, highly intelligent people did not necessarily form the most successful team. The balanced composition of the team was the crucial factor.

Of the *Group 4* team Belbin said, "On the whole this is a well-balanced team with a good general spread of personal qualities, but it is important that each member of the team should be aware of each other's role and potential contribution. This team possesses the strengths to enable it to do a very professional and thorough job. It may have difficulty, though, in seeing itself as a team. Its members could be concerned about the possibilities of overlapping, conflicting and non-existent roles. Therefore special attention should be paid to the question of exactly who does what. If the members are to get the best out of their association, it will also be important for them to appreciate the distinction between individual and group responsibilities."

"The secret of running a team is to keep the six guys who hate your guts from the seven who aren't yet sure."
Mike Brearley, OBE

Merfyn Owen, on *Global Teamwork*, was also determined to display an immediate unity within the crew. Every crew member was given a full set of kit, including a sleeping bag so that everyone was the same. His belief was that a good yacht was a happy yacht and he tried to deal with as many of the organisational issues as possible before leaving Southampton. Food for each leg was purchased, tested and packed in the UK then shipped to each of the stopovers. Merfyn's attention to detail was to be a feature of his performance throughout the race.

Richard Merriweather, on *Commercial Union*, also took his team out for dinner on the first night and followed it with a training session at Salcombe Sailing School. Long days of sailing were rounded off with discussion evenings, where the crew talked honestly together about their expectations and fears of the long months to come. During all the training Richard felt it was vital to involve families and to enjoy the many parties. He singled these out as the best thing they ever did.

James Hatfield, on *Time & Tide*, enlisted specialist help – 'Fast Eddy', Eddy Edrich of the Bulldog Sailing School, who patiently taught the crew the essentials of sail changing and sail trimming, and Peter and Rosie Mackie, from MaST

International, who tackled the problems of sailing as a team. "Participants don't always share a common agenda when they enter a race," Peter explained. "One person may simply want to get round the world safely, whereas another won't be satisfied with anything less than winning. Perhaps a crew member isn't prepared to take any risks – others may be prepared to face danger in order to win. This sort of disparity can lead to conflict if it is not resolved."

James put everyone to work. Fast Eddy had half the crew on deck, sail changing furiously in Southampton Water, while Peter and Rosie and the remaining crew were down below discussing team dynamics on a flip chart. In theory, this was a workable solution. In practice, Fast Eddy was so fast that tacking every few minutes made the yacht heel over violently. The flip chart, Peter and Rosie, were thrown from port to starboard and back again!

Developing a team ethos with a disabled crew was one problem Peter and Rosie had not expected. The reality was that for the majority of this special crew their journey through life had been a personal struggle against adversity; they were not used to working with others. Bringing together such individuals brought complications which were to remain unresolved throughout most of the 10 month race. It is difficult to accept that another's disability is more severe, when you have fought all your life to overcome your own.

Boris Webber on *Courtaulds International* felt he had created the best training programme. He sought advice from Chris Mason of the America's Cup. Boris and his crew trained along military lines. Every weekend together they would start with a 6.30 am run followed by light exercise, then breakfast. Everyone ate together. They spent the day sailing together, constantly changing crew positions. In the evening they would have dinner together, then retreat to the pub, but only if there was unanimous agreement. Otherwise, they would stay in and watch television. Their training covered safety, fire-fighting, a full drop in the ocean and rescue as well as first aid. From day one, everyone did everything on board to ensure a fully rounded crew. Boris felt it essential to explain the 'why' of everything – the successes and the failures. Everyone should always be fully aware of why something had to be done. This training proved to be invaluable, given that his crew had 38 changes throughout the race.

Chris Tibbs had a restricted budget because his yacht had yet to secure a sponsor. This made a huge difference to the amount of training that could be done. The crew learned basic manoeuvres and then trained on dinghies. Chris felt that the most valuable sessions were the end of day analyses and the team building barbeques he held at his house following training. His wife assumed the role of team 'mother' acting as a link between the crew and their families. The crew remained hugely grateful for her unpaid and unsung efforts.

Dave Tomkinson had difficulty pulling his crew together for training. He was also hampered by being one of the last yachts to secure sponsorship. There was no external training; everything took place on the yacht. This lack of an early identity, and absence of team building resulted in the crew feeling they were operating as a group of individuals rather than a team. This feeling prevailed throughout the entire race. Although *3Com* was the 'party yacht' in Rio de Janeiro, there was a lack of unity as a crew. Dave felt that everyone should be allowed to do whatever job they wanted on board, which they did. His quiet competence attracted great affection from his crew but *3Com* never developed the competitive edge of the faster yachts.

One of *Ocean Rover's* crew was the chief executive of MaST International, Humphrey Walters. He arranged for the whole crew to go to the MaST International Training Centre at Kiddington Hall near Oxford for a team building weekend halfway through their training. There they studied the work of Mike Woodcock, whose set of building blocks for effective teamwork, showed them the necessary elements required to produce an efficient working team.

Woodcock believed that without the stron[g] [...]
provided by these blocks, teams would malfu[nction] [...]

Woodcock's building blocks are:
- The identification of **clear goals** and **obj[...]**
  whole crew as well as each individual,
- The allocation of **individual roles** that optimise the
  talent and preferences of the individual,
- The agreement of a set of **values** which the team is
  prepared to adhere to in living and working together,
- The generation of a climate based on **mutual respect
  and trust**,
- The development of a culture that understands that
  interpersonal issues are inevitable but that they can
  only be confronted by a spirit of **openness**,
- An effective **communication** system that is a 360-
  degree process of both giving and receiving,
- The development of **uniform procedures** and **practices**
  whose sole purpose is to improve performance,
- The identification of the leadership needs of the team
  and the provision of **appropriate leadership**,
- The development of **sound inter-group relationships**,
  and,
- The need for **regular review**.

Each of the blocks was studied and assessed individually
and, as *Ocean Rover* sailed round the world, the process was
often revisited to good effect.

Chay Blyth organised specialist training for crew
members on different aspects of the yacht equipment. These
were conducted by Hood for sails and repairs, Perkins for
engine and generator maintenance, Brookes & Gatehouse for
specialist electronics programming and trouble shooting.
Other courses included maintenance of the watermaker and
toilets, plumbing, electrics, mechanics, computers and
software, winches, steering and standing and running rigging.
Some crew members undertook a fire-fighting course, while

others went to the BBC for video camera training, or to Pentax for photographic tips. Others underwent catering courses or travelled to Portishead to understand how to communicate ship-to-shore via satellite and radio.

Every crew member was encouraged to seek out any helpful information that would further their cause.

"The ratio of 'We's' to 'I's' is the best indicator of the development of a team."
Citibank Employee

Skipper Training

One of the criticisms made by many crew members on the earlier British Steel Challenge was directed at the lack of leadership and communication skills of some of the skippers. On one yacht, a near mutiny had resulted in a change of skipper at the end of the first leg. On another yacht, there was not a single crew briefing from the beginning of the race to the end.

One of the unavoidable problems faced by Chay Blyth in selecting The Challenge skippers was that the requirements to have a great deal of blue water sailing experience and a wide experience of managing and leading people were almost mutually exclusive. Many of the long distance sailing competitions in which the chosen skippers had taken part, had been single-handed. As a result, many of the BT Global Challenge skippers had sailed many more miles by *themselves* than they had with other people. Even when there had been other crew on board, they had tended to be dedicated and qualified like-minded yachtsmen and not a disparate collection of relative amateurs. Inevitably, the leadership and management experience of many of the skippers was limited.

Chay consequently decided to make leadership and management training an integral part of the skippers' preparation for this second Challenge race. He commissioned MaST International to design and deliver a week long residential course for the skippers at its Leadership Training Centre at Kiddington Hall. The course was to be run by Peter Mackie and David Dowe from the Leadership Development Team.

> *"The real leader has no need to lead – he is content to point the way."*
> **Harry Miller**

Both Peter and David quickly realised that the skills necessary to lead a yacht and its crew safely round the world had similarities to those required to lead a sophisticated project team to a successful conclusion. Conversely, to deliver a course set in a business context rather than a yachting one would have undermined the course's credibility with the skippers. The end result was a highly practical course embodying a core of management theory, supplemented by practical exercises and examples.

The course was delivered in modular form with each module reinforced through experiential learning. Each skipper was given the opportunity to lead their colleagues in an outdoor problem solving exercise. This apparently high risk strategy, with such a competitive group of people, proved to be largely successful. For many skippers, it was the first time they had ever received feedback on their leadership style; it was a sobering experience for some. The short time on a residential course, away from the demands of ocean racing, resulted in successful team building for the skippers. The final ballista race, modelled on the famous Royal Tournament Field Gun Race, was a model of intense motivation and commitment. A task normally taking civilian managers about 40 minutes was completed by the winning team in 14 minutes. The 'second' team took five seconds longer!

In order to give the skippers an understanding of team dynamics and how to make the best use of their individual team roles, before attending the course they were each asked to complete a self-perception questionnaire using the Belbin model. After taking them through the work of Belbin, they were given feedback.

Learning about the model enabled the skippers to understand where they could most naturally contribute to the team. They were also better able to understand team dynamics, which have such a special part to play in self-management, the management of others and in the resolution of conflict.

The nine team roles currently identified by Belbin are:

PLANT Creative, imaginative, unorthodox. Solves difficult problems.
Allowable weaknesses – ignores detail, too pre-occupied to communicate effectively.

RESOURCE INVESTIGATOR Extrovert, enthusiastic, communicative. Explores opportunities, develops contacts, likes the telephone.
Allowable weakness – over optimistic. Loses interest once initial enthusiasm has passed.

CO-ORDINATOR Mature, confident, a good social leader. Clarifies goal, promotes decision making, delegates well.
Allowable weakness – can be seen as manipulative. Delegates personal work.

SHAPER Challenging, dynamic, thrives on pressure. Has the drive and courage to overcome obstacles.
Allowable weakness – can provoke others. Hurts people's feelings.

TEAM WORKER Co-operative, mild, perceptive and diplomatic. Listens, builds, averts friction, calms the waters.
Allowable weakness – indecisive in crunch situations. Can be easily influenced.

46

IMPLEMENTER Disciplined, reliable, conservative and efficient. Turns ideas into practical actions.
Allowable weakness – somewhat inflexible. Slow to respond to new possibilities.

COMPLETER FINISHER Painstaking, conscientious, anxious. Searches out errors and omissions. Delivers on time.
Allowable weakness – inclined to worry unduly. Reluctant to delegate. Can be a nit picker.

MONITOR EVALUATOR Sober, strategic and discerning. Sees all options. Judges accurately.
Allowable weakness – lacks drive and ability to inspire others. Overly critical.

SPECIALIST Single-minded, self-starting, dedicated. Provides knowledge and skills in rare supply.
Allowable weakness – only contributes on a narrow front. Dwells on technicalities. Overlooks the big picture.

Skipper Team Distribution

When looking at the distribution of the first two natural roles of the skippers it is interesting that no one emerged as a Team Worker. Several skippers actually had this as a role best avoided. All other roles were covered.

Plants – Plants are naturally creative people. Merfyn Owen had a creative approach to strategy and was a prominent contributor to the Challenge Poetry Club that became an unusual feature of this race. A group of poets swapped verses once a week by fax during the voyage. Some of their offerings are included in this book under Chapter 12 'Reflections'.

Resource Investigators – Resource Investigators are essentially creative networkers and are often happiest

47

working outside the team for the good of the team. It was here that James Hatfield came to the fore. As a trustee of the Time & Tide Trust and one of their major fundraisers, he was the only skipper who was also, in effect, a sponsor. Throughout the race James could always be seen on the telephone, frantically trying to come up with ideas to raise enough money to pay for the next stop-over, crew accommodation and other financial commitments. The fact that his disabled crew members ended up staying in the best hotels was very much a tribute to his ability as a Resource Investigator. James promoted the team of *Time & Tide* relentlessly with press and public alike.

Mark Lodge, skipper of *Motorola*, carried his skills as a networker to a natural conclusion when he married one of the girls from The Challenge team!

Shaper – Three skippers emerged as strong shapers - Mike Golding, Chris Tibbs and Richard Merriweather. They are all men with great drive and vision, able to make decisions in a crisis. Of the three, Mike, skipper of *Group 4*, was probably the most focused. His eye was always on the goal and its achievement. He said, "I was not there to be liked, but to make sure that everyone felt they had got something out of the race. I could only drive them that hard because of our success."

Chris Tibbs, of *Concert*, also had great strength of character but coupled this with a soft spoken manner. The way in which Chris and his crew coped with their subsequent dismasting exemplified his strong ability as a Task Leader. Richard Merriweather, of *Commercial Union*, was also intensely competitive but his goal centred drive and vision were complemented by an ability to lead through consensus when appropriate. This is when his secondary ability as a Co-ordinator became apparent.

Co-ordinator – The reason that Mark Lodge, Tom O'Connor and Simon Walker were held in such affection by

48

their crews lay in their ability to understand their crew members, use the crew's talents to best advantage and to delegate effectively. Mark spent hours at the bow of *Motorola* just watching his crew and the different roles that they naturally adopted. He wanted to be sure that, in the event of serious injury, he could reshuffle the pack to best effect. Tom's military training meant that he was a skilled organiser, as was proved when *Pause To Remember* suffered a snapped boom mid-ocean. Co-ordinators are natural social leaders and Simon's ability to delegate and encourage produced one of the happiest crews. That is not to say that *Group 4* were miserable, it was just that words like 'happy' and 'unhappy' were not part of their focused vocabulary – but then again neither was 'losing'.

Teamworkers – Significantly, none of the skippers had Teamworker as one their top two roles. This was not surprising given that they were such competitive people, driven by a need to achieve rather than be a respected team member. For many of the skippers this meant that their natural empathy level was low. This was to be a major limitation for some in dealing with weaker crew members later in the race.

Implementers – Implementers have an exceptional readiness to address the practical demands of a given situation and always like to take a 'hands on' approach. Simon Walker felt that he was a young and active resource within the team and was often up at the bow working in dangerous conditions.

Completer Finisher – Probably four of the tidiest boats during the voyage were *Group 4, Ocean Rover, Courtaulds International and Nuclear Electric*. All were skippered by men to whom attention to detail was a crucial element of successful sailing. When *Group 4's* Andy Girling bought the wrong coloured boots, Mike Golding asked him to change them because they were not in the corporate colours.

Paul Bennett was constantly looking for anything on board *Ocean Rover* that was not shipshape, a trait which had stood him in good stead during his days in the Navy. Completer Finishers are not always good delegaters and impose very high standards on themselves. Boris Webber, of *Courtaulds International,* freely admitted that he had pushed his crew and himself too hard.

Monitor Evaluator – Richard Tudor, Andy Hindley and Merfyn Owen all demonstrated an ability to stand back from the immediate problem and look at the bigger picture. The race proved not to be a happy one for Richard and *Nuclear Electric,* the pre-race favourite, but he earned great respect for his pragmatic view on his misfortunes.

Specialist – Significantly, the biggest group of skippers fell into the Specialist category of the analysis. These men felt that their greatest contribution to the crews lay in their specialist knowledge, acquired from years of sailing experience. Every one of them was to emerge as a master of their craft, but few saw leading and managing others as natural abilities that they had to offer. Communication is very often a weakness of the Specialist.

> *"Real leaders are ordinary people with*
> *extraordinary determination."*
> **John Seaman Garns**

The first real test for the yachts was the Fastnet Qualifying Sail held in June 1996. The traditional course round the Fastnet Rock off the southern tip of Ireland was extended by 200 miles making The Challenge course some 900 miles in total. At the crew briefing, Chay Blyth emphasised that this was to be a qualifying sail and not a race. It was a chance for every crew to experience some off-shore sailing, on a course notorious for rough seas and strong winds. For the first time, crews would be able to work together in their watch teams,

50

under their appointed watchleaders, and get a feel for life at sea. They would devise watch systems, experience sleep deprivation, try the dehydrated and freeze dried foods that they would be eating for six weeks at a time and, of course, test their own level of stamina, endurance and their sailing ability. It was their final preparation for the real thing and would show up any team or personal deficiencies. For many, it was the first shake-down of crew roles. People were able to show their strengths and potential watchleaders were put through their paces. It gave the skippers an understanding of what they were dealing with. Unsurprisingly, several crew volunteers left the race after this sail.

Throughout the summer final preparations were made. Sails were race packed, instruments were calibrated and yacht speeds logged under specific conditions. Some yacht joined forces to complete their training. *Toshiba Wave Warrior* and *Nuclear Electric* engaged in 'twin yacht tuning' – a win-win alliance of joint yacht data gathering and provision of a competitive edge to training. Simon Walker went on to use this method of alliance during the race itself.

For everyone involved, the race preparation had been challenging, demanding, and rewarding. It required discipline, commitment and a certain selfishness. For many, raising the money was the most difficult task, but that was part of The Challenge and the way Chay wanted it to be. After all, he was looking for enthusiasm, determination and commitment and in the majority of cases that was exactly what he found.

By July 1996 he had 14 crews who were ready for the BT Global Challenge.

CHAPTER FOUR

"And gentlemen in England now abed shall think
themselves accursed they were not here."
William Shakespeare

Tears streamed down their faces as they yelled excitedly at the yacht's arrival. The spectators heeled the launch wildly as they strove to get closer to this special 67ft yacht beating up The Solent. *Time & Tide* may have been the last of the 14 BT Global Challenge yachts to reach Southampton, but it was one of the most well-known yachts in the race. Mrs Hatfield joined in the emotional singing of Tina Turner's 'Simply the Best', their adopted theme song, as she witnessed the return of her son's yacht ending its 30,000 mile circumnavigation of the world. She was one of a small group who were an hour south of the race finish to greet the disabled crew home. Around 80 people, many of whom had never met each other before that morning in July 1997, clasped each other, cried, drank champagne and shouted triumphantly. This was the culmination of a dream - it was time for celebration.

SOUTHAMPTON TO RIO DE JANEIRO

Leg 1

Ten months earlier, the big adventure was about to begin. The 'World's Toughest Yacht Race' was due to start at 1.30pm on 29 September 1996 off Calshot Spit in The Solent. Fourteen identical yachts, crewed by a complete cross-section of amateurs, were about to pit their wits and

53

ability against each other and, more importantly, the elements. Most had no real idea what they were going to face or what incidents were about to unfold.

In the days before the start, BT had created a carnival atmosphere at Ocean Village in Southampton with marquees, bands and a permanent filmed display of interviews with crew and shots of crashing seas and spray. The yacht crews were proud of their uniform as it distinguished them from the crowd. The camaraderie between crew members from the different yachts was obvious. Theirs was a unique bond which develops between the participants of great adventures. They moved easily among each other; a handshake here, a quiet word there. There were always smiles and laughter. Who would not want to be part of this atmosphere?

The pontoon area had looked like an army depot. Piles of rope, equipment and food were ready to be loaded onto each of the yachts. Crews were sewing leather over the sharper bits of metal and a number of crew members were working aloft, putting finishing touches to what was to be their home for the next 10 months.

The week leading up to the start day had been hot and pleasant. "This is what sailing is all about," was a frequent comment. "Nice weather, a beautiful yacht and camaraderie."

The Start – Race day dawned. The carnival was over. Skippers and crews waited avidly for the weather forecast:

> *'Wind: southwesterly force 4 or 5, occasionally force 6 around exposed headlands backing south southwesterly, force 6 or 7, perhaps gale force 8 at times in Portland and Plymouth by midday and to south southwesterly force 6 or 7 in Dover and Wight by evening.*
> *Weather: Cloud and heavy rain will spread east to all parts.*
> *Visibility: Moderate or good, decreasing poor in heavy rain with a risk of fog patches in Portland and Plymouth.'*

Low cloud, gale force winds and driving rain greeted the fleet and the relatives of the crews staying in hotels and guest houses around Southampton. The weather attacked everyone with full vigour as they prepared for the start. An armada of private yachts and hired vessels ferried those closely attached to the race to watch the start.

The fleet disappeared into the rain and gale force winds, leaving the marina empty and the bedraggled spectators crouched under the desolate marquees. The mood among those left behind varied. "I resent this race," one wife said. "It has dominated us for three years, taken all our money and now it is going to take my husband away from me and his children for 10 months. How can I feel happy on a day like this? I would rather spend 10 months in gaol."

Among the skippers there was apprehension. How would they cope with the journey and a crew of volunteers who had only been together since January. Late entry of sponsors had posed a problem for some yachts. Whilst most of the crews had had their sponsors all summer and each had a set of crew kit, the crew of *Save The Children* had been known simply as Yacht 29. "Not very motivating; it affected the crew during the build-up to the race," said skipper Andy Hindley. Group 4 crew looked magnificent in their corporate uniform and the yacht was immaculate, a credit to their ebullient sponsor Philip Sørensen, Group 4 Chairman and Chief Executive. "It seems to me that you have to look like winners if you want to do well in such a competitive race. It really is all about starting out on the right foot and getting the correct mental approach to winning throughout the crew," stated Mike Golding, their skipper.

As the yachts motored down to the start line, there was an uncanny silence on board as crews were consumed by their own thoughts. It was, perhaps, a strange feeling in today's jet set world that they would not set foot on the pontoon in Southampton until July of the following year. Would they make it back in one piece? How could they live for six weeks at a time with 13 complete strangers? "I haven't been to sea for more than two days at a time," said Robert Bruce on *Ocean Rover*. "I have no idea what it will be like for six weeks."

More people have been in space than have sailed a yacht round the world 'the wrong way'. The 'World's Toughest Yacht Race' provided a unique combination of challenges. Competition, personal danger, interpersonal and team dynamics, discomfort, fatigue, stress and a hostile and unknown environment would cause heartache, misunderstanding, huge loneliness and fear as well as personal development, unbelievable achievement of goals, excitement and formation of a totally new personal focus. After 30,000 miles, the end would be hugely emotional. No one, neither crew, supporter, organiser nor sponsor would ever be the same again.

"We stand today on the edge of a great frontier – the frontier
of the oceans – a frontier of unknown excitements and perils –
a frontier of hopes, dreams and threats – but, above all,
a frontier of adventure and achievement."
Humphrey J Walters

As the slate grey day struggled with its attempts at summer, Her Royal Highness, the Princess Royal, fired the starting gun from the *Duc de Normandie* ferry. The yachts raced past the Royal Yacht Squadron, a club that has for many years been the symbol of yacht racing and perhaps the elitist ethic which Chay Blyth felt closed yacht racing to the majority of people. It was in an attempt to overcome this discrimination that the BT Global Challenge was created. It was therefore only right that the gracious castellated facade at the very gateway to the English Channel and The Solent should be the starting point for the race.

And so the fleet was on its way in the most horrific of conditions, followed by an armada of spectator boats. Most of the yachts were down to their storm sail configuration, while their hulls which were emblazoned with sponsors' graphics gave some colour to the newsreel helicopters buzzing overhead.

With the wind right on the nose, the yachts tacked down the western Solent keeping the crews on their toes. Most of the skippers had a well-planned starting position for each of the crew but it was clear that others had left it to chance and this was reflected in sloppy tacking procedures with crew members tripping over each other in their haste to satisfy the skippers' demands. The deck of an ocean racing yacht is very crowded with 14 crew, particularly if the conditions make it unstable and soaking wet. In front of their supporters, other yachts and the international media, each skipper was determined to make a good start. However, first across the line was not considered by all to be the best position. Richard Tudor, for example, on *Nuclear Electric* made a cautious, nervous start. "I wanted to keep out of trouble and not get tangled up in a protest early on in this immense undertaking. I needed the crew to work smoothly, rather than rush around like headless chickens." Merfyn Owen, on *Global Teamwork*, was too fast away. Luck was not on his side and he pre-empted the start. He was penalised an hour which was spent bobbing around The Needles in the teeth of the gale. Lying stationary in pouring rain, watching the competition disappear into the gloom, was a devastating start for the crew. Merfyn Owen likened the experience to that of a race horse left behind in the starting stalls.

The first psychological milestone was passing The Needles. It was here that the last of the supporters turned back. It was almost as if the crowd had left the stadium as the supporting vessels and helicopters headed for home. No more horns, slapping of helicopter blades or waving crowds, just silent crews, severe spray and the incessant crashing of waves against the hull, which was to become a familiar sound over the next 10 months.

In preparing for the race, there had been two significant considerations. Firstly, nine of the professional skippers had circumnavigated the globe before, either as skippers or crew in the first British Steel Challenge. Secondly, there were five new yachts. Questions began to arise. Would the new yachts be quicker than the old ones? Would they have smoother hulls and a better shape which would give them a slight edge? How about the rigging and the deck fittings? Would experience be of value? Ocean racing is an extremely dangerous, unpredictable sport. Safety, coupled with the right technique, keeps people alive in such a hostile environment. Had The Challenge Business learned from the British Steel Challenge?

Most of the crews were also concerned about their own personal preparation. They had all been trained to cope with the immense dangers of handling such a powerful, unforgiving piece of machinery. They knew largely which rope to put where and how to handle the winches without losing a hand or injuring a fellow crew mate. But had they trained enough and in sufficient depth?

Due to the weight of the equipment and the size of the yacht, most of the manoeuvres took six to eight people to work in a co-ordinated fashion. When the sea was rough and the wind was blowing at gale force, the team size had to increase and so did the danger. The load forces on the major winches sometimes reached 20 tons which had to be handled by men and women of varying age and strength. Under the worst conditions, would they be able to work together?

"It was an easy decision to go on The Challenge. I had no house, no partner, no job and no cooking utensils."
A Crew Member

Reasons for paying £18,500 in order to be part of such an experience were many, varied and personal. "I have been in a rut for the last 20 years and it's time I shook up the system and my brain," was a common theme among the older crew members. On *Ocean Rover*, there were at least 14 different reasons given by the crew for their participation.

With the average age over 35, achievement of personal goals was high on the list.

The skippers, too, had their own agendas.

For Richard Tudor, it was a chance to prove that he was a winner. He had won the first leg in the last race sailing *British Steel II* before being dismasted in the Southern Ocean halfway to Tasmania. He was now skippering the last winner - *Nuclear Electric* - and he started as firm favourite.

Adrian Donovan aboard *Heath Insured II* had unfinished business. One of his crew, Bill Vincent, was lost overboard presumed to have committed suicide when they were half way through the last leg of the British Steel Challenge and they finished well down the field as a result. It was a sad event for the ultimate professional and it upset him deeply. He wanted to compete again and take his crew successfully round the world.

James Hatfield of *Time & Tide* had been presented with his MBE by the Queen 10 years before the race and, when asked about his next adventure, had said, "I'm going to skipper a disabled crew round the world." He wanted to 'sail the latitudes to change attitudes' - to prove that disabled people are every bit as capable as able bodied people given the chance. Having survived eight open heart surgery operations himself, James was taking with him a crew whose disabilities included blindness, deafness, limb deficiencies and cerebral palsy. It was an immense task.

The Early Stages – It is not surprising that the skippers and their crew members experienced a mixture of sadness at leaving their friends and relatives and apprehension at the task ahead. Some were concerned about their level of endurance and stamina. Others worried about letting their crews down at a critical time. Would they cope with the others in such a confined space? Would they have rows and create personal difficulties?

Even as early as The Solent, seasickness took its toll. Within hours of the start, almost two-thirds of the crews and three of the skippers were suffering from some form of seasickness which many of them never overcame. This caused a significant number of crew changes during the race, particularly in Rio de Janeiro. Roger Arnold on *Global Teamwork* suffered terribly. Although most people recover after two to three days, he suffered throughout the leg and seldom had a day without feeling ill. On *Ocean Rover*, seasickness was a major problem with 10 of the crew incapacitated. The companionway was littered with bodies lying in various positions. Paul Bennett, the skipper, described it as dossing city. Spaghetti Bolognese, the traditional meal for the first day at sea, was eaten by only three of the crew. Paul commented, "I would far rather stay up for two days driving the yacht than feel as ill as they clearly do."

Greeting the yachts were conditions described as storm force. Away from the land, the wind and sea battered the yachts and created a roller coaster ride. On *Save The Children* Rod Stevens was picked up by a wave on the foredeck and hurled onto his head. James Hatfield, skipper of *Time & Tide*, broke his hand between the wheel and the helm stanchion before he had even passed The Needles. A severe injury at this stage of the race could have shattered the dream and three years of hard work. For the disabled yacht, it would also have attracted unfavourable publicity so early in the race. As a result, in immense pain, he battled on in silence. Three days later he sent a message to the rest of the fleet to say that a crew member, Nigel Smith, had broken a leg, leaving the joint horribly exposed. The best the medic could do, he announced, was to give it a shot of WD40, then leave it to the sail repair team to stitch up and bind with duct tape. After an appalled silence, laughter broke out over the radio line as they realised he had broken his *false* leg.

The apparently stream-lined yachts were anything but smooth close up, with jammers and cleats sticking up ready to catch an unwary deckhand unlucky enough to get washed down the deck by the incessant water that swept from the bow to the cockpit. Most of the crews crawled around like small children clutching anything for support. For some of the disabled people on *Time & Tide*, this was a normal way of moving and they could get around the deck with amazing speed.

Deep Sea Sailing – As the yachts approached the north west corner of France, the storms abated and the skippers were faced with their first big decision. Could they risk cutting the corner through the Ushant Channel or should they go round and take on the extra miles to the west? Dave Tomkinson on *3Com* chose the short route and bore down on a lonely French trawler that was busy emptying lobster pots. Faced with a 42 ton racing yacht flying an enormous spinnaker travelling at 10 knots with little manoeuvrability, Dave's broken French and collision rules being called, the trawlerman accepted that Dave, and the ensuing four Challenge yachts had the right of way! Suddenly the amateurs were introduced to the competitive attitude essential to ocean racing. Provided it does not endanger yacht or crew nothing stops the task of sailing the yacht as fast as possible.

As the fleet settled down and entered the Bay of Biscay the first real taste of the Atlantic Ocean swell was felt. The treacherous waters of Biscay are caused by the westerly winds driving the swell into the bowl shaped coast of France. This circulates the water and creates confused waves which can be the most dangerous in the world. The trade winds, on the other hand, gave the yachts the thrill of down wind sailing. With a yacht that is built to cope with sailing into the wind, the instability of the yacht increased dramatically with the wind strength and the resulting size of the swell and surf. With 20 to 25 knots of wind, the yachts were surfing at up to 17 knots down huge rollers with spinnakers flying well out in front. The stern of the yachts could be picked up by the next 25ft high roller and launched forward with terrific acceleration. It was likened

61

to going downhill on a bicycle with no pedals and no brakes and unfortunately no end! In the black tropical nights, the exercise became immensely difficult and totally dependent on the feel and reaction of the helmsman. The direction was sometimes unpredictable and the danger of broaching sideways and being dragged over was always present. The first round of blown spinnakers started as unwary, still inexperienced, helmsmen tried to catch a yacht which had been catapulted from the top of a wave in a different direction. The results were quite spectacular. Not many people volunteered to helm in these conditions which put tremendous onus and pressure on the skippers.

Sail Choice – *Save The Children* popped its huge heavyweight spinnaker when a sudden tropical storm hit the yacht. The wind went from a sedate 15 to 45 knots in an instant and the yacht was thrown sideways, with the spinnaker pulling the whole yacht close to the water. Four of the crew were thrown onto the lower guardrail and were lucky not to go over the side. The effect of having cloth the size of two tennis courts in the water dragging the yacht down was quite dramatic until the sail cloth gave way and the yacht righted itself.

Nuclear Electric and *Ocean Rover* suffered the same fate, resulting in yards of split and shredded material being dragged back onto the deck from under the yacht. With the allocation of only one set of sails for the entire race, protection of the sails was vital. Every boat had two designated sailmakers who had been trained at Hood Sailmakers. On *Ocean Rover*, the sailmaking team consisted of a mounted policeman and a chief executive, who spent four days hand-stitching the cloth back into the side tapes using 10,000 stitches. A total of 100 metres of sewing affectionately known as a "Linford" after the famous UK Olympic Gold medallist, Linford Christie.

Broaching illustrates the power these yachts have when underway. Once, *Courtaulds International* snapped a 20ft long 4 cwt spinnaker pole like a matchstick. Some days later they came across a Spanish trawler who decided to stop ahead of them instead of taking evasive action. This forced Boris Webber to broach the yacht deliberately as the only quick means of stopping.

Group 4 was later to go into the lead by choosing to sail on the most westerly path straight to the corner of South America. It seemed to be an unusual route as most of the speculation was on good winds being close to the coast of Africa. However, with Mike Golding's previous knowledge and his pre-race research, this tactic gave him a clear edge early on in the race.

Ocean Rover was surfing under spinnaker close to the West African coast when there was an immense bang on the hull and the yacht stopped dead in the water with the steering jammed solid. As the yacht was trying to lunge forward, there was a cry from David Kennedy on the helm that the steering had broken. With the yacht in danger of broaching, the sails were released and the yacht lay bobbing in the swell while Paul Bennett tried to free the steering wheel. With no success, it was decided that a team of two should dive over the side to investigate the rudder. As they were about to jump into the ocean, the yacht lurched forwards and a huge 20ft shark floated to the surface behind the stern and rolled over on its belly!

Personal Relations – The day to day issues of people living together, which appear to be trivial on land, caused some major upsets throughout the trip, illustrating to most people how insular their lives had been up to The Challenge. The crews were beginning to realise what life was like on a yacht for extended periods of time. Some found the routine of three hours on watch and three hours off difficult to cope with. Sharing a cabin with two other people, with the continuous crashing and banging of the yacht and constant conversation, was difficult to get used to. It was described as being like, "sleeping in a pub without the benefit of alcohol" and with one of the cabin mates constantly seasick, sleeping became very sporadic. People suffered very quickly from fatigue as no sooner had they gone to sleep than they were woken for the next watch. On *Ocean Rover*, some of the crew had benefited from the advice of a sports psychologist who had trained them how to relax sufficiently to drop off to sleep, a form of meditation which they used for the rest of the race to great effect.

Culinary Delights – Although the emphasis was on driving the yacht, below decks was always a hive of activity. Three meals had to be provided daily for 14 people on a four-burner stove and a caravan-sized oven. The food varied from yacht to yacht but it was always a major element of life on board. *Ocean Rover* had consulted Gerry Goldwire who was a previous BBC Television *Masterchef* winner. *Nuclear Electric* had used a contract caterer and had all their meals prepacked. Most of the other yachts realised the importance of food and had consulted dieticians and caterers to ensure the correct nutritional balance. Adding to the catering problems was the lack of skill of the crew who took turns to prepare the meals. A large proportion had seldom cooked a meal for themselves let alone for a large number of fussy people.

Andy Hindley on *Save The Children* said, "One of my crew, who had no previous cooking knowledge, had avidly watched the previous cooks soak the dehydrated mince before cooking. When his turn came and the menu for the day said 'corned beef hash' he duly opened up the five tins of corned beef provided and left them to soak in a large pan of water. He was somewhat nonplussed when the chunks of corned beef didn't expand!"

James Hatfield, on *Time & Tide*, himself a restaurateur, believed that one of the hardest parts of circumnavigating the world was coping with freeze-dried food. His crew faced the added difficulty of precision timing of food intake for certain crew members who needed to eat and rest regularly for medical reasons.

64

"People," he said, "acted like children over food. I placed 14 pieces of fruit cake on the table one day and said there was *one* piece each. They were grabbed immediately and 'named'. The next day I placed another 14 pieces of fruit cake on the table and said that everyone could help themselves - only six pieces were taken!"

Jocelyn Walters, on *Nuclear Electric*, said that although her yacht had probably the best food in the whole fleet, it was seldom appreciated. Despite having been prepared and cooked under the most arduous of conditions, it was consumed within seconds in animal-like fashion.

Fresh water was desalinated through a watermaker at a rate of three pints an hour. To most people it tasted brackish compared to the recycled and chlorinated water drunk on land. It affected the taste of the tea and coffee.

Crew members who were normally used to clear routines and standard diets were suddenly thrust into freeze-dried food, disturbed sleep patterns, a hostile environment, differing personalities and the prospect of 10 months away from home. No wonder some found it difficult to cope with this 'Challenge of a Lifetime.'

As the fleet headed south in beautiful weather and trade winds, they approached the Equator. The crews were beginning to sail the yachts well and gain confidence. On crossing the line King Neptune traditionally invites new subjects into his kingdom. This usually takes the form of a ritual during which the subject is anointed with a revolting brew for the absolution of all sins. And so it was for those crew members who were now crossing the Equator for the first time. A concoction, made largely from left over food with a custard base, provided the necessary brew!

The End Of The First Leg – As the fleet approached Rio and the finish, there were inevitable flare-ups and some people realised that the 'Challenge of a Lifetime' was not for them. On *Nuclear Electric*, a crew member had been unhappy as early as the third week and he was to leave.

Merfyn Owen on *Global Teamwork* confessed to an autocratic style which had left a huge communication gap between him and his team. Boris Webber on *Courtaulds International* was feeling the strain of trying to handle amateurs from all walks of life. He was to gather the whole crew together in Rio and examine his leadership style. The result was a complete change of style from autocracy to consultation. Whether this caused a significant change in performance or not, the fact was that on the next leg *Courtaulds International* moved from last place to fifth.

Some crew members missed their families too much, some never overcame their seasickness and this contributed to nine people disembarking in Rio.

The arrival into Rio was to provide a final frustration for many of the crews. With no wind and glassy seas for the last mile along the Copacabana beach, *Motorola* took seven hours to complete the final mile and *Heath Insured II* and *Ocean Rover,* who had battled for the last 2,000 miles, arrived at the final turning buoy 50 yards apart. *Heath Insured II* went out to sea and *Ocean Rover* stayed near the beach. The surf nearly spelled disaster for *Ocean Rover* as it launched the yacht towards the sand. A final small puff of wind saved the yacht from running aground, but *Heath Insured II* had covered the last mile two hours earlier. There is nothing more frustrating than trying to control a yacht with no wind. Very different conditions to the weather which had battered the crews some 5,000 miles earlier at the start of the voyage.

"You know what makes good leadership? It's the ability to get men to do what they don't want to do and like it."
Harry Truman

WHAT MADE THE DIFFERENCE

As this was the first leg, many of the crews had not settled into any firm behavioural pattern. However it was interesting that even at this early stage in the race, some crews displayed the necessary cohesive qualities required for the race.

Thinking

This is the key to strategy formation and the highest contribution to performance. In many organisations, it is the least developed and least recognised. The three behaviours in this cluster are Information Search, Concept Formation and Conceptual Flexibility.

Information Search – The High Performance Behaviour of Information Search is about a structured and disciplined approach to the widespread collation of all possible information relevant to a problem. For the skippers, the three areas in which their ability to search for information were yacht performance, sea conditions and weather. All were tested to the full.

Each of the 14 different yachts carried 12 sails, each designed for use in different wind conditions and direction, and capable of being hoisted in a number of combinations. Consultations with the sail designers, yacht designers and sailing strategists allowed each skipper to formulate his own unique set of data indicating which sails to use, in which combination and when. A number of yachts formed 'win-win' alliances during the work-up period to allow the effects of various subtle changes in sail and yacht trim to be analysed against the benchmark of another yacht with identical sail set, sailing alongside.

One such alliance was between Simon Walker, a computer systems analyst and skipper of *Toshiba Wave Warrior*, and Richard Tudor, a professional sailmaker and skipper of *Nuclear Electric*. Inevitably Simon took a systems approach to the problem of identifying best sail

67

combination and trim, whereas Richard took the more pragmatic approach of the master sailmaker and experienced mariner. Their respective yacht crews spent hours in The Solent sailing on parallel courses with one yacht keeping trim as constant as possible and the other testing the effects on overall speed of subtle, and sometimes infinitesimal trim changes. The resulting information collated by both skippers proved invaluable in a race in which three seconds ultimately separated two yachts after 30,000 miles.

The next area requiring comprehensive information search was that of the combined effect of wind and current. The average speed of the yachts over the whole race was about eight knots. The effects of even a two knot current are obvious, giving a potential speed over the ground of between six and 10 knots; a big difference if one skipper got his yacht in the right current and another the wrong one.

Far out at sea, current trends are widely tracked and fairly predictable, but closer inshore local information becomes critical when tidal eddies around coastal formations produce strange and unpredictable currents. Before the race and at each stopover, some skippers were to be seen in quiet, private huddles with local fishermen and sailors, desperately trying to glean local information on current patterns. The more diligent the skipper, and in some cases his delegated crew member, the greater the data bank available when the time came to make that critical decision as to the course to take inshore.

The collation of weather information was an even more daunting task. During the race, each yacht had access to the same weather forecasts using radio frequencies and computers. The real differential lay in how much data skippers and crew had managed to acquire in advance of each leg.

Accurate weather data on global weather patterns has been collated for many years. The prediction of weather patterns has become big business, particularly for defence purposes, oil exploration and the space programme. The advent of weather satellites has allowed the collation of global weather data of great accuracy.

One of the challenges facing the skippers throughout the race was how to place their yacht in a more favourable weather pattern than that of their competitors. This was the main reason why individual yacht tracks varied so greatly and why the winning skippers were often the ones who had more predicted data available to them. During the race, one split emerged between the yachts: those who had access to private weather and current strategists, or 'routers' as they were called and those who did not. These armchair strategists, with vast data banks of weather data available to them, allowed skippers to get scenario analyses in advance of each leg. Sometimes there was almost too much information available and then the ability to interpret this data became crucial.

There is no doubt that Information Search in all its dimensions was to prove to be a race winning factor. There were those whose diligence and determination took them to the relevant waters before the race. There were those who found the best router they could to gain the necessary information. There were those who felt it important to have information from more than one router. There were those who had the information but never analysed or used it. There were those who never sought it, sometimes for financial reasons, but not always.

Conceptual Flexibility – If Information Search is about basing decisions on the widest possible information, Conceptual Flexibility is about exploring all of the options in depth before taking a decision. A winning combination of Information Search coupled with Conceptual Flexibility prompted Mike Golding to take the most westerly route, straight to the corner of South America. It seemed an unusual route but Mike's breadth of knowledge on both weather and currents plus his attention to detail gave him a clear edge even at this early stage. *Group 4* was soon in the lead. "I knew that the same thinking and preparation that had won the last race wouldn't be enough to win this one," he stated. "The chances were that previous skippers would follow the same route that they sailed last time. I knew that it would be a hard grind to outsail them. I had to out-think them."

Simon Walker used two totally different kinds of routers as he planned his path round the world on *Toshiba Wave Warrior*. He felt that by so doing he would be able to analyse both very varied concepts and then make a decision. This was Conceptual Flexibility working to great effect.

Developmental

This cluster of behaviours is critical to flat flexible team based structures. These behaviours help build ownership, involvement and commitment. They ensure that the contributions of each team member are recognised and nurtured. The three behaviours in this cluster are Empathy, Teamwork and Developing People.

Empathy – Several of the skippers had a real problem in empathising with their amateur crew members. To a professional sailor, with thousands of miles of sailing experience, this behaviour was almost inexplicable. As tiredness and seasickness took their toll, it almost seemed as if all of the training before the race had either been a complete waste of time or largely forgotten. Merfyn Owen compensated by trying to do everything himself. Boris Webber admitted to an enormous frustration which often surfaced as harsh correction of faults being made. It was only after a three hour debrief with his crew in Rio, during which the crew complained bitterly of Webber's short fuse, that he started to understand the totally different demands of skippering an amateur crew. This process was to continue until arrival in Boston. The development of Boris' relationship with his crew inspired their improving placings during the race.

Teamwork – The first leg also provided the first real opportunity to test the extent to which the crews were able to operate as teams or whether, individually, they would withdraw into their own private world as the going got tough. Some of the skippers had invested considerably more training time in developing team dynamics within the crew than others. This investment started to pay off immediately. Two particularly cohesive crews from the outset were those of *Concert* and *3Com*. In both cases, the skippers Chris Tibbs and Dave Tomkinson had adopted an almost patriarchal style of leadership from the start. The climate on both yachts was one of quiet confidence and encouragement rather than the volatile blame culture that emerged on some other yachts. The fact that both Chris and Dave were two of the older skippers, whose sailing careers included many voyages skippering large charter boats with paying guests, contributed largely to their quietly competent approach. Significantly, by the end of the race not one of Chris Tibbs' crew could remember him raising his voice in anger.

Another crew which had identified a set of values to which they adhered for the rest of the voyage was that of *Toshiba Wave Warrior* skippered by the youngest skipper in the race, Simon Walker. Simon's self-effacing enthusiasm coupled with a natural empathy and charm found great favour with his relatively young crew. The crew's confidence in its own ability grew rapidly under Simon's quiet coaching and encouragement. The spirit that emerged was to be the mainstay of the yacht's performance throughout the race. Simon himself experienced a level of homesickness that surprised him and others but he quickly adopted a self discipline whenever loneliness struck - he went down below and washed the dishes! This quiet return to domesticity and working for his new family seemed to do the trick and he

71

would soon be back on deck. Teamwork can take many forms.

Developing People – The whole ethos of The Challenge was to have "ordinary people doing extraordinary things." To describe the crew volunteers as "ordinary people" would be a disservice but for many crew members, personal development was high on their agenda for the race. Many of the skippers also realised that the key to success lay in developing the crews to their full potential quickest. On several yachts, not only were the skippers developing their crew members through continuous and painstaking coaching, but, more interestingly, crew members were cross-training in the various specialist skills that they had picked up in the pre-race training. One skipper admitted that eventually his crew was teaching itself through shared experience rather than depending on him; he did not complain.

Building Confidence – One of the differences between the skippers that emerged early on in the race was their perception of the extent to which crew members needed recognition of their efforts on the yacht. At one extreme, one skipper never gave praise because he expected total dedication and professionalism at all times. Several skippers introduced a more structured approach – one jelly baby for a good job, two for an outstanding one. This may appear to have been a simplistic and condescending approach but such was the level of banter and humour developed on these yachts that the jelly babies were seen for what they were — a visible token of recognition.

It is interesting that several skippers, completely independently, reached the same conclusion. The absence of 'thank you' and 'well done' was to be a real sadness for some of the crew members throughout the voyage. For others, the public humiliation of being shouted at by a tired and frustrated skipper proved a bitter pill to swallow, particularly when so many crew members held positions of great responsibility themselves in 'civilian' jobs. Equally, several skippers commented that whereas they tried to praise their crew when appropriate, the crew never praised them. Those yachts who arrived in Rio well down the rankings had to pick themselves up and start again – another test of a skipper's ability to instil confidence for the leg ahead.

Achieving

These behaviours are crucial for making things happen and blasting through bureaucracy. They ensure that the tasks are structured and that plans and ideas are implemented. They ensure that people are given responsibility and encourage continuous attention to be paid to improving the performance of all aspects of the team.

Continuous Improvement – Every tack, every sail change and every meal provided an opportunity for debrief, reflection and improvement. Not every skipper grasped those opportunities. Some yachts did not have a single crew debrief on the whole leg. Others painstakingly analysed every bad move as well as every good one to see what could be corrected and improved. On *Toshiba Wave Warrior*, Continuous Improvement almost became a way of life – a classic demonstration of a Level 5 behaviour at its best (see page 29). The end result was a steady and sustained improvement in performance which resulted in *Toshiba Wave Warrior* being consistently one of the front runners throughout the race. Significantly, the bulk of the Continuous Improvement had been initiated by the crew rather than by the skipper.

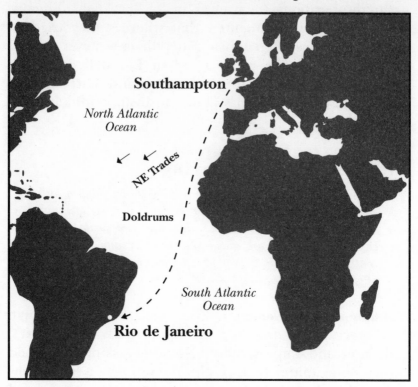

LEG 1 RESULTS

Position	Arrival Time (GMT)	Leg Time D H M S	Overall Position
1 Group 4	25 Oct 14:52:15	26 03 47 15	1
2 Toshiba Wave Warrior	25 Oct 17:01:11	26 05 56 11	2
3 Concert	26 Oct 01:57:23	26 14 52 23	3
4 Save The Children	26 Oct 09:10:39	26 22 05 39	4
5 Commercial Union	26 Oct 18:03:49	27 06 58 49	5
6 3Com	26 Oct 20:39:38	27 09 34 38	6
7 Motorola	27 Oct 01:35:55	27 14 30 55	7
8 Heath Insured II	27 Oct 03:37:03	27 16 32 03	8
9 Ocean Rover	27 Oct 05:34:48	27 18 29 48	9
10 Nuclear Electric	27 Oct 07:35:15	27 20 30 15	10
11 Global Teamwork	28 Oct 06:48:23	28 19 43 23	11
12 Pause To Remember	28 Oct 21:41:10	29 10 36 10	12
13 Courtaulds International	29 Oct 08:19:58	29 21 14 58	13
14 Time & Tide	29 Oct 10:45:33	29 23 40 33	14

CHAPTER FIVE

*"Victories that are easy are cheap. When they come
as a result of hard work, they are priceless."*
Henry Beecher

Chay Blyth assembled the crews and told them what
they could expect to face. "You are now embarking on
the first interesting part of The Challenge," he said
addressing the crews in the Rio yacht club cinema. "You
will start with a pleasant sail down the coast of South
America with the winds coming across the land mass
which will give you protection from heavy seas. Then
you will turn right and hit the ferocity of the Southern
Ocean with seas that have been churning round the
world's surface uninterrupted by any major land mass.
The westerly winds, continuous storms and currents,
coupled with the rotation of the earth, mean that huge
seas build up, with rough waves on top of massive swells.
Once this energy hits the constriction provided by Cape
Horn and the land mass of Antarctica, it combines with
a depth reduction from 10,000 to 1,000ft. The water
piles up on itself which produces even larger seas and
much shorter troughs. It is a bit like a concertina that is
suddenly squeezed together. During storms, these
swells will be travelling at you at between 15 and 18
knots on a collision course with your yacht travelling
the other way at eight knots. You will find that some of
the waves have no back and your yachts will fall into the
trough some 30ft below with a tremendous crash. The
first time you hear this sound, you will think that the
yacht will never survive the impact. However, remember
that these yachts have already been tested through
these waters and are built to withstand anything the sea

75

can throw at you. "I offer you two pieces of advice. Keep one hand for the yacht and one for yourself, and get into deep water as fast as you can.   Good luck and see you in Wellington."

RIO DE JANEIRO TO WELLINGTON

Leg 2

The crews had a terrific send-off in Rio de Janeiro with a party and prize-giving organised by BT at the Iata Club of Brazil.

Peter Vroon – The fleet had been saddened a few days earlier by the sudden death in Rio of Peter Vroon who worked for the sailmakers Hood. Peter had been in charge of repairing all of the sails the fleet had blown in the voyage from Southampton.

A Dutchman, Peter had a wonderfully cheerful disposition and all the fleet knew him. He had established a sail inspection area at the yacht club and was always chatting with passing crew members and helping them to inspect sails for damage. He was taken ill in his hotel on a Saturday evening, collapsed at 3am in the foyer of his hotel and died the following evening from meningitis.

The Challenge Business reacted quickly and all of the crews were told of the tragedy on the Monday. There was then the mammoth logistical task of getting all of the crews and families vaccinated. This required a search of the pharmacies of Rio to obtain as much vaccine as possible and further supplies to be flown in from Europe. The fleet's doctors then set up a vaccination clinic and completed the task within the deadline, while everyone mourned Peter's death.

The following poem was written by a crew member on *Ocean Rover* perhaps reflecting what Peter might be saying.

> *Do not forget me*
> *Dear lost companions*
> *Now that my soul*
> *is turned to the west.*

I see your faces
Lit by the sunset
Friends of The Challenge
Dearest and best.

In memory of our friend Peter Vroon

Many of the crew attended a service held in the yacht club chapel. This included an address by Andrew Roberts, the Race Director, who had worked very closely with Peter Vroon, and a poem written and recited by Susie Goulder, a crew member on *Courtaulds International.* It was a very sad day for the whole fleet and particularly for Mark Lodge on *Motorola.* He had been a good friend of Peter's and had been with him the day he collapsed.

The Re-start – The crews were anxious to get going. The initial part of The Challenge was over. The first leg was the dress rehearsal. Now they faced the terror of rounding Cape Horn and 6,600 miles across the Southern Ocean which was, by reputation, the most barren and fearsome part of any ocean in the world. To most crew members this was the real Challenge.

There was a lot of anxiety on the dock as the yachts and crews prepared to leave. No-one seemed to know what was in store for them. The six skippers who had been before were constantly being asked what Cape Horn and the Southern Ocean were like. The crews all knew that Chay Blyth had been round Cape Horn four times and on the last trip had been overturned in the trimaran *Beefeater* spending 19 hours on the upturned hull in massive seas and freezing waters before he had been rescued. He was indeed lucky to be alive. Would the same catastrophe occur this time? The Challenge yachts were not trimarans and so the risk of sinking was greater.

Two hours before the yachts were due to leave their moorings, a crew member on *Motorola* decided he could not face another leg and told the skipper he wanted to get off the yacht. Mark Lodge escorted him forlornly to the shore in a rubber dinghy and he sadly walked away. The yacht duly left the mooring an hour later than they had planned, one crew member short. One hour later, the reluctant crew member radioed that he had changed his mind and would like to return to carry on with the race. He was placed in another dinghy and motored out to rejoin the yacht. This may have seemed bizarre behaviour, but with such apprehension and the unknown Southern Ocean ahead, it was perhaps understandable.

The yachts left Rio in the same still, glassy conditions that they had arrived in, except that it was now raining with low cloud. Without doubt, all the crews and skippers were glad to leave and get into the start of the real Challenge.

Group 4 made a terrible start and was seen close to the beach as the other yachts ghosted around the same critical buoy that they had rounded on arrival at the end of the first leg. Such was *Group 4's* reputation for professionalism and tactics that the rest of the fleet could scarcely believe its initial course and thought there was some cunning plan afoot. In reality, it was a miscalculation on Mike Golding's part; he took the yacht too close to the beach and was affected by the swell which stops a yacht dead in light winds. Even the experienced make mistakes but it was not long before Mike and *Group 4* reasserted themselves and sailed through half the fleet.

The westerly wind which had come from the Pacific over the land mass of South America blew briskly once the fleet was south of Rio. With warm weather, the race was continuing in pleasant conditions. The crews enjoyed the sunshine and shorts and T-shirts were the order of the day. It was hard to believe that they were heading for the Southern Ocean and the cold.

The racing was closely fought down the South American coast with half the fleet going out to sea to get local tidal streams and the other half forsaking tide for the shorter route. The decision to take the inshore route also

78

risked falling foul of the slight wind shadow from the land; a series of compromises and calculations that are a feature of ocean racing.

As the fleet approached the Falkland Islands, the sea temperature suddenly dropped some 14 degrees centigrade in as many hours as the Antarctic current swept around Cape Horn and up the Southern Atlantic. Close behind this drop in sea temperature came the first gale and, with 40 knots of wind, the first huge seas. It was a baptism of fire as suddenly the crews had to don all their battle dress for the first time and get used to the critical safety procedures which were to become an automatic and essential way of life for this leg.

All of the crews wore four basic layers to keep them warm and protect them from the spray and water that would continuously drench them. Underwear comprised silk long johns and a long sleeved vest. On top of this were long thermals, covered with a third layer consisting of a fleece-lined jacket and trousers. The bright yellow or bright red yachtsman's foul weather gear, so familiar in any yachting photographs, was the final layer.

"Here I am, dressed up in black silk long johns looking like ballet dancer," commented a 6ft 2 inch 15 stone ex-rugby playing crew member on *Ocean Rover*. "If my friends back home could see me dressed like this, I would never be taken seriously again."

In the freezing cold with the yachts crashing and banging in the hostile ocean, few crew members undressed beyond their foul weather gear. Many who had never worn silk before became converted by its warmth and capacity to dry quickly.

Off the South American coast, *Heath Insured II* hit a massive wave while changing a sail which effectively wiped out the crew on deck and caused extensive injuries. Four people on the foredeck were washed into various sharp pieces of deck equipment and three suffered injuries ranging from cracked ribs to a fractured collar bone. The skipper Adrian Donovan ended up wrapped around the mast and the force of the water was such that the new sail, which was lying on the deck, was washed into the cockpit. Angus McPhie was wrenched off the helm and ended up against the guardrail while Sally Stewart, who was manning the mainsail, was thrown across the cockpit.

This was a sample of the hostile environment which was to become a feature of everyday life in the weeks to come.

Surprisingly, some crew members resented being called on deck to do sail changes when they were officially off watch. Being woken after one hour's sleep caused a lot of bad tempers. The crew had come from all walks of life; some were used to a fairly predictable and regimented environment and began to resent the upheaval and unpredictability of racing a yacht over long distances in such a competitive environment. There was also a lack of understanding of what actual racing entailed. All of the crews had been taught how to handle the equipment, but days at sea with the frenetic activity essential to make a yacht travel consistently fast was a new discipline.

"I was woken up halfway through my sleep to be summoned on deck to change a sail," said a crew member. "By the time I'd got dressed, the wind had eased and I was told this change was not necessary. I really resented this at first but later on in the race I began to understand that sailing the yacht fast was the primary objective and weather didn't wait for shift changes."

One crew member remarked later in the race that he found it significant that people who had been self-employed reacted differently from those who were used to working for big organisations. When some of the leggers joined the yachts, they found it took time to adjust from a working environment which was organised and predictable, to the uncertain environment of ocean racing. The leggers joined for one leg courtesy of their employers and sponsors and they tended not to be self-employed. They were representative of many corporate employees. It became a

Andrew Dare

n board the BT training yacht, crew volunteers undertake navigation work,
arning how to use a sextant and take sun readings.

ctualling the yacht was an essential part of race preparation. Freeze-dried food
d boil-in-the-bag meals were selected for longevity and ease of preparation.

Mark Pepper

HRH The Princess Royal and Sir Peter Bonfield, Chief Executive Officer of BT, brave the lashing rain and gale force wind on race start day along with hundreds of spectators.

The *Duc de Normandie*, moored in The Solent, from which HRH The Princess Royal fired the race start gun at 1205 hrs on Sunday 29 September, 1996.

Mark Pepper

ind speeds reach 37 knots as *Nuclear Electric* battles her way out of the The Solent.

Mark Pepp

Global Teamwork's crew line the rail as they enter the English Channel.

Hello!   Andrew Fernandez

Goodbye!   Andrew Da

Wildlife accompanies the fleet as it crosses the Equator.

Richard Langdon

he Statue of Christ welcomes *Commercial Union* to Rio de Janeiro.

Humphrey Walter

After rounding Cape Horn, the yachts head south into the Furious Fifties and Screaming Sixties.

Festive cheer and high spirits as the crew of *Ocean Rover* celebrate Christmas at sea.

Humphrey Walter

Robert Bruce

typical day in the Southern Pacific Ocean – life at an angle!

oom dipping – the helmsman's nightmare.

Humphrey Walters

Mark Pepp[...]

A happy crew, an unhappy yacht – the dismasted *Concert* arrives in Wellington.

An ocean racer's washing line – drying out at the end of the first Southern Ocean leg.

Stephen Munda[...]

part of the crew's banter that the leggers operated by the clock and if it was not their shift they were not particularly concerned about a sail change or some other yacht manoeuvre. The self-employed people seemed to accept the regime more easily and resorted far less frequently to clock watching or shiftwork. Nevertheless, the leggers also brought a freshness and enthusiasm which helped the morale on the yacht and they almost always proved to be popular.

Some of the crew experienced a new concept of who was responsible for what. The Challenge ethos was for self-sufficiency. There was no outside help available to help the crews repair something when they were 2,500 miles from land. The talents within the crew were the only resource available.

One night, the sidetape of one of the bunks broke, sending the sleeping occupant to the floor with a mildly bruised shoulder. The indignant crew member went to skipper Mark Lodge "My bunk is broken Mark," he said. "So?" replied Mark curtly as he walked to another part of the yacht. There was no bunk department to ring up, no facilities manager to complain to, no warehouse to ring up and order a replacement - just needle and thread or no sleep. Welcome to the world of self-sufficiency.

A Meeting With The Royal Navy And Demonstrations Of Human Frailty – Nearing the Falklands Islands came the first signs of human vulnerability. Kurt Kinast on *Save The Children* became ill. Andy Hindley, the skipper, had put out an emergency call to get help. The procedure was both simple and efficient. Whenever there is a medical emergency at sea, all ships in the area are notified and obliged to render assistance if they are able to provide the help that is required. *HMS Lancaster*, a Royal Naval warship, was in the vicinity on exercise and immediately came on the radio to offer help. From the ensuing conversation, it was clear that the ship was prepared to evacuate Kurt Kinart and give medical help on board from their ship's doctor. Once the situation had been assessed they would then arrange for the appropriate medical assistance.

They dispatched a fast rubber dinghy with two sailors on board and came alongside *Save The Children*. They quickly plucked Kurt from the deck into the dinghy and were gone. Kurt was eventually sent to Montevideo and evacuated back to Austria. He did not rejoin the race.

Paul Bennett, the skipper of *Ocean Rover*, had been in the Navy for 20 years and could not resist some naval conversation with the Captain.

"Hello Captain, this is Paul Bennett, skipper of *Ocean Rover*, fast on your starboard bow."

"Hello skipper, this is the Captain of Warship Lancaster."

"I thought I would give you a call. I am ex-RN 20. The Ark. Middle East MacV. commficer.proc.3rd class med ptrl 69-75 weapon specialist 6."

"Oh that's interesting. I wasn't MacV Middle East. But saw Ark. Was 2nd Lute Pinnacle then navicer Porpoise windies patrol 78."

"Roger, then I went to C sat comm. D procurement. CPC Intl/Pacific then finally to Mono sat prem. class with 1st MG Plym."

"Roger all that. I am presently Captain 22 class stlth warship classified code 43/456 A code red status South Atlantic."

"Well it's been nice talking to you Captain. This is Paul Bennett standing by on channel 16."

"Thanks skipper and good luck to you all. This is Captain HMS Lancaster standing by."

A totally unintelligible conversation to all of the crew but perhaps an illustration of the camaraderie and help, as well as the joy of jargon, which is a feature of life at sea.

The human dramas continued just 36 hours later with Rhian Jenkins of *Global Teamwork*. She had been ill for a couple of days but the crew had no idea how serious the problem was. The symptoms indicated a suspected ulcer and should she get worse while the yacht was deep in the Southern Ocean with no hope of evacuation, the situation could become critical.

John Scott, a dentist who was the medical officer on board *Global Teamwork*, was liaising with the fleet doctor as well as the Naval Hospital at Haslar in Portsmouth. The decision was made to evacuate Rhian Jenkins to Port Stanley. There were two options. The first was for the yacht to divert and drop her off, the second was a helicopter evacuation from the deck of the yacht. Rhian was adamant that the yacht should not change course and lose crucial time in diversion so the RAF offered to send out a helicopter and winch her off the deck.

Elaine Adams, who was a Royal National Lifeboat Institute member from Poole in Dorset, was put in charge of the evacuation. *Global Teamwork* had practised such an emergency in The Solent before the race started, and Elaine had been involved in several simulations with the coastguard before so they were not worried about the actual evacuation procedures. What worried the crew more was the loss of a fellow crew member and a good friend.

"I tried to imagine what Rhian was feeling," said Elaine Adams. "The only word I could come up with was devastated. The evacuation itself went very smoothly, exactly as we had practised. The crew of the helicopter was a little shocked when the skipper Merfyn Owen told them that we were racing and did not want to slow down. They made a couple of passes to assess the speed of the yacht before they lowered a crewman.

The pilot plucked Rhian off the deck and then made a second pass to pick up her bag. We approached the task just like all the major procedures we carried out on *Global Teamwork*. We planned it, allocated tasks and just got on with it. I will never forget Rhian's face at the window looking down at the yacht for the final time before she was whisked away. I had to finish the washing-up with my eyes full of tears. Then we got back to racing again."

The whole crew of the yacht was very impressed by the speed and efficiency of the operation and they only learned later that it was the pilot's first rescue from a yacht at sea.

Rhian recovered completely, rejoined the yacht in Wellington and completed the race.

The Yachts Round Cape Horn – After the Falklands, it was a mere 200 miles before the yachts reached Staten Island. This marked the last landfall they would see as they entered the Southern Ocean and rounded Cape Horn, named in 1616 by the Dutch discoverer, Willem Schouten, after the town of Hoorn, his birthplace in Holland.

The fleet had been warned that when they turned the corner past Staten Island into the Straits of Magellan it would look and feel like a lock gate opening. So it was to prove.

The disappointment for most of the crews was that they passed some 60 miles south of Cape Horn and never saw the treacherous piece of land that they had talked so much about. The aim of the yachts was to go south, the shortest route to the deepest water and less turbulent seas. It was not long before the fleet encountered the severe gale force winds, storms and massive seas of which they had been warned.

Working on deck changing sails in 40 knot winds and freezing water, on a yacht which is crashing through massive seas at a 40 degree angle is a daunting experience. The fear created by facing these conditions, with the worst of the weather seemingly at night, took its toll on the crew. Would the wind increase and make a sail change necessary? Would they get through their watch without the dangers of a sail change? The on-watch crew would be transfixed by the wind speed gauge looking for a change in wind speed.

The approach to the Falklands had also been a testing time for James Hatfield on *Time & Tide*. The leg down to Rio had not been a happy one for his inexperienced and under-trained crew of disabled people. Three crew members had retired from the race in Rio for personal reasons and had been replaced by even more inexperienced sailors. Although the crew started to settle down again on leaving Rio, James Hatfield was still not convinced of their ability to deal with the rigours that he knew lay ahead. The combination of disabilities within the crew resulted in every sail change and every course change taking several times longer than the rest of the fleet. Should James take them beyond the last outpost of the Falklands or retire before the inevitable disaster struck? After detailed discussions with his first mate Chris Ogg, James decided to continue. The look of joy and satisfaction on the faces of his crew arriving safely into Southampton eight months later proved him right.

Safety discipline became paramount as the combination of wind and sea became progressively more intimidating. One crew member on *Heath Insured II* confessed to being physically sick when asked to go on deck in these conditions.

"Clip on before you leave the safety of the companionway and come on deck," shouted Mike Golding on *Group 4* to crew member Andrea Bacon. "I was hanging on with both hands trying to climb on deck," she described. "The yacht was heeling over at 35 degrees and the effort to get up the steps was beyond belief. Terrified and speechless, I huddled low, clipped on, and held onto the nearest secure object as the waves crashed over my head. The one thing I was dreading was having to let go and do something."

Surviving More Than Sailing – As the yachts entered the Southern Ocean and sailed through the most remote part of the planet, rigging failures began to occur. The first indication of problems was with *3Com* who reported that its forestay had broken with a crack like a rifle shot. This was a major blow as it was the primary wire stay which held the mast up.

Skippers were suddenly reminded of poor Richard Tudor

and *British Steel II* which had been dismasted in the last race at almost the same position. Five days later disaster struck. The yacht *Concert* suddenly reported that its entire rig had collapsed like a pack of cards and snapped the mast some 15ft above the deck. Luckily the crew managed to cut all the rigging away before any major damage was done to the hull by the pieces of mast clattering against the side in the rough seas.

This failure caused all the yachts to send people aloft in horrific conditions to check all the rigging. Every yacht was affected and the worst sufferers seemed to be *Heath Insured II* and *Toshiba Wave Warrior.*

The dangers of long distance yacht racing and the effects of the hostile environment jolted the amateur sailors into the reality of the 'World's Toughest Yacht Race'. Equipment *did* break and disaster was likely to happen at any moment. The essence of The Challenge was to be prepared for such eventualities and for the crews to use all available skill and ingenuity to look after its resources.

Suddenly The Challenge had more to do with survival than sailing.

Adrian Donovan on *Heath Insured II* had the mammoth task of keeping his yacht from losing its rig in an identical way to *Concert.* A gentle giant of a man standing 6ft 5in, Adrian spent the best part of three days hoisted up the mast, replacing parts of the rigging. It took five of the crew to hoist him skywards and they kept sending cups of coffee aloft in a bucket rather than allow him below as the crew felt he was too heavy to hoist back up again. Given the freezing conditions and the size of the sea, which caused the mast to sway some 40ft from side to side, it really was a Herculean effort.

Simon Walker on *Toshiba Wave Warrior* had kept very quiet about his rigging problems but had had to replace one complete side of the rigging. He had given the crew a pep talk and told them that they must helm the yacht very carefully on the opposite tack, as the rigging was only holding up one side of the mast.

"Just remember," he warned the helmsman with a

rueful smile, "if you make a mistake while I am up the mast I will crash down over the side with the mast and entire rig on top of me."

Paul Bennett on *Ocean Rover* showed similar courage. He had found some strands of broken wire and had to dismantle the forestay from the top of the mast, lower the entire length of wire onto the deck and refit the screw fitting. After a team on *Ocean Rover* had wrestled for six hours in the galley to remove and refit the masthead fitting, Paul was winched aloft to refit this crucial length of rigging.

"We only had one securing pin which was the final part to fit to complete the repair. If anyone was going to drop it I thought it should be me!" stated Paul after the successful reinstallation.

Every yacht successfully maintained and repaired all its rigging and, save for the unlucky *Concert*, managed to complete the journey into Wellington unscathed. A wonderful indictment of the courage, ingenuity and professionalism which was a feature of The Challenge.

These incidents took their toll on the crews. Being continually battered by the fierce seas and winds, and having to live in a cold dank atmosphere, inevitably produced interpersonal problems.

Boris Webber, skipper of *Courtaulds International*, was attacked by a crew member with a knife.

Boris described the situation: "I discussed a plan of action with our medic and it was decided that the crew member needed a course of tranquilisers to help him settle down. However he would have been suspicious if we had offered him some pills to take. I knew he liked porridge and so I decided to cook some for breakfast, put the tranquilisers in one bowl and then eat with him.

Inevitably, I was called on deck at the crucial time leaving the two bowls sitting on the galley table. On my return, I found both bowls had been moved ready for us to eat. I was now unsure which bowl contained the tranquilisers. I suggested he ate both bowls which he did and he was effectively knocked out in his bunk for four days. It would have been interesting if I had eaten the wrong bowl in this part of the Southern Ocean," Boris added.

Before the start of the race, Chay Blyth had planned for problems such as this and each skipper had a secret code. He arranged for a coded message to be sent to them all, warning them of the situation, and asking them to be vigilant for any similar breakdown on their own yachts.

The crew member from *Courtaulds International* left the yacht in Wellington and returned to the UK for medical help.

The Dismasting Of *Concert* – Back on *Concert*, the crisis with the rigging had bound the crew together into a very tight unit. Once they recovered from the shock of the dismasting, they set to work to ensure they would reach Wellington and bring the yacht safely home. Chris Tibbs, a veteran of two Whitbread Round the World Races, had been busy calculating the amount of diesel he would need to motor to the closest landfall, Chatham Island, situated some 600 miles east of New Zealand. The strength of the Challenge fleet lay in the expertise of the skippers and the camaraderie between the crews. Here was a yacht in trouble and the whole fleet responded to bring one of their own to safety.

Concert had enough diesel to take her 800 miles and it was worked out that she would need three refuellings along the route. These had to coincide with her tanks being empty so that she could get the maximum mileage before refuelling. The yacht needed to keep ahead of the fleet so that it could get fuel before everyone disappeared over the horizon.

The first rendezvous was arranged with *Motorola* which proved to be an outstanding feat of seamanship. *Motorola* transferred 100 gallons of diesel to *Concert*, four gallons at a time, with both yachts motoring some 40ft apart in a rolling sea.

88

Mark Lodge recalls: "The first problem we had was to find *Concert*. Despite our satellite navigation systems a dismasted yacht in such a big sea with deep troughs and massive swells is very difficult to find. Eventually we saw her and were shocked at the sight of this beautiful yacht in such a crippled state - a really sad sight.

However we soon got to work to rig a transfer system which enabled us to relay the diesel cans between the yachts. It took us two hours and the whole operation went faultlessly despite the difficulty of keeping the yachts close together. With no mast, *Concert* was very unstable and rolling badly. We were more stable.

Concert wanted to give us a present which I refused as quite unnecessary and also on the grounds of 'receiving outside assistance.' Chris then told me it was film for Reuters which they wanted delivered as *Motorola* would get in before them. Having received the package we discovered it was in fact chocolate. We sent over a bottle of malt whisky which I discovered two days later was our last bottle!

We then watched them motor off into the distance as we resumed sailing. There wasn't a dry eye on either yacht and Chris Tibbs told me in Wellington that they had felt very small but not alone."

The next rendezvous was with James Hatfield and *Time & Tide*. This time it was *Time & Tide* that was in need. James Hatfield was desperate for antibiotics for an injured crew member and *Concert* turned back retracing some 100 miles to participate in a drugs for oil deal in the South Pacific Ocean. *Concert's* final rendezvous was with *Courtaulds International* when a further 80 gallons of diesel were exchanged for chocolate, a Fortnum & Mason Christmas cake, dumpling mix and cigars! Southern Ocean bartering at its best. *Concert* was now 400 miles from Chatham Island and confident that its fuel supplies would last. Skipper Chris Tibbs increased the pressure on the throttle and, to the delight of his crew, the yacht speed increased from five to eight knots an hour.

Chris and the crew of *Concert* celebrated New Year's Eve on Chatham Island. The rest of the fleet received a fax from the Commodore of the Chatham Island Yacht Club which read : "We have just said good-bye to *Concert*. Please note that you don't have to be dismasted to come and visit us!"

Hurricane Fergus – Just before the fleet arrived in New Zealand, there was a final sting in the tail for some of the yachts. The fleet had been monitoring the movement of Hurricane Fergus which was sweeping through the tip of the North Island of New Zealand. It was expected to continue travelling south west which meant that some of the yachts would benefit from the wind on the periphery of the hurricane to blow them home. As often happens once it had left the environment of the land it turned due south forcing the majority of the fleet to sail straight through the middle.

There was nowhere else to go.

With this news came the normal trepidation within the crews that the skippers were finding so difficult to handle. After the dismasting of *Concert* everyone was concerned about the mast and rigging. Would they last? What happens if we get dismasted?

"I had already been dismasted in the previous race and here we were again with the prospect of a similar problem. The one bit of good news for us was that we were closer to land and probably had enough diesel to make it if disaster struck," said Richard Tudor aboard *Nuclear Electric*.

All the yachts carried out rigging checks and reinforced the rigging with any available halyard. The inter-yacht chatshow was dominated by skippers sharing information on what they had done to reinforce their rigging. As competitive as the racing was, no-one wanted another yacht to suffer the disaster of losing the entire rig, let alone expose the crew to danger.

The camaraderie created an environment of mutual support demonstrated so ably by *Motorola*, *Time & Tide*, and *Courtaulds International* coming to the aid of *Concert*.

The hurricane started to hit the yachts during the afternoon of New Year's Eve with the wind reaching 60 knots within three hours. The one bizarre difference was that the water was relatively warm and for most of the crew it seemed strange to be helming in a storm with no gloves on.

On one yacht a crew member went happily off watch greeting the new team with a "Happy New Year and Good Luck." Three hours later he was thrown out of his bunk.

A Happy New Year indeed.

Jon Hirsh on *Ocean Rover* described the conditions. "Once we were in the teeth of the storm I found the size of the scenery quite remarkable. It seemed to me the whole world was uphill with enormous undulating hills of water with massive valleys. It seemed to be more permanent than water. The waves colliding provided foam which turned aquamarine once the initial boiling fury had settled. Every few minutes a rogue wave would come in from the side and collide with a terrific impact; helming through this turbulence was a case of hanging on and hoping for the best."

Despite all the skill that had now been acquired by the helmsmen there were some impossible conditions. *Ocean Rover* was hit by a 70ft rogue wave which picked the yacht off the surface and threw it some 50 yards sideways onto its port side.

People below started emerging like hedgehogs ending a hibernation, wondering what had happened. Some sleeping crew had the entire contents of the opposite cabin deposited on their bunks and objects in the galley were flung from one side to the other.

The computer printer, secured firmly in its own closed cupboard, ended up in pieces against the opposite wall. This was followed in the opposite direction by a saucepan the size of a bucket, full of spaghetti, flying off the stove and landing firmly embedded in the bookshelf. The safest place in such weather was on deck. At least the crew could see what was coming at them and had a chance of protecting themselves."

On *Nuclear Electric,* the thought of going through the hurricane after Richard Tudor's concern for the rig was a daunting one. Its track took it right through the middle.

"We survived the first half of the hurricane and came to the eye of the storm - something I had read about but never really believed. Sure enough we suddenly came into the lull. A bizarre sight with the big seas and no wind. Then the mayhem started again and we shot out the other side as though we were being spat out by some enormous wind god. The crew were more relieved to see me relax than they were about the conditions!"

The Arrival In New Zealand – Finally the first leg of the Southern Ocean was coming to an end. Some 30 miles off the coast of New Zealand, Lyn Guy on *Ocean Rover* described how she could smell land and, in particular, new mown hay.

"In the beginning I felt disbelief. I thought I was imagining things with no sight of land. Then I saw a line of low clouds and began to realise I was actually looking at the mountainous coast of New Zealand. I felt tremendous euphoria that I had made it. I had never been exposed to such conditions before and felt an inner pride that I had been able to cope. Yes, it was a good feeling!"

Yet again, most of the yachts were becalmed trying to get into the rocky approaches to Wellington Harbour.

Ahead of the crews was the prospect of a meal, a beer and the euphoria that comes with the welcome they knew was in store for them when they arrived at the dockside. After all they felt proud and it is good to be treated as a hero once in your life.

"My crew are heroes to have endured such a journey. I am proud of what they have achieved," Paul Bennett, skipper of *Ocean Rover*, commented.

Just behind *Ocean Rover*, came *3Com*, followed closely by *Time & Tide* in 11th position. The latter's arrival was eagerly awaited. A huge crowd had gathered on Wellington waterfront to welcome these heroes in. But the sight of an ambulance parked on the dockside brought a tear to many eyes. Two crew members had suffered many weeks in pain, one having lost more than two stone, and another having broken his only leg after a fellow crew member had been thrown across the deck and landed on him. Both were taken off the yacht, one on a stretcher, and transported to the local hospital. Brendan West's bones mended quicker than expected and he rejoined the yacht in Cape Town. John Rich sadly never rejoined the yacht. He recovered sufficiently to return home to Sydney and enthusiastically meet the yachts on their arrival at the end of the next leg.

To bring this leg of The Challenge to an end the fleet expectantly waited for the arrival of *Concert*. For Richard Tudor this was a special moment. Although *Nuclear Electric* had been deliberately dismasted in port to have new rigging fitted he insisted on motoring out to escort *Concert* home. It was bizarre seeing two dismasted yachts coming in side by side with *Concert* looking like an Arab dhow with her jury rig.

On the dockside, there was a tremendous throng of crew sitting waiting in the sunshine. As the yacht motored slowly round the corner to sirens and fog horns there was hardly a dry eye.

For Chris Tibbs and his crew the reception was some consolation but their race was run. Satisfaction for them perhaps that they had used their ingenuity to arrive safely, and had become a close knit crew who will never forget the experience. Extreme frustration, however, for such a veteran competitive sailor as Chris to have any chance of winning sadly taken away from him.

Dare anyone say to him or his crew,"That's what The Challenge is all about."

WHAT MADE THE DIFFERENCE

This was the leg in which many individuals finally discovered their true potential. Fear was a wonderful leveller which stripped away all pretension. The less flamboyant crew members often proved to be the more resilient under stress. Equally, the contribution of the crew jesters in the cold sullen world of the Southern Ocean often lifted spirits of those numbed to the core. Mutual respect developed through the shared conquest of the angry seas. Nothing binds individuals together more strongly than shared and conquered fear - and the Southern Ocean was the ultimate threatening environment.

Thinking

Information Search – Skippers were now delegating more of this all-important task to crew members who avidly took up the challenge. Richard Merriweather on *Commercial Union* appointed two meteorologists and two navigators who worked together for five days before leaving Rio to collate information. He also used a private router. An important side effect of all of the information collecting that went on was that there is little doubt that knowledge dispels fear. Those crews who knew what to expect were undoubtedly less apprehensive than those who did not, however horrific that prospect was.

Developmental

Empathy – Mutual respect and trust had developed during the first leg and at the same time so had the levels of empathy among most crew members and skippers. One major issue was that of mutual respect between male and female crew members. Many of the men changed their initial chauvinist dismissal of the lack of physical strength of some of the women to an admiration of their sailing skills and resilience under pressure. Andrea Bacon was very concerned on being allocated to the crew of *Group 4* as she thought Mike Golding might not appreciate female crew in his highly competitive team. She realised that the converse was true as evidenced by Mike assigning Amanda Tristram as one of the two watchleaders.

Communication also became a problem in a world dominated by survival and cold. Richard Merriweather made a special effort to ensure that the lines of communication among his crew always remained open and he and his watchleaders paid particular attention to ensuring that no-one was left out or allowed to withdraw into depression. On the other hand, personal privacy had to be respected. A 67ft yacht could quickly become claustrophobic. Skippering the yachts became as much about successful counselling as it did about sailing.

Teamwork – Teamwork again emerged as a race winning factor. Some skippers felt that they almost had to start building their teams again on leaving Rio de Janeiro because of crew changes. Seven yachts had crew changes at Rio and *Time & Tide* had three new members which made James Hatfield's already demanding task more difficult.

One dimension of teamwork was the great variance in how skippers organised their crew. Their first decision was whether or not to have a mate. Most did not, but the role of *Time & Tide's* mate, Chris Ogg, was vital. It is one thing for a skipper to make life threatening decisions, but for the skipper of a disabled yacht to make those same decisions it requires the counsel of a good mate. The next decision was how many watches to have. Most favoured two main watches with a small supplementary 'motherwatch' to cover housekeeping below decks. Others, including Tom O'Connor, favoured three watches as it allowed him to have more people on deck for crucial sail changes without totally disrupting sleep patterns.

A major issue was whether strong competition between watches was healthy or not. Several skippers admitted that they allowed healthy rivalry to get out of hand with the result that watches barely talked to each other. However, Dave Tomkinson on *3Com* insisted on a 15-20 minute debrief, tactical discussion and handover between watches. These proved to be the most creative sessions of the whole voyage. Mike Golding also found watch changeover the best time for communication. On other yachts differences between watches were caused by interpersonal problems between watchleaders and several changes had to be made before the best combinations emerged. There was inevitable disappointment on some yachts when crew members were not selected, or were subsequently demoted. They too had to be brought back into the team through empathetic discussion and handling. Chris Tibbs had allowed his crew to select their own watchleaders before the start and significantly the positions remained unchanged throughout the race. Another interesting aspect of team development was the extent to which the crew of *Concert* grew as a consequence of their dismasting. Up until that point in the leg, the crew admitted that they were not totally pulling together but, as is often the case, adversity focused their performance. The team became totally confident in its ability to handle whatever the race threw at them and were to remain totally cohesive both in and out of port for the rest of the voyage.

Developing People – By the end of the first leg, it was very clear as to what individual roles within the crew were going to be most appropriate for the remainder of the voyage. Andy Hindley on *Save The Children*, recognised quite rightly that everyone including the skippers themselves developed personally throughout the voyage, but some skippers adopted a more structured approach than others. Richard Tudor believed that cross-training among the crew members themselves was a valuable method of encouraging development, particularly as the teacher was developed as much as the student. Simon Walker set out a strategy that would allow him to spend the last leg in his bunk! He did not, but always maintained that he could.

An element that upset several skippers was the continued reference in the media to their 'amateur crew'. By the time the yachts finished even this second leg, many of these so called amateurs had developed a professionalism of which many professional sailors would have been proud. They had also successfully overcome weather conditions that many professional seamen would never experience in a life-time at sea.

Inspirational

Influence – The scene for this leg had been very much set by Chay Blyth's presentation to the skippers and crew beforehand. He had pulled no punches and had told the crews exactly what to expect. All too often leaders try to play down difficulties which they expect to encounter, but this can be a dangerous tactic when individuals are then caught off guard. No-one who left Chay's briefing had any illusions about what they were about to face. This hard-line approach was to influence the whole attitude of the crews for the remainder of the leg.

Building Confidence – The biggest challenge now for the skippers was to persuade their crew members that they really could cope with the horrors to come. Bravado was very quickly replaced by apprehension as the conditions grew steadily worse approaching Cape Horn. Those nine skippers who had been round the Horn before had the obvious advantage of being able to describe the experiences ahead to their crews. James Hatfield had warned his crew that they were about to move from racing mode into survival mode - an approach with which his disabled crew readily identified.

Two features in building confidence in individual crew members had been those of recognition and of shared success. Andy Hindley commented that you could almost watch crew members physically grow when they received praise for a particular job well done. Merfyn Owen allowed his foredeck crew to develop their own sail changing drills which he freely admitted were different from his own. However his subsequent praise for the improved timings achieved with the new drills ensured that their approach thereafter to sail changing was one of total confidence because they owned the process.

Motorola's crew found the biggest boost to their own confidence came from their skipper. Mark Lodge's ability to encourage and coax and to recognise when individuals needed a personal boost in confidence was one of his greatest strengths. Adrian Donovan's heroic efforts to save the rig on *Heath Insured II* inspired his crew and built up their confidence in the crew's ability to succeed. Paul Bennett also provided similar inspiration for his crew.

For the skippers themselves, the problem was somewhat different. "No one expects me to be frightened," said Richard Tudor. Boris Webber commented that at times, when confidence sagged, many individuals seemed to appreciate physical contact. The quiet pat, handshake or hug brought people back out of their self-defensive shells. Even Boris, a rugged South African, admitted that on occasion he had particularly appreciated a comforting hug in recognition of the loneliness of command. Without family and loved ones, physical comfort is a scarce commodity. Dave Tomkinson admitted that he sometimes felt more lonely on this race than he had with single-handed sailing. The leader also needs his confidence built.

Lastly there are some wonderful examples of the merits of leading from the front when the time is right. On the first leg many crew members had rightfully criticised their skippers for not delegating and trying to do everything themselves. Merfyn Owen had admitted to only taking two hours sleep a day. Suddenly however the boot was on the other foot. Making repairs to the damaged rigging proved so perilous that skippers like Adrian Donovan and Paul Bennett felt unable to ask anyone else to tackle such a dangerous task and did it themselves. This proved inspirational to those who watched these brave and skillful mariners battling to save their yachts. No-one would ever question again their skipper's ability to cope in a crisis. The moral seemed to be to let others have a chance when the situation allows it but to lead by example when it does not.

RIO DE JANEIRO – WELLINGTON

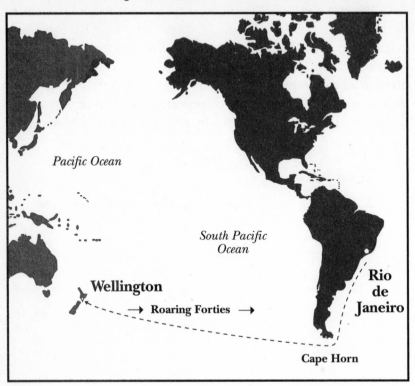

Pacific Ocean

South Pacific
Ocean

Wellington

→ **Roaring Forties** →

**Rio
de
Janeiro**

Cape Horn

LEG 2 RESULTS

Position	Arrival Time (GMT)	Leg Time D	H	M	S	Overall Position
1 Group 4	30 Dec 00:16:30	39	07	16	30	1
2 Save The Children	30 Dec 03:08:13	39	10	08	13	3
3 Motorola	30 Dec 23:06:08	39	21	09	08 R	4
4 Toshiba Wave Warrior	30 Dec 14:27:23	39	21	27	23	2
5 Global Teamwork	31 Dec 08:05:24	40	15	05	24	7
6 Commercial Union	31 Dec 08:15:32	40	15	15	32	5
7 Pause To Remember	31 Dec 13:23:30	40	20	23	30	10
8 Nuclear Electric	31 Dec 20:55:37	41	03	55	37 P	6
9 Ocean Rover	01 Jan 16:05:12	41	23	05	12	9
10 Time & Tide	02 Jan 06:16:18	42	06	42	18 R	12
11 3Com	02 Jan 05:46:43	42	07	42	43 R	8
12 Courtaulds International	02 Jan 06:49:56	42	11	54	56 R	13
13 Heath Insured II	03 Jan 16:29:06	43	23	29	06	11
14 Concert	10 Jan 06:48:00	50	13	48	00	14

P Penalty   R Redress

CHAPTER SIX

"If you wish to succeed in managing and controlling others, learn to manage and control yourself."
William J H Boetcker

"It is difficult to describe the smell on board after a few days at sea. It had nothing to do with personal hygiene, although that posed its own demands. The problem was rather that clothing, when washed and pegged on a line below deck to dry, reacts with the salt air to give off one of the most unpleasant odours. Everything became distinctly whiffy."

HRH Prince Michael of Kent

WELLINGTON TO SYDNEY

Leg 3 – 'The Executive Leg'

The New Crews – Affectionately known as the 'Sprint', this leg was to prove popular with the senior executives from the various sponsors. Inevitably there were the usual jokes about those who had joined for this short seven day leg :

"Not too long, not many decisions to make and a chance to get away before any damage is done," was a popular comment or, "I've flown down from head office to come and help you."

In fact nothing could have been further from the truth. A typical crew member for this leg was Dr Alan Rudge, Deputy Chief Executive of BT. He was joining *Global Teamwork* and no sooner had he arrived than he donned his crew kit and immersed himself in crew work.

A few days before the race start, Alan was having a snack on shore with skipper Merfyn Owen when a senior executive of a major Asian telecommunications company came over to chat to him. After the initial greeting, the executive suggested they have dinner that night at Alan's hotel. "Fine," said Alan. "We're all staying in the YMCA; the food's not bad, shall we make it 8 o'clock ?" Somewhat taken aback, the executive suggested they make it breakfast the next day at his luxury hotel.

Alan was to prove to be a very enthusiastic and hard-working crew member and why not? After all, the spirit and ethos of The Challenge was to create an environment for people from all walks of life. There was no room for prima donnas.

"You cannot be a leader and ask people to follow you unless you know how to follow too."
Sam Rayburn

Another welcome guest was HRH Prince Michael of Kent who had been an enthusiastic follower of the fortunes of *Ocean Rover*. He had seen them off at Southampton, after meeting the crew at an on-board tea party the week leading up to the start of the race. It was in Rio that it was suggested that he ought to take part in a leg. The gauntlet had been thrown down and he duly accepted, much to the delight and apprehension of the crew. "Britain has always been a very adventurous nation; this generation is no exception. I am excited and proud to be playing a small part in that adventure," he said.

"What should we call him? Should he clean the loos and do the cooking?" were questions being asked on board *Ocean Rover*. In the event, just like Alan Rudge, he was to be a popular crew member taking and giving the relaxed banter that was a feature on both yachts.

Commercial Union had on board Ian Reynolds, General Manager, Life Assurance, while *Save The Children* had Richard White, Chief Executive of Serco Group Plc. *Group 4* was joined by Loek Malmberg, a Senior Vice President from The Hague and Mark Baker, Chairman of Magnox, was aboard *Nuclear Electric*. Michael Buerk, the *BBC News* presenter, joined the crew of *Toshiba Wave Warrior*. Journalist Mike Calvin, who joined *Motorola*, was later to find seasickness one of the worst problems he had to face. "I fought hard to get over a little gremlin in my stomach." he said.

The Preparation – The yachts had become very much the central focus in Wellington during the previous six weeks. A special pontoon had been constructed at the waterfront close to the central business district, and with the enthusiastic support of Mayor Mark Blumsky, the whole Challenge fleet had become a talking point in the town, as well as in the local newspapers.

The bravery of the crew of *Time & Tide* had caught the imagination of the people of New Zealand. A television programme about disabilities was broadcast from the yacht. A song was written for them by an admirer and they even had their own wine. James Hatfield had established a 'good drinking relationship' with one of New Zealand's leading wine producers, Hunter Wines, on a solo circumnavigation trip in 1987. During the BT Global Challenge stopover, Hunter Wines held a fund-raising barbeque selling *Time & Tide* labelled wine, autographed by crew members. James was given a further 24 bottles of wine, labelled for *Time & Tide,* with strict instructions to auction them back in England, in aid of the *Time & Tide* Trust.

The yachts had all been totally re-rigged in Wellington to ensure that there was no further danger of a dismasting. All the steering wheels had been reinforced as most of the spokes had become loose through cracks in the original welds. This was largely due to the helmsmen bracing themselves against the waves, rather than the forces on the wheel from steering the yacht through massive seas.

Courtaulds International lost the crew member who had threatened Boris Webber with a knife. With four other yachts also losing crew members, there was a total of nine crew changes.

After the comparatively long stay in New Zealand, the crews were ready to take on the Tasman Sea, a sea with a reputation for being vicious. For The Challenge crews who had previously completed a 40 day leg around Cape Horn and across the Southern Ocean, this was just a short sprint across to Sydney. This 1,200 mile hop was expected to take a mere seven days and consequently give all the crews a chance to show their racing skills.

This was a marvellous opportunity to take some real risks and see what could be achieved. The downside to risk taking was fairly limited because even the weather would not make a tremendous difference to the finishing times throughout the fleet.

Andy Hindley on *Save The Children*, who had gained a 4th and 2nd place in the previous legs was determined to go for a win. As part of his preparation for this leg, he had competed in the 1994 Sydney to Hobart race and had immersed himself in local knowledge before leaving Wellington.

"I knew that I needed to get away from Wellington and use the advantage of the current and the eddies through the Cook Straits. I had also been told never to approach Sydney from the south, although that seemed to be the logical direction. The Tasman Sea in between was fairly straightforward so I realised exactly where I needed to concentrate my efforts. Not exactly very complicated, but it amazed us how few yachts seemed to take the local advice we had been offered."

The whole leg really belonged to Andy Hindley on *Save The Children* and Boris Webber on *Courtaulds International* who took chances and stuck to their guns, even when all seemed to be lost.

"A decision is the action an executive must take when he has information so incomplete that the answer does not suggest itself."
Admiral Radford

The Re-start – Race re-start day arrived. A grey, overcast day with light rain and winds gusting 30 to 35 knots. It was going to be another frenetic start in far more restricted waters than in Southampton and Rio. It was also going to be crucial to get round the buoys, out of the harbour and into the Cook Straits in a good position.

The New Zealand Navy added to the carnival atmosphere by anchoring the frigate *Waikatu* at the end of the start line, resplendent with a full set of flags from stem to stern.

Motorola did not trust itself to its own fortune and sailed with a traditional Maori blessing. The ceremony, which was conducted with due solemnity on the foredeck of the yacht, took place just before the start.

As the start cannon sounded from the deck of the *Waikatu*, *Nuclear Electric* went into the lead past the first buoy. The start was a real switchback ride with the fleet routed around a series of buoys in a large triangle. This gave the supporters and spectators on the headlands around the beautiful Wellington harbour a grandstand view of the impressive Challenge yachts and their awe-inspiring sails.

The jostling around the tightly placed buoys had yachts manoeuvring within inches of one another. Anxious shouts for 'starboard' and 'water at the mark' could be heard across the harbour and the little red protest flag was hoisted on the backstay of *Group 4* as *Save The Children* failed to give way on starboard. A 720 degree penalty turn was taken once *Save The Children* was clear of the harbour and *3Com* reported back to race headquarters that it had, "missed *Commercial Union* at one mark, by a coat of paint."

Given the enormous support that the Wellingtonians had shown The Challenge yachts and crews, it was no surprise to see so many spectator boats and helicopters following the yachts out of the harbour.

With the stiff breeze and short sprints between each buoy, sail changes were frequent in the first 10 miles. *Heath Insured II* got off to a cracking start and led the fleet out of the harbour and into the Cook Straits. Less than an hour out *Nuclear Electric*, blew its spinnaker in full view of all the spectators. It was a magnificent sight bursting like a huge balloon with the light green cloth streaming in the water and the head of the sail hanging off the mast head like a man on a gibbet. The crew, including Mark Baker, Chairman of Magnox, quickly pulled the remnants back on board while they hoisted one of the trusted golden sails which seemed to be capable of handling anything.

The yachts rounded the outer mark while the support vessels, including a magnificent three masted sail training ship, turned around to return to port.

Phantom of the Straits, (formerly *New Zealand Lion*, an ex-Whitbread racing yacht) did not turn back. Her crew had befriended the fleet during its stay in Wellington and had become so involved with the race that they had chartered their yacht and were accompanying the fleet across the Tasman Sea to Sydney. On board were several sponsors and partners of some of the crews who were trying to emulate life on board and experience The Challenge. They had formulated their own watch systems and rotas for cooking and cleaning and followed in the wake of the fleet.

Once again The Challenge crews settled down to the business of ocean racing in an atmosphere of anti-climax. A crew member on *Pause To Remember* commented, "I hate the starts. I am as keen as anyone to get going but the atmosphere changes so rapidly and ends up with a massive anti-climax. We arrive on the yachts as celebrities, walking tall in our crew kit. There is all the commotion on the dock with family and friends and crew members on other yachts. We spend time fiddling with last minute details on the yacht, which are usually unnecessary. Then the goodbyes and we leave the dockside with applause, cheering and hooters, only to mill around for some three hours looking at the course. Then comes the frenetic activity of the start and all the shouting that seems to be a part of yacht racing. And suddenly after all this, the spectators leave and we are on our own and I have to worry about cooking spaghetti for 14 people. It is the worst let down in the world."

A mile out of the harbour and the fleet began to separate.

A Short Leg To Sydney – *Global Teamwork* followed its much studied strategy and kept under the lee of the shore. Where other yachts were further out, battling against four knots of tide, *Global Teamwork* was benefiting from two knots of tide. It was all going well until it was hit by eddies and at this point it tacked behind *Time & Tide*, crossing the fleet at 90 degrees to reach the northern side of The Straits. Bemused by *Global Teamwork's* chosen course, James Hatfield, skipper of *Time & Tide* offered some friendly advice, shouting and pointing across, "Hey Merv, Sydney's that way!"

Steaming along, *Global Teamwork* was positioning itself to take the lead, but unfortunately for the crew, they failed to capitalise on their position early enough and stuck to the right-hand side just a little too long, losing a few miles and passing Cape Farewell in second position.

With the winds increasing to gale force nine, the first night proved to be particularly busy and extremely lumpy. Short confused seas between the North and South Islands took their toll on the crews who were struggling to find their sea legs once again. For the new 'executive' leggers it was their first introduction to real racing and what The Challenge was all about.

On *Ocean Rover* a number succumbed to seasickness as they struggled to change sails with water sloshing down the deck. A particularly large wave came and sluiced four of the crew into the mast area. Although the water was relatively warm, the Tasman Sea still carried the aggressiveness that can damage anyone unwary enough not to hold on tight and show some respect. Soft flesh against the steel obstacles that litter the deck do not mix well. 'Pinball alley', as it was known, ripped two sets of foul weather gear and badly

107

damaged one crew member's shoulder.

Out into the Tasman Sea and the tacking duel started. For the first time in the race the yachts were sailing in sight of one another throughout most of the leg. With only 21 miles separating the first and last yacht, the racing was extremely intense and concentration levels were even sharper given the close proximity. "We have never been out of visual contact with at least one other yacht and that certainly sharpens your reactions ... the benefits of every bit of trimming are readily apparent which is a great motivator," reported a crew member of *Global Teamwork*.

Two days out of Wellington and *Heath Insured II* was still leading the fleet. A jubilant crew reported that although it had been hit by a bout of food poisoning, spirits on board were high and the crew was still racing to full potential.

A dubious chilli left half the crew operating a new form of rota. Skipper Adrian Donovan was on the helm when suddenly a shout came, "Take the wheel, I'm going to be sick." Without waiting, he dived to the back of the yacht and hung out over the rail, leaving another crew member to wrestle with the wheel. A few minutes later, this helmsman was suffering the same fate and the pattern continued for a four to five hour period with a rota of helms all taking it in turn to be ill over the stern.

As the fleet moved across the Tasman Sea, *Group 4* clawed its way into the lead. At this stage, it was the most southerly yacht in the fleet, while *Save The Children* continued to head north. The further *Save The Children* headed north, the more it dropped towards the back of the fleet. Within four days it had dropped from 6th to 11th position but the crew was elated and excited. Andy Hindley had fully briefed his crew on his tactics before leaving Wellington.

Courtaulds International was now lying in 14th place, some 46 miles behind the leaders, in a fleet that was slowly beginning to expand. The morale on board *Courtaulds International* was low as it languished at the back of the fleet.

108

At this stage, skipper Boris Webber, who had also chosen to take a more northerly route, needed to rally his crew members. They needed to be reassured that this strategy was really going to pay off and Boris reiterated that they must be patient and the benefits would soon become clear.

Sticking to its guns, *Save The Children* continued on its northerly course remaining 11th in the fleet for two days before the strategy finally paid off. After an atmosphere charged with excitement at the prospect of taking a risk that could possibly pay dividends, the crew became worried and tense as it fought to take the lead. The yacht's meteoric rise from 11th to 1st place in 36 hours left them completely terrified. Now that they had the lead could they possibly hang on to it and make it in first across the line?

"To win without risk is to triumph without glory."
Pierre Grueille

The "Executive Leg" provided some of the best and most exciting racing of The Challenge.

HRH Prince Michael of Kent, aboard *Ocean Rover*, was reported to be "a demon main-sheet trimmer and putting some of us to shame," according to fellow crew member Humphrey Walters. "Prince Michael is on the helming rota and guiding the yacht very smoothly. He has also turned his hand to sail repairs and has joined the sail repair team, toiling away in the galley."

As *Save The Children* took the lead, the rest of the fleet were languishing in a huge high pressure ridge which had engulfed them just 100 miles outside of Sydney. A concertina effect occurred during Saturday night as the yachts at the back of the fleet caught up with the leaders. *Group 4* watched helplessly as, one by one, the fleet sailed over the horizon and into the same parking lot. With virtually no wind the yachts were drifting aimlessly and crews were unable to even keep the yachts pointing in the right direction.

Courtaulds International, however, was capitalising on its northerly position and was able to avoid the ridge of high pressure by sailing right round it. Within a 12 hour period it had moved from 11th to 2nd position.

Meanwhile, Mike Golding skipper of *Group 4* was formulating a different strategy, knowing that he was unable to move fast enough to cover the attack on his position. He pointed his yacht in the opposite direction to Sydney and sailed south in an attempt to get out of the north-moving ridge first. With so little wind and virtually no boat speed, he and his crew drifted south while the rest of the fleet overtook him as they made headway towards Sydney. *Group 4* fell back into 12th position and things did not look good.

However, after many frustrating hours of slow progress, the decision paid off. The breeze started to build from the south and *Group 4* was able to regain lost ground against the majority of the fleet, crossing the line beside Sydney Opera House in 2nd place, some two hours 10 minutes behind *Save The Children*.

> *"Do something. If it doesn't work do something else.*
> *No idea is too crazy."*
> **Tom Peters**

Entering Sydney Harbour proved tricky for many of the fleet. Five of the yachts entered the harbour nose to tail, with a mere 100 yards between them all. Hoping to gain a position or two amidst this mêlée, *Motorola* decided to cut the corner and sail in tight to the rocks, following hard on the heels of *Ocean Rover*.

In 35 knots of breeze with spinnaker flying, a sudden bang heralded *Motorola's* arrival on the rocks. One crew member flew from the staysail back into the cockpit, another went sprawling and suffered a cracked rib.

Luckily for the embarrassed skipper Mark Lodge, the tide was coming in and this abrupt stop lasted only a couple of minutes. With boom right out to catch the wind in the

110

mainsail, *Motorola* was soon off the rocks and heading in towards the magnificent Sydney Harbour Bridge and Opera House.

Nuclear Electric skipper, Richard Tudor, was overwhelmed by the sight before him as he rounded the corner. "It was a great privilege to arrive in front of Sydney Opera House," he commented.

The welcome into Darling Harbour was tremendous. With the lights of the city illuminating the skyline and the cheers from the dockside, the crews arrived in one of the most spectacular cities in the world. The fact that all the yachts arrived within a six hour period added to the magic of the night. As each yacht arrived, the welcoming crowds on the pontoon grew larger, each crew wanting to welcome the next one in. The atmosphere was electric and the crews were ecstatic. It was a sight which would have moved anyone on the dockside that evening.

Reflections From Mark Baker, Chairman Of Magnox And Crew Member *Nuclear Electric* – Mark Baker, Chairman of Magnox was overjoyed when John Collier, the late Chairman of *Nuclear Electric* and orchestrator of the *Nuclear Electric* sponsorship called him into the office to break the news that Mark was to sail from Wellington to Sydney on the 'short and hairy' Executive Leg of the BT Global Challenge. Mark had never sailed a yacht before but had followed the British Steel Challenge with much passion. He and his wife Meriel both became emotionally involved with the yacht and its crew, their partners and families and their triumphs and defeats.

At the age of 56, he was pleased that he had kept himself trim enough to fit into a Challenge yacht bunk. He enthusiastically undertook the arduous mid-winter training, although he admits he wondered what he was doing.

"It was bloody rough, bloody cold and bloody nasty beating our way up to Dartmouth. The wind was howling, it was a north easterly blowing in from Siberia," he recalled.

Like all The Challenge crews, the executives undertook

111

the physical training programme as well as the sail training. It was the responsibility of Martin Ley, training skipper, to ensure that they were fit enough to participate.

Mark Baker remembers that well. "Then there was the early morning run along Plymouth Hoe at some ungodly hour in the morning. It was dark, cold and there was snow on the road. I eventually fell about laughing as I thought back to the stories my father used to tell me about how tough his days at the Naval College in Dartmouth had been when the cadets had been made to go for similar runs – 70 years earlier!"

To really get to grips with sailing, Mark chose to undertake a dinghy sailing course and spent a couple of weekends with the core crew aboard *Nuclear Electric* training in The Solent.

"The Challenge training was very good and very realistic, although I'm not so sure that there was really enough time during the summer of 1996 for the core crew to settle in and prepare themselves for such a trip," commented Mark.

Joining the yacht in Wellington, he felt quite vulnerable. "I knew my abilities were limited and was glad that skipper, Richard Tudor, assigned me to the winches in the cockpit. I really wouldn't have felt happy up on the foredeck.

The crew members were brilliant, they helped me along and were great at explaining exactly what was going on," he reflected.

"I was, however, a little embarrassed about the sleeping arrangements. Usually the leggers are allocated the coffin bunk in the aft cabin but before I arrived Hakan Rodebjer had swapped bunks and I spent the week in his old bunk, staring at his girlfriend's love message in Swedish stuck on the wall!"

Just like any other crew member, Mark got stuck in with the jobs on board, the general cleaning as well as the heads. "They didn't allow me into the galley to cook but I did take on my fair share of tea and coffee making," he joked.

Blowing the spinnaker just outside Wellington Harbour

gave Mark his first insight into the vagaries of sailing. "We were just on the point of hardening up round the headland and we were ready to get the kite down. Hakan went up to the end of the spinnaker pole and was there ready with the spike to let the corner of the kite go when we heard a terrific bang and the kite was in tatters. Just a minute earlier and we would have saved it," he added.

"I didn't really enjoy the first two nights out of Wellington. It was dark, cold and rough and everything was new to me. I felt pretty clumsy and was concerned about my abilities on deck, particularly in the lumpy weather we were experiencing through The Straits. Physically, I was exhausted. I'd never slept so well and my legs were battered and bruised."

Popping Stugeron, an effective seasickness remedy, several times a day to combat the feeling of nausea, Mark became quite woozy and recognised that his movements were slower than usual.

"I invented some new words for the English language – stugefaction, stugefied and stugid – words which described the way I felt and probably acted on board."

Working in an industry which prides itself on high standards of safety, Mark was appalled at the conditions in which the crews had to work. "In industry, no way would you work in total darkness five feet from a major moving hazard on a platform that was at an angle of 25 degrees or more, with unmarked objects scattered around beneath your feet. It is a tribute to Richard Tudor's standards of safety on board that the crew has not been injured and they have all returned safe and well."

One thing that struck Mark during the leg was the importance of clear communication. "I was amazed at the degree of difficulty of communication on board. In howling winds it was impossible to hear what was being said even in the cockpit, let alone from one end of the yacht to the other. Simple commands seemed to take ages to get through and were easily misinterpreted."

113

The arrival into Sydney Harbour was quite exhilarating. Five yachts approached the finish line together. *Nuclear Electric* battled it out with *Ocean Rover* who finally crossed the finish line just two minutes ahead.

Mark was elated. He had successfully completed the leg and proved himself capable of the task. Awaiting him on the dockside were his wife, his daughter from Sydney and his son who had flown in from Hong Kong. "It was the first time that the family had been together for two years and I felt euphoric."

In summing up the leg Mark said, "What impressed me most on the leg was the team spirit on board. There was an amazing day-to-day banter, something unique to the environment and I was touched by the degree to which the crew took care of each other. It was second nature to them to check each other's safety gear or stop someone in their tracks if they could foresee a potential incident."

Reflections From Michael Buerk, BBC News Presenter And Crew Member *Toshiba Wave Warrior* – "One of the things that struck me most about racing on board *Toshiba Wave Warrior* was the 'inclusive' culture that was characteristic of the crew. Coming into an established team at that stage in the race, after the strong bonding that one imagines would have taken effect in the dangerous and horrific conditions of the Cape Horn leg, I was wary. Here I was, a familiar nightly face from the BBC, but an outsider and an amateur sailor too. I need not have worried.

Not only was I struck by how they included *me*, but there was *not* a single crew member who they did not include. The whole team was smashing. That really struck me as something quite unique.

I have been in intense situations at various times throughout my working life when levels of tolerance are pushed to the limit, when the pressure is really on, when individuals are completely fatigued, physically weak and living in discomfort. In those situations, I have seen people 'lose it'. But aboard *Toshiba Wave Warrior* everyone was

114

cheerful, there was not an inkling of resentment despite the conditions and the physical demands.

The yacht was managed in such a way that everyone had a chance to try everything. Even I, with little experience of sailing apart from flotilla holidays in the Aegean, took a turn on the helm. What I lacked in other areas I tried to make up for in wild, uncritical enthusiasm and brute force. I felt included and very much part of the team.

Skipper Simon Walker had a fantastic management style which was low key and inclusive. He was very accessible and companionable, yet had an air of authority and generated enormous enthusiasm among the crew. He was very clear and extremely articulate. Before any manoeuvre, he was careful to brief the crew, clearly defining what was to be done and by whom. He always left it open for ideas, suggestions and encouraged contributions from crew, though managed to maintain authority.

I took a turn at all the other jobs on board from cooking to cleaning. In fact I prepared the first meal of the leg which was pretty difficult in the choppy conditions we experienced through The Straits. I kept going up on deck every few minutes to take in some air.

For me the things that really stood out were the comradeship, the fact that everyone was included and treated as an equal, the amazing team spirit and the outstanding tolerance levels.

The Challenge was special. It was a race, it did matter who won and although these were amateurs, there was a sense of purpose and a driving ambition to do well."

Reflections From Ian Reynolds, General Manager Life Assurance, Commercial Union Head Office And Crew Member *Commercial Union* – Ian Reynolds was thrilled to be able to take part in the 'Executive Leg'. The decision was made by the toss of a coin with Cees Schrauwers Managing Director, UK Division who was also keen to take part. "We asked Sean Blowers to toss the coin, and luckily I won," Ian recalled. "It wasn't until then that I suddenly realised how much I really wanted to take an active part. I suppose it was in my blood as my grandfather had rounded The Horn and had often talked to me about it when I was young."

As with all senior people who sailed on this leg, Ian was anxious to be treated as part of the crew, particularly as the core crew had been together for a long time already and he felt he was a newcomer.

> *"Nothing creates more self respect among a team than being included in the process of making decisions."*
> **Judith Bardwick**

"I wanted to be treated as a crew member and really play my part in helping the team. Richard Merriweather was very good at making me feel that I was contributing and I was assigned to the winches in the cockpit section – a job which Richard felt I could do well so that I didn't feel inept.

On one occasion, the crew suggested I take the helm but after 15 minutes it was quite clear that I was not as proficient as the regular helmsmen and I asked to be relieved. It was a nice gesture from the crew, but I felt it was important to allow the experts to do the expert things. That is what I hope happens within my own organisation.

By Australia, it was clear that for the crew of *Commercial Union* getting round the world was no longer really the objective. To win a leg was a definite goal that the yacht was striving for. There was an ethos provided by Richard to allow people to achieve more than they felt they were capable of and this created an atmosphere of allowing people to learn – particularly from each other.

I found that Richard was very good at giving praise.

It was clear what a lonely life being a skipper was and Richard had few people he could turn to. In business, we at least have the luxury of time away from it and partners with whom we can discuss issues. On a yacht there is no such luxury and I wanted to leave the crew with the thought to

116

praise the skipper now and again. I hope they took my advice – certainly they were a very happy bunch and we are proud of what they did for themselves and for *Commercial Union.*"

The icing on the cake for Ian was to celebrate his wife's birthday in Sydney, albeit one day late.

"I suppose being a day late for one's wife's birthday was excusable in the circumstances. I told her that I got there as soon as I could!"

Reflections From Dr Alan Rudge, Deputy Chief Executive, BT And Crew Member *Global Teamwork* – "I knew it was essential for me to immerse myself into the team and, before joining the crew of *Global Teamwork* on Leg 3, I thought through quite carefully how it might best be done. The fact that I was the BT Board Member responsible for the overall race and had organised the sponsorship of *Global Teamwork*, and also *Concert*, was not a help. I felt it was likely to compound the problem of my being accepted as 'one of the team'.

I needed to demonstrate to the crew that I wanted to be one of them. So on my arrival in Wellington I shared the crew shore accommodation before we sailed and was an early volunteer to clean the heads and the galley on the yacht. I was aware that it would take a while for me to find my place in the team and that I was going to be the most junior member. Nevertheless, I hoped that the crew would read my signals and appreciate that I was keen to take part on their terms.

Many businesses today apply matrix management methods and make extensive use of project teams. They have moved away from the single-axis hierarchical structure and toward project matrices, where teams of people with the necessary blend of skills are brought together to perform a given project. Within the project structure, it has to be recognised that the most senior person is not necessarily the best leader. It's rather akin to a tribe of Red Indians. In camp the Chief is clearly the boss, but when they go hunting the best leader is the guy who can run the fastest. The project team approach gives great flexibility in business and there are many similarities in the teamwork necessary on board a racing yacht. I am a long term champion of the project matrix approach in business, and that is why I believe that sailing is such a great training environment for business and managers.

As a senior manager joining the race, and one with a vested interest in its success, I was particularly interested in observing its effectiveness. Here was a classic example, with a disparate bunch of people, all from differing backgrounds, thrown together in a challenging, competitive and physically uncomfortable environment.

On *Global Teamwork*, it was clear from the start that skipper Merfyn Owen had done his management homework before setting out on the race. He told me that he had stressed to the crew, at the outset, the type of problems they would experience and had tried to create an environment into which he felt the team would best fit. His style produced a very happy yacht with a certain 'Celtic spirit' and an abundance of poetry reverberated around the yacht. The crew had a deep affection, as well as respect, for Merfyn and it was clear that his team would tackle anything for him.

In business it is equally important to have your people with you. With the wholehearted support of your team it is possible to get out of many difficult situations. I worked for five years as the manager of an organisation which contracted to perform R&D projects on a commercial basis and during this time, we did not have a single project which failed. Contract R&D can be a difficult business to get right and I made my share of mistakes. But whenever we hit a problem, my team would be there for me, burning the midnight oil, until we had sorted it out.

A good skipper, like a good manager, builds up some sort of credit or reserve with his team, on which he can draw in difficult times. On *Global Teamwork*, there was never a sign of hesitation if a change of sail was called. Whatever the conditions, day or night, the crew went forward to carry out

118

the task without complaint. This was a true reflection of the leadership skills of Merfyn – he had created an amazing atmosphere on board, such that his crew were motivated to do difficult, often uncomfortable, and sometimes dangerous, tasks with a will.

I observed very similar characteristics on the yacht *Concert*, on which I completed the final leg, from Boston to Southampton. This was another happy yacht, well led by its skipper Chris Tibbs. While the culture on board differed in detail, the basic leadership, management and teamwork principles were very similar, and Chris had won the total commitment of his crew.

Being on board *Global Teamwork* and *Concert*, I had the opportunity to observe the complex interplay of management techniques and human behaviours. This experience reinforced many of the fundamental management principles which I have learned, sometimes the hard way, throughout my career. I was able to note the things which were done well and the mistakes made by the less experienced managers among the crew. Too often as senior managers, we forget some of the key factors which influence the performance of people within our organisations. I believe that it is a very healthy exercise to be reminded of them in such a direct way – in effect to be back on the receiving end.

Undertaking both legs confirmed my original belief that the BT Global Challenge was not primarily about yachts and sailing, but about people. Indeed this was the premise which inspired me, and then BT, to undertake the race sponsorship. I can recommend the experience to anyone who has the desire to better understand the real potential of people, and to gain some insight into what leadership and management are all about."

Reflections From HRH Prince Michael Of Kent – Crew Member *Ocean Rover* – "I accepted the invitation to join *Ocean Rover* as a legger because it was going to offer me the opportunity, probably once and forever, to take part in an

119

ocean race. My longest previous voyage in a yacht had been a cruise to Deauville 30 years ago.

The thing about *Ocean Rover* that made the most impression on me was the close harmony of the crew members. They came from every kind of background and gave as good as they got. The tougher the conditions, the more acute the sense of humour.

One of the skills I was able to practise at length was sail repairing. Leaning over the saloon table with a staple gun, trying to ignore the smells of porridge and soya mince, legacies of an earlier meal, made this a novel activity, and an object lesson in teamwork.

It is difficult to describe the smell on board after a few days at sea. It had nothing to do with personal hygiene, although that posed its own demands. The problem was rather that clothing, when washed and pegged on a line below deck to dry, reacts with the salt air to give off one of the most unpleasant odours. Everything became distinctly whiffy.

The most frustrating thing was to have absolutely no wind. On my leg, that only happened once for a few hours, but the Doldrums must have been ghastly. Crews had to put up with dead calm for days on end, their computers lowering morale still further by indicating that the yachts were actually going astern. *Ocean Rover,* resourceful as ever, carried some excellent music which we blasted out at full volume, much to the delight of the whales and other animals who came to enjoy the fun.

The organisation of the race was first class. I have never seen the efforts of sponsors so well repaid, in that all the crews went out of their way to fulfil sponsors' requests. Everyone was willing and an atmosphere of exuberance abounded. It was a terrific show.

The BT Global Challenge lived up to its name. Everyone involved can be justifiably proud to have participated in such an uplifting and demanding competition. This was especially true of *Time & Tide*. I raise my hat to all their crew who proved that, disabled as they were, they could cope. At the end of the Sydney to Cape Town leg, the toughest of all, James Hatfield brought them in ahead of four of the other boats, with only 12 crew where the others all had 14. What a compelling story!

The Challenge will go down as a shining example of human endeavour. I am very proud to have played a small part in it."

WHAT MADE THE DIFFERENCE

This leg was short, fast and tactical. It was a leg in which the Thinking cluster of behaviours was critical. Those who displayed high levels of competency in Information Search, Concept Formation and Conceptual Flexibility were in the best position.

Thinking

Information Search – *Save The Children's* skipper Andy Hindley had participated in the 1994 Sydney to Hobart race to obtain experience and information on sailing in Antipodean waters in general and in the approach to Sydney in particular. Armed with this knowledge, Andy felt better placed to make the right strategic decisions.

> *"It takes vision and courage to create – it takes faith and courage to prove."*
> **Owen D Young**

He had fully briefed his crew before the start of the leg. He had wanted full support in the high risk strategy he was aiming to undertake and he had received it. He had explained that, while the rest of the fleet would inevitably head south, he wanted to go north. This, he warned them, would put them at the back of the fleet for a while until they reaped the benefits from the current as they came down into Sydney. Boris Webber, on *Courtaulds International* had also done his homework and decided on a similar northern strategy.

The crew members of *Global Teamwork* who had arrived in Wellington in 5th position, were keen to get a good result on this leg and had spent much of their time ashore researching local currents and wind patterns in the Cook Straits. They had even spent a day under motor, tracing the start out of the harbour and along the coast monitoring the effect of the current in the shallow inshore waters. As a result, Merfyn Owen elected to adopt a strategy on the exit from Wellington to keep under the lee of the shore. While others battled midstream against the tide, *Global Teamwork* forged ahead and, despite a brief tactical error, passed Cape Farewell in second position.

Concept Formation – Mid-voyage, Mike Golding, who was leading the body of the fleet, faced a different problem. When the wind died, one by one the other yachts caught up, leaving *Group 4* in a windless hole. At the same time, those yachts who had taken a northern route suddenly started to overtake the rest of the fleet. Mike decided to head south away from his destination but towards better weather coming from the south. The strategy paid off with *Group 4* finishing in second place, only two hours behind *Save The Children* after approaching Sydney from a totally different direction.

Developmental

Teamwork – By this stage in the voyage, teamwork on nearly all of the yachts had reached an advanced level. Without exception, all of the executive leggers expressed their apprehension at being accepted into the highly cohesive crews to which they had been assigned. What differentiated the really successful teams was the desire and ability to incorporate these newcomers into their ranks very quickly. It is not sufficient to form an exclusive club if this deters newcomers from inputing their talent; the high performing team quickly recognises and assimilates additional talent as a value-added behaviour. The accounts of the executive leggers in this chapter show just how successful some skippers and crews were, and how honoured the executives felt at being used to good effect rather than as decoration.

Achieving

Continuous Improvement – For Mike Golding, not winning Leg 3 was the best thing that could have happened. The margin of coming second was not sufficiently great to threaten *Group 4's* ability to win the race overall. However after winning the first two legs with apparent ease, Mike's biggest fear was complacency. Coming second ensured that the crew's determination to win overall was revitalised. Mike's philosophy had always been 'when we gain a mile we've had better weather, when we lose a mile we've sailed badly.' Contribution from everyone was vital. It was never his intention to make friends but to ensure that everyone on board got something out of the race. "We prepare more than anyone else. It's long, over the top, but mentally we attune more. Everyone has individual roles, the key players are in fixed positions and are spared motherwatch. This works because the crew's attitude is that whatever they do they do for the good of the team. We have eight days rest in a port, then two days of training and a roster for boatwork."

> *"A man who wants to lead the orchestra must turn his back on the crowd."*
> **James Crook**

Mike knew that the vibes about *Group 4's* professionalism were not always good. Sometimes being out in front was lonely and frustrating. He knew that he was the focus of everyone's attention.

For Andy Hindley's crew the reaction was totally different. Having come 4th and 2nd in the previous legs, at last a win was theirs. "We always knew that we could do it, but this win made us even more determined to win overall," said Andy. "We had thoroughly analysed our performance in the first two legs to see where we could improve and we enhanced our performance during this leg. Even though we had won, we knew that we could still do better and we had to identify exactly where."

WELLINGTON – SYDNEY

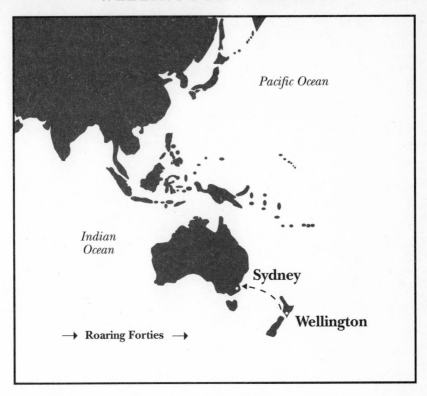

LEG 3 RESULTS

Position		Arrival Time (GMT)		Leg Time D H M S				Overall Position
1	Save The Children	16 Feb	07:32:58	07	07	32	58	3
2	Group 4	16 Feb	09:50:44	07	09	50	44	1
3	Courtaulds International	16 Feb	10:51:45	07	10	51	45	13
4	Global Teamwork	16 Feb	11:05:03	07	11	05	03	7
5	Pause To Remember	16 Feb	11:17:41	07	11	17	41	10
6	Concert	16 Feb	11:18:32	07	11	18	32	14
7	3Com	16 Feb	11:19:05	07	11	19	05	8
8	Ocean Rover	16 Feb	11:33:47	07	11	33	47	9
9	Nuclear Electric	16 Feb	11:35:34	07	11	35	34	6
10	Toshiba Wave Warrior	16 Feb	11:39:30	07	11	39	30	2
11	Motorola	16 Feb	11:41:44	07	11	41	44	4
12	Heath Insured II	16 Feb	12:01:01	07	12	01	01	11
13	Commercial Union	16 Feb	12:55:11	07	12	55	11	5
14	Time & Tide	16 Feb	13:13:48	07	13	13	48	12

CHAPTER SEVEN

"They can conquer who believe they can."
Virgil

"The sunset tonight was truly awesome – spectacular. We sailed down a sunbeam giving chase to the sinking orb as it ran for the horizon. Despite full sail and 10 knots of speed, we could only dance our way through the platinum pathway of waves as, once again, it beat us to the edge of our world. The warmth of its beauty made up for the chill in the air. Not too uncomfortable today, but when the wind builds, the chill factor turns this ocean into a harsh wilderness complete with huge islands of ice, and sea monsters that blow plumes of mist high into the air. At times I wonder if we are not sailing across one big Jurassic Park. There is a purity and honesty that transcends modern mumbo jumbo. Prejudices are blatant. It's not colour, creed or sex that is discriminated against. It is humans in general. We are trespassing across another's territory. Like refugees we carry our homes with us. Too late to go back for that which was forgotten, yet along the way we will harvest memories that will feed and enrich us for the rest of our lives. On arrival at the next port, we will be able to measure the magnitude of our achievement."

James Hatfield, Skipper *Time & Tide*

SYDNEY TO CAPE TOWN
Leg 4

"Never in my life have I seen anything so hostile and power so awesome. It is trying to kill me and is all around me every

127

minute. I am convinced that there will never be a problem so severe in real life that will compare with surviving in the Southern Indian Ocean." So described Paul Bennett, Skipper of *Ocean Rover* on completing Leg 4.

"The leg from hell. We are trying to take on a part of the ocean where ships do not venture. Yet we have chosen to tackle this ocean head on in a 67ft open-decked racing yacht. It is a really terrible place to go," wrote Humphrey Walters in his personal log close to the Kerguelen Islands halfway through the leg.

The crews had been warned. The first Southern Ocean leg from Rio de Janeiro to Wellington had been hostile enough but was a mere dress rehearsal for the conditions that the fleet would meet during this leg.

The statistics showed what the yachts and their crews endured.

The conditions were the toughest ever encountered by The Challenge fleet. It was without doubt the ultimate test for the yachts and their crew. Although the leg was 6,200 miles in length, the winning yacht *Group 4* sailed 7,500 miles at an average speed of eight knots. The severity of the conditions and the fact that the realistic top speed of these yachts in good conditions is 10 knots, illustrates the degree of expertise required.

The weather conditions were far more extreme than those experienced during the 1992/3 race and the highest recorded wind speed was 86 knots. The fleet also noted an unusually large number of icebergs and 'growlers' – large chunks of ice which form part of the debris of icebergs and lie just below the surface. Growlers can hole a racing yacht and are especially dangerous because they are invisible to radar and crew are unable to see them, particularly at night. They tend to float in the vicinity of icebergs but, in extreme storms, can drift some miles away and thus increase the hazard when sailing for extended periods so close to Antarctica and the ice belt.

Global Teamwork came into contact with a growler which

128

only showed up when the hull was examined in Cape Town. Other than the anti-fouling layer being badly scraped there was no further damage. A 60ft fibreglass yacht would have been holed by such an encounter and sunk without trace.

On this leg it was the weather which occupied the minds of skippers and crew. The real root of the problem lay in the two land masses of Australia and Antarctica. These two vast continents have huge high pressure systems sitting over them which, because of their size, are fairly static. The low pressure systems which swirl around the globe are squeezed between these two land masses and back up against each other in a weather traffic jam. They then deepen in intensity and accelerate before they are released to unleash their fury on the ocean. This results in huge seas and intense winds with very short lulls between storms, giving no time for the seas to settle and develop the more rolling swells encountered in the first Southern Ocean leg.

There was tremendous apprehension among the crews that they had another endurance leg before they were to reach Cape Town. They had been warned, but no-one could have prepared them for what was to come or the ferocity of the weather.

There had even been drama on land before the crew embarked on this dangerous leg. Paul Stephens from *Ocean Rover* had decided to visit the Sydney Aquarium by the dockside. Having hit a shark on the first leg, Paul was curious to find out more about sharks, see what they were like and what size they were. As he was standing by the first tank, the thick glass exploded, tons of water swept him off his feet leaving sharks flapping helplessly around the entrance to the aquarium. He picked himself up to find he had a six inch gash across his forearm, caused by a shard of the glass, which had severed some muscle tissue. He was taken to hospital for 20 stitches. This was a real blow, for after three years of preparation, he was unable to complete the next leg. Paul Clifton, a Rover employee and a legger scheduled to sail on the last leg, was asked to join *Ocean*

Rover at the last minute. It was to be an unhappy leg for him as he suffered from chronic seasickness and was confined to his bunk for several weeks.

The Re-start – For the contestants, the re-start in Sydney was the most congested that they had encountered. The harbour was full of small yachts and boats of all sizes. The sheer size of the golden sails of The Challenge yachts made them stand out against the white sails and colourful boats and ferries that were carrying the hundreds of supporters.

There was a small exclusion lane which was supposed to be the marshalling point for the yachts to manoeuvre prior to the start but, due to the intense interest of local yacht enthusiasts, became a viewing lane for them to take a closer look at the yachts and their crews. There was friendly banter between The Challenge crew and local boats until the start gun went and the racing was on for real.

Courtaulds International had a very close encounter with a 20ft yacht which bounced off the side of the hull. Skipper Boris Webber duly used the traditional yachtsman's language which was later subject to a protest as it was captured by the yacht's camera and inserted into a BBC programme. The charge was "ungentlemanly behaviour and bringing the sport into disrepute."

In reality, had it not been for some outstanding seamanship by Boris in such a confined space, the small yacht would have been sunk and the four people in it in grave danger of being run over by all the following craft.

Fortunately for Boris the jury dropped the charge with a warning, but this was after an agonising week where he was told at one stage he would have to fly to Kiel in West Germany to face the judge and jury. A real storm in a tea cup but sufficient to cause Boris unnecessary stress in Boston where the charge was made.

For the supporters, the start was one of the most beautiful and the most moving. It was the first time many of them had seen the yachts actually racing. How different they looked from the fleet of 'dressed overall' yachts lined up like soldiers on the pontoon.

"The start in Watson's Bay was fast and furious with bright sunshine and a good wind," said Rosie Mackie from MaST International, on board the *Time & Tide* support ferry. "With the backdrop of the Sydney Opera House and Sydney Harbour Bridge, The Challenge yachts looked majestic. The crews, now starting their fourth leg, displayed real professionalism in their quietly efficient behaviour. We were able to sail alongside the fleet until they reached North Head at which point our ferry captain told us he could go no further. As he turned the boat to port in order to head for home, the fleet turned to starboard, sailed through The Heads and was gone. The roar of the crowd ceased, the helicopters returned to base, the well-wishing was over.

Suddenly the yachts seemed very small and alone, surrounded by the ocean.

We watched them in silence, aware that the Southern Ocean lay between us and our next rendezvous in Cape Town. We all said a silent prayer for the line of yellow sails disappearing over the horizon. It was probably the most emotional start of the whole race."

"All things be ready if our minds be so."
William Shakespeare

The Fear Of The Known – The first part of the journey was, literally, the calm before the storm, very much as they had found when leaving Rio de Janeiro for Cape Horn. The yachts were very close as they sailed down the South Australia coast with positions changing all the time. It was almost like a match race around a harbour and at night it was always possible to see the lights of several other yachts nearby.

As the fleet sailed south they carried on past the island of Tasmania to avoid the wind shadow that creates a lull just

131

to the south of the coast. This meant entering cold water and the rim of Antarctica which brought the yachts once again into iceberg territory and desolation. The last sight of land was to be two giant pillars of rock sticking out of the ocean south of Tasmania, which have defied the pounding seas for thousands of years.

As soon as the fleet passed Tasmania it was hard to starboard to enter the fury of the Southern Ocean and the reality of the next leg to Cape Town. Once again, the balmy sailing was over and the severity of the Southern Indian Ocean was about to take its toll. Every yacht suffered breakages and knockdowns in this the most frightening and arduous leg of The Challenge.

There was added apprehension for sailing this ocean as recently it had been the scene of two remarkable rescues. One, the rescue by the Australian Navy of Tony Bullimore after four days in his upturned yacht, and secondly, the rescue of Raphael Dinelli by Pete Goss, both competitors in the Vendée Globe. Pete had turned his yacht, *Aqua Quorum*, around to sail back 200 miles, against the winds and seas, to rescue Raphael from his sinking yacht.

Pete Goss had trained most of The Challenge crews so it was very much a personal story which they all shared. The sight of Raphael Dinelli standing on the upturned hull of his yacht in freezing conditions certainly focused the minds of The Challenge crews. The scale of courage which Pete Goss showed is perhaps understood when it is realised that his entire yacht weighed the same as the keel of a Challenge yacht. To turn round a yacht which looked more like a giant surfboard and which had been designed and built as a 'downwind' yacht, into the pounding that the Southern Indian Ocean gives, and survive, is a truly remarkable piece of seamanship.

The crews carried these two incidents in the back of their minds as the yachts sailed back into the Southern Ocean.

The only constant companions to the yachts were the albatross. They would desert the fleet prior to extreme storms and return just as the wind abated. These giant birds, with a wingspan of some 10ft, wheeled around the yachts in a constant pattern. They used the lift generated by the gale force winds and skimmed inches from the rough sea in a demonstration of precision flying at which the crews marvelled.

"Somehow when we sailed in the Southern Ocean without sight of land or another yacht, the sight of the albatross accompanying us through these hostile waters gave us some comfort," wrote Humphrey Walters. "They were our only companions and it seemed to us that if they could survive we had a chance too. They would accelerate up to the yacht as steady as a glider and give us a stare with their beady yellow eyes almost as if to say, 'What are you idiots doing down there putting yourselves through hell when you could be up here steady as a rock making use of the power of the wind.' Then, suddenly, they would be gone and we knew the expected wind was going to increase to 50 or 60 knots and we would be alone. There was never a sight more welcoming than the return of our friends and we felt they were telling us that the wind was going to abate and we would have a short respite from the terrible weather. I have to confess that I became more interested in watching for the albatross than viewing the weatherfax. I feel nature is more in tune with these conditions than satellites and forecasters.

Watching these wonderful birds, I did make one resolve. If I was ever to return to the Southern Indian Ocean it would be by jumbo jet at 35,000 feet. Maybe I did learn something after all !"

The first storm hit the fleet as they rounded Tasmania. The weatherfax showed this to be 3,000 miles across – more than the width of the North Atlantic Ocean – and had isobars so tight it looked like a giant thumbprint on the map. With a massive high pressure system situated over Australia – some 6,000 miles across and the same weather conditions over Antarctica – the low pressure area was going to be squeezed through the narrow gap like a giant venturi and accelerate the wind to storm force conditions.

The effect on the sea state was going to make the conditions very different from those encountered on the first Southern Ocean leg. It caused waves of enormous height which seemed to lift up to some 60 to 80ft in front of the yachts and accelerate at them with a terrifying force. Gone were the majestic swells with long valleys forming 150ft troughs which the fleet had coped with in the first Southern Ocean leg. Instead they met waves so steep and sharp that it was possible to see through the top 20ft with a clarity of green liquid glass as they came snarling and curling at the yachts. The waves would then crash down and leave an aquamarine stain with the foam dissipating slowly until the next wall of water arrived.

The technique for helming in these violent conditions was to steer the yacht diagonally up these massive waves, 'aim off' or 'bear away' at the crest, and slide the yacht sideways down the back of the wave and then set the yacht up for the next wave. A sort of weaving motion to avoid the full ferocity of the force of water. With the yacht bow climbing at a 45 degree angle, similar to a jumbo jet landing, it was difficult to see the exact crest and the helm had to judge when to aim off. Too early turning the helm, the yacht would have tons of water crashing over it and if too late, the yacht would take off and crash into the trough below with impact and sound of a violent car crash. The strain on the mast and rigging was tremendous, with the top of the mast whiplashing forward and backwards, relying on the stays and fittings to keep everything in one piece.

Each wave had a different shape and configuration and the concentration and physical strength required to cope meant that the on-deck crew was changed every half an hour in the watch system. The sea temperature dropped to three degrees centigrade and with the wind chill factor meant that every inch of flesh needed to be covered up.

"Helming in these conditions is a constant challenge, with each wave being a different shape and coming at you from a different direction," said one of the crew. "I try and thread my way up the wave to find the path of least resistance and hope I don't get it wrong and take the yacht airborne to crash into the trough below. I have everything zipped up and my face mask secured so that no part of my body is exposed to the spray which shot blasts our skin and makes life unbearable. On top of my face mask I wear goggles to protect my eyes. It's a bit like looking through a letterbox which restricts my vision but it is the only way we can cope in these conditions."

"It's like throwing your heart over the next wave and launching the yacht to try and catch up with it."
Humphrey J Walters

Upstairs, Downstairs – Down below it was extremely difficult trying to sleep, cook and clean the yacht. With 14 extremely hungry people, it was essential that meals were prepared to a strict menu and timetable so that no-one was kept waiting for food which would either delay them on deck or prevent them from getting the precious sleep they needed. Cooking proved to be a hazardous occupation and it was a bizarre sight seeing the cooks wearing their foul weather gear to protect them from hot food and flying pans, when the helmsman got it wrong and launched the yacht off a wave. Given that the yacht was also at 35 degrees most of the time, the cooks braced themselves against the cooking area as they prepared the meal.

Bread was baked daily and proved to be very good, as well as popular. The smell of freshly baked bread wafting through the air gave everyone a great psychological boost. James Hatfield on *Time & Tide*, himself an experienced chef and former wine bar owner, was the envy of the fleet with his adventurous attitude to catering. "Here's one for all fast food pizza places," he said heeling over in the Southern Ocean. "In the same pan we can achieve both thick crust deep pan pizza and thin crust pizza!"

135

At the beginning of the race, few people had ever cooked for so many people in such conditions, but a lot of initiative and trouble was taken by most crews.

Meal times provided an important opportunity for people to meet, discuss the situation and exchange friendly banter. The quality of the food was crucial in order to create the correct atmosphere. Despite this being 'The Challenge of a Lifetime' and very much an adventure in adverse conditions, some crew members were extremely fussy about the food they were prepared to eat, and in some cases, were not prepared to alter their stance. This naturally caused some ill feeling within the crews and also exasperation for the individuals tasked with victualling the yachts. It seemed that 'The Challenge of a Lifetime' did not extend to eating rice and pasta when one was used to meat and two veg or chips with everything.

As the temperature dropped and the ocean pounded the yachts more and more, water and condensation seeped in. Crews had already become used to sleeping in clothes wet from spray which found its way through the foul weather gear, but below deck, water was beginning to drip incessantly from the ventilation dorades which in normal circumstances were completely waterproof. On *Pause To Remember*, one bunk had water two inches deep sloshing to and fro and on *Ocean Rover*, water was seeping through the floor boards, soaking the crew bags which were stored on the floor. The incessant dampness began to have an affect on morale and to make matters worse, the diesel heaters on some of the yachts had filled with water and were impossible to re-light.

At last the weather abated and the sun came out. The crews could hardly believe it after 10 days of continuous storms. They came out of their burrows and some of the yachts became Chinese laundries with wet clothes over all the guardrails and rigging. The crew of *Ocean Rover* had been receiving iceberg warnings yet, unlike the other yachts, had seen nothing. Suddenly on the radar there

136

appeared an enormous blip which was either the next storm clouds or an iceberg. As if to order, a huge shape appeared out of the haze on the horizon which looked like a huge cliff face. *Ocean Rover* sailed serenely past this enormous edifice which was the height of the cliffs of Dover and some half mile square.

This was the lull before the next series of storms. The yachts were to suffer further arduous weather on their way to the Kerguelen Islands which served as a psychological turning point in the journey to Cape Town's calmer climate.

It was Cassius who advised Caesar to "Beware the Ides of March" and indeed the fleet was hit by the worst storms during this period. A total of six yachts were knocked flat by huge unstable waves which knocked them on their sides with the mast and rigging below the horizontal. These knockdowns caused considerable damage to sails as well as the radar struts which were normally some 12ft above the waterline.

Save The Children lost most of her electronic instrumentation and radio during a knockdown and *Global Teamwork* was hit by another huge wave which injured the cockpit crew and washed the compass away. Perhaps the worst damage was inflicted on *Group 4* which was knocked flat on the 19 March. Crew member Andrea Bacon described this incident as one of the most terrifying moments of the entire trip.

"I had just finished supper and was about to use the computer to write my daily reports, when there was a terrific violent bang and the yacht started to tip over. For the first time ever, I thought my life was about to end, as I believed we had struck an iceberg and the yacht was about to sink. I was thrown across the galley and pinned against a wall as every unsecured object hurtled towards me. All the cupboard doors flew open and released hand-held radios, books, the medical kit and anything else that was loose. A large heavy floorboard flew up across the galley and jammed itself behind the sink. It was a miracle it didn't hit anyone.

137

Bill Shuff was at the sink washing up the supper plates and suddenly he was pinned on his back on the ceiling, which now became the floor. The remains of the meal, mashed potato, chilli, pickle, coffee, tea, cheesecake and washing-up water was everywhere. Suddenly the yacht righted itself and all the items were flung back across the yacht again. It was absolute carnage below but the mess didn't matter. I was very relieved when I ran up the steps to look out and see the mast, sails and rigging still intact."

"The test of an adventure is when you're in the middle of it, and you say to yourself, 'Oh now I have got myself into an awful mess; I wish I were sitting quietly at home.' The sign that something is wrong with you is when you sit quietly at home wishing you were out experiencing an adventure."
Humphrey J Walters

Group 4's radar dome was smashed from the 12ft strut which supported it; it looked as though someone had bitten out a large piece. Water had poured into the yacht and drenched the sleeping areas as well as sleeping bags and clothes. The computers were also water-logged, and to make matters worse, the heaters became flooded which meant that there was little likelihood of drying anything out for some time.

Despite the severity of these knockdowns, there was absolutely no structural damage to any of the yachts which was an indictment to their strength and design. The only sign of damage was some panel indentation to the decks, which is hardly surprising considering the battering they took and the relentless way the yachts were being driven.

Man Overboard – On *Ocean Rover* an event happened dreaded by any person going to sea – a 'Man Overboard'. In heavy seas, one of the most dangerous areas of a yacht is the lee rail, the side of the yacht nearest the water. *Ocean Rover* was heeling over at 35 degrees with the wash boiling past

138

the side of the yacht. Paul Bennett was beneath the mainsail trying to secure one of the reefing lines, when a huge wave cascaded down the yacht and washed him over the side. Jon Hirsh, on the helm at the time, describes the events:-

"I was trying to protect Paul from the waves but they eventually conspire against you and a huge wave came down the length of the yacht, picked Paul up and deposited him over the side. I felt a moment of panic as I thought he wasn't clipped on and we had lost him. I cried 'Man Overboard' and this call brought more response from other people than anything I will ever do in the rest of my life. Within a flash we had the emergency procedure working, which included putting on the engine and pressing the satellite navigation button which would guide us back to the exact spot where the accident occurred. I was helpless to go to Paul's aid as I had to helm the yacht. However some members of the crew came on deck and we had Paul back on board within two minutes. It was a tense time and an endorsement of the excellent training. Everyone worked brilliantly and we saved a disaster."

> *"Seamanship is about keeping the man in the ship*
> *and the sea out."*
> **John Chittenden**

After this crisis on *Ocean Rover* there was a notable improvement in the performance of the yacht. Up to this point the crew were beginning to feel overwhelmed by the conditions. Once they had recovered from the shock of nearly losing their skipper, there was a new resolve and the crew started to take on the conditions. The old adage of using a crisis to galvanise the focus and efforts of the team seemed to work.

Boom And Bust – On 23 March, *Pause To Remember* was to suffer a serious setback. It was sailing along in 20 knots of wind and a reasonable sea when a bang was heard, similar to a wave crashing on the yacht. When the crew members looked down the deck, they saw the boom snapped in two just by the vang; this supports the boom and provides some rigidity to stop it bouncing up and down with the waves. The crew were incredulous as they removed the mainsail from the two halves and sat on deck next to this massive 1/4 inch thick piece of aluminium tubing. There were two options; either to motor to the Kerguelen Islands some 750 miles away and get help to repair the boom on land, or to carry out a repair at sea and keep sailing. By motoring they would incur a heavy time penalty so Tom O'Connor and the crew decided to repair the boom at sea and keep racing as best they could.

The engineering team aboard *Pause To Remember* dragged both sections of the boom below and started work to join them together. They hacksawed the two ragged ends, cut off a foot section from one and used this to form a sleeve over the shortened boom. They then used some bolts taken from a bar in the bow section of the yacht to bolt the two halves and the sleeve together. Unfortunately the drills they had on board were too small for the bolts so they had further work by hand filing the holes so that they fitted the bolts. After 48 hours of non-stop work they had completed a repair which the rest of the fleet marvelled at when the yacht finally arrived in Cape Town. Once the conditions improved they were able to hoist the complete boom on deck which emerged from below with half an inch clearance. Luck was finally on their side.

"Talent is cheaper than table salt. What separates the talented individual from the successful one is a lot of hard work."
Stephen King

The Kerguelen Islands marked the next major psychological and physical turning point for the fleet. The crews were hoping that passing these islands would bring them warmer water, more favourable conditions and less hostile seas.

140

These islands form an archipelago made up of the main Kerguelen Island (also known appropriately as Desolation Island) and 300 other islets which together cover 2,700 square miles. Discovered by the French navigator Yves Joseph de Kerguelen-Tremarec in 1772, they were frequently visited by whalers and seal hunters. James Cooke, the British circumnavigator, also explored the islands. In 1950, a permanent scientific base was established there as well as a French meteorological base which helped previous round the world yacht races. These islands sit on a shelf known as the Kerguelen Plate, with shallow water similar to Cape Horn, which can cause extremely rough and turbulent seas.

The race organisers had placed an imaginary waypoint north of these islands to keep the fleet away from the Kerguelen Plate and avoid the shallow water. In the event, the fleet was to experience endless stormy conditions and further breakages.

Working on deck changing sails in these ferocious conditions was never a pleasant experience. For those crew out of action through injury there was a feeling of helplessness. They felt they were letting the team down by being unable to contribute on deck.

Jo Dawson, on *Toshiba Wave Warrior* had suffered a broken arm and was having to stay below decks while her colleagues battled with the harsh conditions. "Confined below decks through some of the worst Southern Ocean storms may sound like an easy ride, but the mental anguish can be just as intense as physical exhaustion, as you feel you are letting the team down," wrote Jo. "The wind gusted up to 70 knots and one of my watch was thrown off the helm by a huge wave which bent the wheel back four inches. Then another huge wave crashed down from 45 feet sweeping everyone in its path down the deck to the end of their life lines. The hurricane force wind then ripped the small storm mainsail from the track on the mast and left it flogging violently. Another dangerous task for the crew to get the flogging sail under control and removed from the mast. This took them an hour in freezing conditions. While this mayhem was occuring on deck, I was below in the relative warm, feeling helpless. All I could do was to offer them moral support and hot drinks when they came below to thaw out. I performed the below deck 'Mother' duties until we arrived in Cape Town. I was surprised when a bunch of flowers was brought out by our supporters boat and given to me from the rest of the crew as a gesture of thanks for looking after them.

It sounds melodramatic but at that moment I was very moved and felt privileged to be part of the team. I am not sure if I have ever felt quite as privileged on dry land, but hostile conditions bring the worst and certainly the best out of people – I shall miss them all!"

"I learned a long time ago that minor surgery is when they do an operation on someone else – not you!"
Dr John Walters

On *Group 4* Amanda Tristram, a gynaecologist and the yacht's doctor, had been having severe toothache from a broken tooth, and as there were at least 10 days before the yacht was due to arrive in Cape Town, emergency treatment was necessary. Amanda finally decided that she had had enough. A radio link-up was made to *Global Teamwork* which had John Scott, a dentist, on its crew. Instructions were relayed to *Group 4* crewman Andy Girling, a marine biologist and environmental scientist, who was picked to perform the operation. This involved injecting Amanda and pulling the broken half of the tooth out with forceps. Andy confessed that the only injection he had ever given was to a fish at university some years before, but he administered the anaesthetic and performed the extraction after three attempts. Mike Golding, skipper of *Group 4*, had retreated up the mast and could hear the screams of pain 80ft in the air. The final act of dentistry was to fill the

142

remaining half of the tooth with a sealing paste. Unfortunately they had forgotten to ask how to mix the paste and the best technique to apply it. As often happens at sea the radio link for further information from John Scott failed but, undaunted, *Group 4* contacted *Toshiba Wave Warrior* which had Ciara Scott – John's daughter and also a dentist – on board. Ciara provided the information so that Andy Girling could apply the finishing touches.

It was a link between three yachts, two dentists – a father and daughter – giving instructions by radio. The operating theatre was the seat in the saloon area. The operation was performed by an environmental scientist who had only injected small fish and all the time the yachts were racing flat out. The National Health Service would never believe it, but such was the ingenuity that was shown continuously throughout The Challenge.

The final drama was to be played out as the leading yachts approached Cape Town. Two yachts, *Concert* and *Group 4*, had been continuously swapping positions in the four days up to the finish. As the coastline of South Africa approached, *Group 4* could see *Concert* eight miles to the west heading out to sea. Mike Golding went below. For two hours he sat on his bunk and studied. Perhaps he read David Houghton's book *Weather at Sea*, he looked up the relevant pilot book data, weather faxes and the latest fleet plots, and he re-read the Bracknell data. He decided to head inshore and hope that an offshore breeze would develop to take them in; a brave decision based on homework, but needing a bit of luck. As they approached the coast, the wind died and the yacht sat helplessly while the crew morale plummeted with the inevitable shaking of heads. Was the leg now lost to *Concert*? Would the wind pick up or was this an outrageous gamble? Slowly the offshore breeze picked up and *Group 4* finally won the leg by 0.9 of a mile after sailing 7,500 miles. Surely one of the closest finishes ever in an ocean race and an indication of how well-matched the yachts were in terms of performance.

143

The skippers and crews had endured so much during this leg. Their commitment to each other was summed up by James Hatfield's fax to Mike Golding on his arrival.

"Attention Mike and crew. You have all raced a fantastic leg. Crew and I admire your stamina. Just a few more miles. Press on. Can't believe it's match racing still after all these miles. Utmost respect to both *Concert* and yourselves. See you in the bar."

This was by far the worst leg the fleet had encountered. During the 41 days at sea there had been 12 days on which wind strengths were more than 60 knots and 28 days of gale force winds. Most of the yachts experienced the wind rising from 25 to 60 knots in the space of three minutes. This necessitated very rapid changes of sail. The risk of extensive sail damage was always present. Some yachts recorded as many as 13 sail changes in a 12 hour period which was very arduous on the crews and also very dangerous.

"Man is the only creature that strives to surpass himself,
and yearns for the impossible."
Eric Hoffer

By the time the fleet arrived in Cape Town, 103 out of 168 sails had been damaged but, due to the seamanship and resourcefulness of the crews, only one sail was ultimately replaced. Five of the storm trysails were damaged but this was mainly due to wave action. It is difficult to comprehend how wave action could damage a sail which was set so much higher up the mast but indicates the ferocity of the conditions.

Six of the yachts suffered complete knockdowns caused by huge unstable waves throwing the yachts onto their sides with the rigging below the horizontal. Three compasses were knocked over the side, washed from their binnacles in front of the wheel by massive waves.

All in all it was a miracle that no-one was lost over the side and that there was no severe damage to the masts or

Mark Pepper

...affic jam in Wellington Harbour as the fleet jostle for position round ...e tightly placed racing buoys.

...RH Prince Michael of Kent takes to the winch on the 'Executive Leg' to Sydney.

Humphrey Walters

Chris Kapetan

A jubilant crew aboard *Save The Children* as they approach the finish
line in Sydney and prepare to celebrate victory.

Leaving Sydney Harbour and The Opera House, bound for Cape Town.

Mark Pepp

Humphrey Walters

...et and sunshine – the vagaries of the weather in the Southern Indian Ocean.

...n Goddard inspecting the damaged boom shortly after disaster struck on
...*use To Remember.*

Henry Pritchard

Helmet protection, an additional item of battle dress worn on board *Toshiba Wave Warrior.*

Day after day of white frothing foam and freezing spray.

Humphrey Walters

he albatross' beady eye watches the crews as they battle against the elements.

breathtaking sight – a Southern Ocean iceberg the size of Wembley Stadium
oms out of the greyness.

Humphrey Walters

Simon Walk

Crashing off a wave means yet another dousing in the cockpit.

Foredeck crew hang on as another icy wave engulfs the yacht.

Robert Bru

ruggling on the foredeck during a sail change.

orking conditions – sea temperature 1°C.

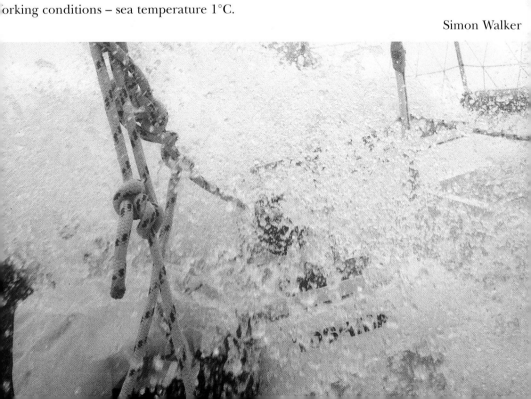

Joanne Wats

Skipper of *Toshiba Wave Warrior*, Simon Walker, preparing the milk.

rigging. This was a further endorsement of the strength and design of the yachts which had now covered over a million miles since the prototype was launched.

For the crews, Cape Town was a most welcome sight. James Hatfield on *Time & Tide* was elated to have brought his brave crew of disabled yachtsman through these terrible waters. It had not been an easy leg. They had sailed with 12 instead of 14 crew and early on Paul Hebblethwaite, their bowman and watchleader, had been thrown down the deck and injured badly. Lesley, the yacht's medic, had had to stitch him internally, using the galley table as an operating theatre as the yacht rose and fell continuously in horrendous seas. On arrival James joked and said that before the leg began he had told anyone who wanted to moan on this leg to do so to their watchleaders, not him. The watchleaders, Carolyn and Paul, were both profoundly deaf! He added, "Coming in 10th is wonderful, but we didn't know how to welcome in other yachts – we soon learnt!"

For Adrian Donovan on *Heath Insured II* it had been another terrible leg and a poor result despite all the hard work he and the crew had put in. A series of breakages and misfortunes had piled one on top of the other and their ingenuity had been tested almost every day. A proud man, he wanted to be alone at the finish and remained below decks while the rest of the crew celebrated their safe arrival.

Tom O'Connor and his crew were justifiably proud to have brought *Pause To Remember* home with such an excellent repair to the boom. This had remained intact despite sailing through five further gales and one storm with wind speeds of 70 knots.

The most consistent comment among the crew was, " I wouldn't have missed it for the world, but never again!" and perhaps the sight of Jane Corfield of *3Com* kissing the pontoon on all fours – before she had a drink – said it all!

"Difficult is the excuse history never accepts."
Anonymous

145

WHAT MADE THE DIFFERENCE

This was the most testing leg for all the crews. Although they were racing, most yachts had gone into survival mode. Chay Blyth's words were on most of their lips – anticipate, detail, speed.

Do it fast
Do it now
Do it right

Thinking

Information Search – In their Information Search before the race, some skippers had gone to extraordinary lengths. Merfyn Owen had visited Boston and Cape Town at his own expense in 1995 in order to gain as much knowledge of the local coasts and currents as possible. He had collected all of the weatherfaxes from the Southern Ocean for the 12 months before the start. In conjunction with a private router he had produced a complete set of "what if" alternative strategies for *Global Teamwork* during the leg.

Merfyn was not alone in his continual quest for more information. Such was Boris Webber's focus that his bedtime reading throughout the race was a vast collection of sailing, weather and pilot books that he had bought at his own expense. Mike Golding's adherence to a strict policy of comprehensive information search before making a strategic decision resulted in him winning the leg, albeit by a frustratingly close margin for Chris Tibbs.

Concept Formation – At one stage in the race Merfyn Owen elected to sail 120 miles off course in search of better weather, much to the disquiet of his crew, but the strategy paid huge dividends. On another occasion after the mainsail was seriously damaged Merfyn changed the whole watch system from 6 + 6 + 2 crew on motherwatch, to 3 + 3

146

+ 3 crew on motherwatch with five on sail repair. This calculation tried to balance the reduction in race speed from a smaller crew on deck with the necessity of getting the mainsail back in action as soon as possible.

Developmental

Empathy – This was the leg in which the emotional lows were at their nadir. To enter the Southern Ocean for a second time required a huge amount of bravery. In Rio, most crew members had not known what to expect from the Southern Ocean; now, armed with that knowledge, they were going back there. There was inevitably a price to be paid for this courage. The effect of the emotional pressure on individuals varied enormously and there was no predictable pattern. For the skippers, their powers of empathy were stretched to the limit as they tried to cope with the emotional complexities of 13 individuals coping daily with sheer terror. Some crew members suffered brief emotional breakdown and had to be relieved of all duties for a couple of watches. Some cried in despair and were comforted by the crew, others withdrew to their bunks in exhaustion and slept for 48 hours. Others needed to be alone. It was the successful understanding and handling of these varying needs that made the difference. When a high level of empathy was displayed as a behaviour on board a yacht, mutual respect flourished and individuals felt encouraged to give of their best.

One skipper said that, "Everyone was terrified but mutual support was huge. When the chips were down, I gave people a couple of watches off. Their space was respected and the crew became very cohesive. If someone was really scared, they could work in the galley rather than on deck."

Teamwork – This was the leg in which a crew's ability to work as a team was vital. The effects of cold wind and wild

147

water combined to make even the simplest task an almost Herculean effort. Sail changing was probably the worst. The duty watch of six crew members had to demonstrate total co-ordination and commitment despite their being unable to hear one another, and being constantly immersed in huge volumes of freezing water trying to sweep them overboard. For the foredeck crew, the problem was compounded by trying to do all of their highly physical task on an open, slippy and sloping deck that was rising and falling 40ft at a time. The mutual respect that evolved between participants in such a manoeuvre was intense, particularly when one false move from any of them would have directly threatened the lives of the others. Individual crew members could operate at Level 3 (see page 29) by being good team players but it took a whole crew to demonstrate Level 5 behaviour in which teamwork was an ethos rather than a way of working together. Only some of the crews ever reached Level 5 and these reaped the benefit in the Southern Ocean. Interestingly, when the race was over, it was the Level 5 crews who found the transition to 'normal' life most difficult. They realised that they had experienced a level of total inter-dependence and mutual commitment that they were unlikely ever to see again.

Developing People – After the disappointment of dismasting on the first Southern Ocean leg, Chris Tibbs felt it vital on this leg of all legs, to lead from the front. He helped with all sail changes. At one stage, when they were lagging far behind, Tibbs knew that he had to give his crew at least one tangible success. They succeeded by tackling one yacht at a time and instilling the belief that they could do it. They stuck to their goals without risking people. Success bred success and everyone became motivated and moved up a gear.

Mike Golding felt that it was up to the watchleaders to develop people. Both watches did all their own training.

148

Their leadership styles were very different but both successful. One of his watchleaders developed four good helms and delegated that key function to them, whereas the other helmed himself and delegated the other crew duties.

James Hatfield said that the most successful crews were the ones where as many responsibilities as possible were delegated. Merfyn Owen delegated the whole method of sail changing to the crew. "I'll give them tips, but they own the yacht."

Boris Webber felt that the successful development of people was all about the development of attitude. "Before we left Southampton we agreed to save weight on board by only eating freeze-dried food. Similarly there was no alcohol and we were light on clothes. Yachts carrying junk are at the back. It's the mind set of freeze-dried food that matters."

Inspirational

Influence – For Mike Golding it was a race for those who really wanted to race. "It is all about passion. Passion creates success." His obvious passion influenced the crew to push the yacht to its limits. At one stage *Group 4* was lying in 2nd position, 15 miles behind *Concert*. In order to recover some miles Mike elected to sail with far too much sail for the conditions – full main, No 1 Yankee, and staysail, in 40 knots of wind. Only five crew members were physically strong enough to helm. It was a huge risk and the yacht was totally unstable. They went from catching up the fleet two miles every six hours to 10 miles every six hours. Mike admitted, "The adrenalin rush on the helm made it terrifying for 15 minutes, thrilling for another 15 minutes and then you were totally exhausted and had to be replaced." It was a gamble that paid-off, but it was the influence of Mike's passion to win that inspired his crew to follow suit. A leader who has no passion cannot expect passionate commitment from other team members.

149

Building Confidence – Building confidence in a crew was a result of three factors:

> **Recognition**
> **Shared success**
> **Mutual respect**

Throughout the race, those skippers who recognised that praise to crew members was motivational food received a response of improved performance. Mark Lodge's crew was particularly responsive to his continual efforts to build up self esteem; Richard Tudor's own quiet self confidence inspired confidence in his own crew members. The view that if it looks right it probably is right, was the driving force behind those skippers whose particular focus was on keeping the yacht as meticulous as possible at all times; this inspired confidence in the yacht's ability to cope. Untidy yachts failed to inspire confidence.

As the miles slipped by in the most appalling conditions the overall confidence in the fleet grew as the crews conquered day after day. This growing confidence was an almost unavoidable by-product of the conquest of the Southern Ocean. Overcoming challenge is a time-honoured method of developing individual and team confidence. Equally the way in which a skipper addressed and treated his crew had a profound effect. "My crew is anything but amateur. I treat them like professionals so they behave like professionals," said one skipper. Another skipper admitted that in the earlier legs his crew had behaved like children so he had treated them like children. By the end of the leg most of the crew volunteers were behaving like the seasoned professionals they were and they disembarked in Cape Town with their heads held high. Some skippers elected to maintain these professional standards even when ashore. "We never relax totally when we are in uniform," said one skipper, but this attitude ensured that the mutual respect and cohesion among the crew was maintained throughout the stopover. Some members of the other crews let their hair down too much and this became divisive as they lost the respect of their fellow crew members.

"Winning isn't a job, it's a way of life."
Mark Lodge

SYDNEY – CAPE TOWN

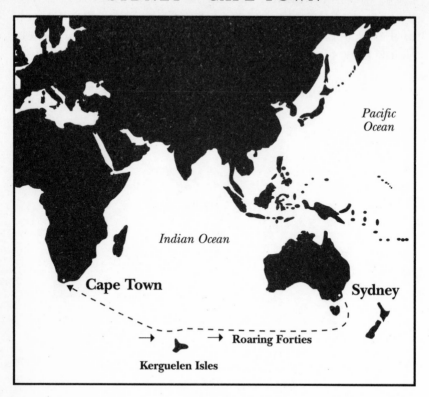

LEG 4 RESULTS

Position	Arrival Time (GMT)		Leg Time D H M S	Overall Position
1 Group 4	09 Apr	01:35:05	37 23 05 05	1
2 Concert	09 Apr	01:55:26	37 23 25 26	14
3 Toshiba Wave Warrior	09 Apr	05:41:30	38 03 11 30	2
4 Commercial Union	09 Apr	21:19:23	38 18 49 23	5
5 Motorola	10 Apr	05:55:27	39 03 25 27	4
6 Save The Children	10 Apr	09:53:39	39 07 23 39	3
7 3Com	10 Apr	16:13:30	39 13 43 30	7
8 Global Teamwork	10 Apr	16:48:51	39 14 18 51	6
9 Ocean Rover	11 Apr	07:45:43	40 05 15 43	8
10 Time & Tide	11 Apr	22:07:29	40 19 37 29	12
11 Nuclear Electric	12 Apr	08:07:24	41 05 37 24	9
12 Courtaulds International	12 Apr	11:43:30	41 09 13 30	13
13 Pause To Remember	12 Apr	12:33:33	41 10 03 33	10
14 Heath Insured II	12 Apr	12:55:48	41 10 25 48	11

CHAPTER EIGHT

"To win without risk is to triumph without glory."
Pierre Grueille

"We have lost 250 miles to the leaders after being becalmed for 60 hours. We have watched the yacht in 4th place overall come from 150 miles behind to be 200 miles in front and had our other nearest rival sail up to us from 95 miles astern and then sail round us within sight while we sat still. I am totally running out of explanations for the poor crew."

Andy Hindley, Skipper *Save The Children*

CAPE TOWN TO BOSTON

Leg 5

Race Preparation – "This, guys and gals, is the 'Paradise Leg' – dolphins, sunshine and gin and tonics – that's what the Cape Town to Boston leg is all about," bellowed Chay Blyth at the pre-leg crew briefing. "You may even get to see some mermaids – if you're lucky!" he added.

On a more serious note, he reminded the crews that races are won and lost in light airs. This leg was going to be somewhat different to the ferocious storms and gales the crews had faced for 40 odd days down in the Southern Ocean, but speed was paramount. The presentation continued and Chay's favoured maxim appeared yet again on a slide – 'TRIM, TRIM, TRIM' – three simple words that could make the difference between a first and a second!

And so the scene was set for the start of the next leg. A

153

leg that had not been included in the previous British Steel Challenge, but one that provided great scope for yachts to make some big gains and dramatic changes in overall race position. In terms of mileage, this was the longest leg of the race - some 7,000 miles.

At this stage in the race, the crews were far from amateurs. They had now sailed nearly 20,000 miles round the world and were totally familiar with the yachts. They were now well tuned racing teams that worked together in total synchronisation, gybing and peeling spinnakers with relative ease and pushing the yachts to their limits, knowing the optimum speeds and wind angles and able to capitalise on wind shifts.

What was going to make the difference, therefore, were the tactical decisions made on board based on the information available. Whoever chose the best route, was best able to interpret the weather information, reacted the quickest and took advantage of the ocean currents would benefit the most. These decisions were largely down to the skipper of each yacht and, for several reasons, this was the leg on which they would have more time to think, leaving the competent crews to race the yachts.

Mike Golding, skipper of *Group 4*, commented, "On this leg I could relax. I had confidence that my crew members were capable of handling the yacht and themselves and this left me free to focus on the tactical issues. My mind was clear to allow me to make critical decisions."

"Executive ability is deciding quickly, and getting someone else to do the work."
John G Pollard

The major considerations of this leg were entering the Doldrums, tackling the Azores or the Bermuda high pressure system and crossing the Gulf Stream. All could impede the progress of the yachts, but if well researched, considered and acted upon, could bring massive benefits to the speed and performance of the yachts on their journey to Boston.

It was not surprising therefore that before leaving Cape Town, many of the skippers and crews took the time to monitor the weather patterns and the movements of the high pressure systems, to research the local currents and to assess the Gulf Stream current, its strength and direction.

Skipper of *Toshiba Wave Warrior*, Simon Walker said, "We gathered more information for this leg than for any other. At the end of the day, all the information pointed towards going west but we thought everyone would do that so we wanted to try something different. We called on Roger Badham, our weather guru, who ran a couple of simulations for us on which we based our final route."

Mark Lodge, skipper of *Motorola*, also did his homework. It was time very well spent considering the amazing results he achieved on this leg. Not only did *Motorola* arrive into Boston in 2nd position, but the crew managed to improve its overall race position by reducing the time between *Motorola* and *Save The Children* from 26 hours to just 15 minutes!

"We knew we could never make up the hours on *Save The Children* if we were to sail the same route and we were therefore keen to do something different. If we got it wrong we could put ourselves back into 5th position. But so what - 4th or 5th, what's the difference? However, if we took the chance we could possibly bring ourselves up into 3rd place overall," commented Mark Lodge.

"It was important that the whole crew was involved in this major decision. We all sat down and I discussed with them the two potential strategies:-

i) We sail the Great Circle route on which we could possibly make miles on others but not enough to make a difference to our overall position, or
ii) We take a westerly route and try something different.

The crew knew we would be taking a gamble but they were all for it," added Mark.

155

Ligia Ripper, crew member on *Motorola* recalled, "We were all keen to take the risk and understood the consequences of our initial move west. I warned my father before leaving Cape Town that he would see us at the back of the fleet for a while, but told him not to worry that that was all part of our strategy."

So, armed with information and differing strategies, the skippers and crews prepared themselves for race re-start day.

Cape Town was a tough stopover for the crews. After a physically and mentally challenging leg from Sydney to Cape Town, the crews had had to work tirelessly throughout the stopover in order to ensure that the yachts were fit to continue.

The wave damage to the hulls of the yachts was quite considerable, while on deck, rigging, deck blocks, jammers and stanchions needed to be replaced. Several of the yachts required new pulpits, steering cables and wheels and *Group 4* required a total radar unit – strut and dome – following the loss of the previous one in the Southern Ocean knockdown.

Pause To Remember required a boom to replace her makeshift one and modifications were made to all the booms to ensure that such a breakage could not happen again.

Down below in the galley, seats needed to be refitted to the floor, cupboard doors needed re-hinging and woodwork needed repairing. Computers which had been completely ruined after being damp for weeks or covered in chocolate powder, chilli or milk had to be replaced and all the electronics needed retuning.

Preparations were still underway late into Saturday evening, less than 18 hours before the race was due to resume.

HRH Prince Michael of Kent had arrived in Cape Town to see the start of the next leg and was keen to give a helping hand aboard *Ocean Rover*. He would really have liked to have undertaken the leg but instead busied himself aboard joking with the crew as they finalised preparations.

The Re-start – On Sunday 4 May at The Waterfront, beneath Table Mountain, Archbishop Desmond Tutu blessed the 14 yachts. A huge crowd had gathered to bid farewell to the fleet who had received tremendously open and warm hospitality throughout their stay in South Africa. Jazz bands played, while children paraded along the quayside and the Cape Minstrel Troupe performed in an environment buzzing with excitement and anticipation.

The crews looked good in their kit as they stood on the foredecks waving to the huge crowds who cheered loudly as the yachts slipped their lines and left the marina basin. It was a magical atmosphere which brought tears to the eyes of the families and friends who watched their loved ones leave.

The spectators took to the water and followed the fleet out to the start line, bobbing around in all size of craft, waving and cheering. Table Mountain formed the most magnificent backdrop to the event and was a sight which the crews enjoyed until late into the evening when the sun went down.

Everything looked to be perfect to the onlooker, but 10 out of the 14 yachts had several crew suffering from a severe bout of South African belly. Aboard *Group 4* Martin Hall was suffering to the extent that he was incapable of taking up his pre-start position. He lay in his bunk, sweating hot and cold, while others in the crew sat on deck shivering and shaking despite the heat of the day. Start positions had to be re-allocated to accommodate the crew members who were too weak to grind the winches or hoist the sails.

With winds gusting up to 30 knots from a south easterly direction, most of the fleet decided not to hoist a headsail until the last moment As the race officer counted down the final 60 seconds before the start gun, the crews started to haul up the headsails. *Courtaulds International* shot away across the line in what was described as one of the fastest and most aggressive starts of the race. Under the command of South African skipper Boris Webber, it led the fleet around the first buoy closely followed by *3Com*, *Nuclear Electric* and *Commercial Union* but as they turned to head north to the second buoy, the wind died away.

In the lee of Table Mountain the yachts wallowed around with only six knots of breeze, spinnakers collapsing. *Heath Insured II* crept through the congestion and rounded the second buoy in 1st place, leading the fleet out towards Robben Island, where Nelson Mandela had spent many years in prison.

In the 1700's Robben Island had been established as a penal colony by the British. It was then a leper colony before becoming the home of political prisoners as well as some of the most violent murderers and criminals in South Africa. There was no segregation, something that the political prisoners found more difficult than the spartan conditions in which they lived. Up until the 1970's one large room housed some 300 prisoners for over 18 hours a day, in three tier bunks with no lockers or space for personal possessions.

By the time Nelson Mandela was imprisoned there, the inmates were living in separate 8 x 5ft cells, each with its own raffia mat on the floor, a felt overblanket, a jug and bucket. Mandela was privileged enough to be allowed a bed, table and chair.

The President had been rumoured to visit The Challenge fleet before its departure from South Africa. However, the weekend of their departure he was called away for an offshore meeting with the heads of all the African countries concerning the troubles in Zaire and the future of President Mobutu. A couple of weeks later the fleet heard on the BBC World Service that Mobutu had disappeared and that the rebel leader Kabila had taken over Zaire renaming it the Democratic Republic of the Congo.

A Different Kind Of Racing – Gybing around the island, the fleet waved a final goodbye to the spectator boats and left South Africa behind.

As Table Mountain faded into the distance, the yachts

started to split. *Courtaulds International* and *Global Teamwork* stuck close to the coast, heading north, while *Motorola* began to show the first signs of her pre-leg strategy keeping out to the west of the fleet. In the middle of the pack the majority of the yachts vied with one another, watching and waiting to see who was going to do what.

Less than six hours out from Cape Town *3Com* fell foul of the breeze which was building. A wild broach was watched by many of the yachts before *3Com's* brand new 2.2oz spinnaker blew out, leaving them to gather up the bits, bundle it below and start a mammoth stitching job. With their heaviest spinnaker now flying they were off again but sadly not for long. Later that evening they blew this kite and a couple of days out a third, quickly earning them the name '3Gon'!

This was not the only problem that *3Com* was to face that first night. Already suffering the loss of two spinnakers, a huge patch of seaweed then became entwined around the rudder of the yacht, forcing her to stop for several hours while the crew frantically tried to cut themselves free. As a consequence of the time lost from these problems, *3Com* dropped back to 13th position and never fully recovered for the remainder of the leg. The crew did eventually manage to patch two of the shredded spinnakers together to make one.

3Com was not alone, however, in its spinnaker fate – *Save The Children*, *Nuclear Electric* and *Ocean Rover* all blew a kite within the first few days.

Each yacht had been issued with a brand new 2.2oz spinnaker before departure from Cape Town. This had not been the original intention of The Challenge Business. When the yachts were issued with their race sails back in May 1996, crews were told that these were to see them through training and round the world, enduring the passage of time and the effects of the Southern Ocean storms. There would be no new sails en route.

One of the big differences between The Challenge and professional round the world yacht races is the fact that The

Challenge yachts are issued with only one set of 12 sails, while the professional racers are issued with as many replacements as they require, sometimes as many as 150 to 200 a race. If a yacht blew a sail in any other yacht race it would get a new one. If a yacht blew a sail in The Challenge, it had to be repaired or a penalty was incurred.

Any damage had be repaired either by the crew on board or in the sail loft in each port of call. If a sail was deemed beyond repair, the yacht was subject to a severe time penalty which differed depending on the sail that was ruined. Preserving sails was a key objective throughout the race and a decision to change a sail took preservation into consideration as well as the speed and performance of the yacht. Getting the balance right was essential.

An Airborne Farewell – The first night out from Cape Town the crews were given an unusual and unexpected chance to say a final goodbye to their families and friends. The evening British Airways flight Speedbird 58 from Cape Town to London was filled with families, friends and sponsors, and piloted by an ex-*Time & Tide* legger, Mike Austin. As the plane crossed the path of the fleet, Mike called up each yacht in turn and, one by one, relatives and sponsors were called to the cockpit to take part in the link-up.

Ocean Rover received a call from HRH Prince Michael of Kent. He talked and joked with skipper Paul Bennett before wishing the crew all the best. The next link up was with Philip Sørensen, Chairman and Chief Executive of Group 4, followed by a number of parents, partners and friends.

"It was quite amazing to think that we had all been talking ship to plane," commented a crew member from *Time & Tide*.

Seafaring Emergencies – Day two and the smell of bacon wafted across the South Atlantic. James Hatfield, skipper of *Time & Tide*, had delivered bacon to all the yachts before

160

leaving Cape Town, a gesture much appreciated across the fleet as most of the crews were used to living on freeze-dried meals once out at sea.

With *Group 4*, *Concert* and *Commercial Union* all sharing the lead, the race looked like close match racing all the way to Boston. Some 170 miles now separated the fleet east to west with *Motorola* still the most westerly yacht.

The fleet had been asked to keep a look out for a vessel that was missing within the area in which they were sailing.

On day five *Heath Insured II* spotted a drifting yacht with no crew visible on deck. It immediately changed course to investigate. Nearing the yacht, it began to sound its fog horn to try to attract the attention of anyone who might be below. As they cautiously manoeuvred themselves alongside, the crew spotted two bodies lying on the cockpit floor. Shouting and sounding the fog horn again they eventually saw movement and two heads popped up. The yacht had a steering problem but all on board were fine and they did not require help. *Heath Insured II* then resumed its original course and sent a note back to race headquarters claiming redress for the time they had lost.

Global Teamwork meanwhile continued on its northerly track, the most easterly yacht just 380 miles off the coast of Namibia. *Courtaulds International* was struggling with two new French crew members. In an environment in which communication is crucial it was important to understand that Pierre Saint-Jours calling 'Bees, bees' was not an indication of the approach of a swarm of stinging bees but the need for a spinnaker sheet ease.

Ten days later *Heath Insured II* made another detour. This time it headed towards St Helena to evacuate crew member Andy Pilkington who was suffering from suspected appendicitis.

"When it became obvious that Andy was suffering from more than a stomach upset, I undertook several tests and contacted the fleet doctor urgently," said Sally Stewart, the medic on *Heath Insured II*. "Andy's temperature was high and

161

he was in such excruciating pain that I couldn't touch his stomach without him jumping out of his bunk," added Sally.

"I couldn't relate to the pain. It was so bad that I thought I was going to die and at one stage I even asked for some paper to write a note to my family," reflected Andy Pilkington.

After consultation with *Heath Insured II* skipper Adrian Donovan, Chris Price the fleet doctor, the medics at Haslar – the Naval Hospital at Portsmouth, and The Challenge Business it was agreed that Andy needed to be taken off the yacht.

"I set up a drip to administer antibiotics and tried to make him as comfortable as possible as we motored full steam ahead toward St Helena," recalled Sally Stewart. "It was a really difficult moment breaking the news to Andy that he was going to have to be taken off the yacht to get proper medical attention. He was devastated and I felt so guilty, but knew it was the right thing to do."

"Seeing Andy being taken off the yacht was one of the hardest moments for me to cope with on The Challenge. He was a very popular crew member who had the ability to boost morale on board and keep us all going when times got tough," said watchleader Dave Bracher.

"As a mark of respect, we all dressed in our smart crew gear, usually saved for our arrival into port, and we sent Andy off with three loud cheers. One thing that we just couldn't bring ourselves to tell Andy, however, was that there was no airport on St Helena. We sailed away quickly before he had time to find out!" added Dave.

St Helena is a small island in the middle of the South Atlantic where Napoleon Bonaparte was exiled and was later to die. Today, with the demise of the flax industry, just 5,000 people inhabit the island. Of these, the majority are female with a ratio of women to men of 7:1.

Without an airport, there is limited transportation to and from the island but a supply ship delivers goods and mail at regular intervals. With the introduction of television in 1996, the inhabitants are now more in touch with the outside world than ever before. An inhospitable coastline makes it almost impossible for ships to land and the long South Atlantic rollers sweep in making it treacherous for any vessel unfamiliar with the coast.

With no safe harbour, it was therefore not advisable for Adrian Donovan, skipper of *Heath Insured II*, to take the yacht in. He arranged for a boat with medical staff and a customs officer to come out to meet them.

On the island Andy underwent a series of medical tests, but nothing untoward was discovered. He kept himself occupied and was once caught fishing with two nurses out of the back of an ambulance. On another ocassion, the doctor's wife caught him drinking in the pub! On discharge, he was taken by the last remaining mail ship across to Ascension Island where he was almost arrested after inadvertently wandering into the US Airbase to watch the landing of the Challenger spacecraft! He was then flown by the RAF back to the UK where he was reunited with his family. Andy later flew out to Boston to rejoin the crew of *Heath Insured II* for the last leg. His wife joined the crew of *3Com* as a legger for the final sprint home. Two weeks after his arrival in the UK Andy was rushed into hospital where his appendix was removed!

Relative Comfort Sailing North – The contrast between Leg 4 and Leg 5 could not have been more marked. Flat calm seas, bright blue sky and brilliant sunshine meant the crews were able to wear light clothing for almost four weeks. Unlike the lengthy and extensive dressing-up period required between waking up and going on watch in the Southern Ocean, this leg entailed pulling on a pair of shorts and T-shirt just 10 minutes before going up on deck. Moving around was easy. The yachts were level and there was no need to grab on to the nearest secured object while below or above deck. Using the heads was bliss, cooking was a piece of cake. Sleeping was no longer a hazardous occupation since there was no danger of waking up on the

163

floor or in someone else's bunk!

In the words of *Concert's* skipper Chris Tibbs, "What we experienced on Leg 5 were the most perfect sailing conditions in the world - what all sailors dream of but which most will never experience in their entire life."

Sail changes were few and far between. The wind direction and speed remained unchanged for days, meaning the same spinnaker could be flown for long periods of time. But for many of the crew this was torture. After the hectic days of the Southern Ocean they could not adapt to this new way of life. They felt guilty not to be busily changing or packing a sail, continually trimming the sails or struggling to keep the yacht on course to prevent it from crashing off a massive wave. They were not used to the ease of life on board, the long periods of inactivity, the abundance of energy, the time to think.

And as these conditions continued, day after day, week after week, the skippers began to experience problems with their crews that they had not previously encountered. The crews all knew what they were doing, they knew how to work together and how to sail the yacht but they did not know how to handle these long periods of quiet and many of the crews found it impossible to occupy their time. They were finding the leg tedious, and were desperate for some form of entertainment. The need for reassurance, pep talks and morale boosters was noted across the fleet and skippers had to take on a role that did not come naturally.

> *"Why is one man richer than another? Because he is more industrious, more persevering and more sagacious."*
> **John Ruskin**

Andy Hindley, skipper of *Save The Children*, reported, "Everyone is hating this leg. Having previously said they would never go back to the Southern Ocean, they are now saying they will never go ocean racing again."

There was a similar feeling aboard *Concert*, "This leg is

the worst one, it's just too easy and we're not enjoying it. We're bored and we know we are not sailing the yacht very well," commented one of the crew. "This is the closest we've been to a crew blow-up," reported Chris Tibbs.

Crew relationships on many of the other yachts became strained and on *Ocean Rover* two of the crew ended up in a punch up. Humphrey Walters, sleeping in the forward cabin, was woken by raised voices and heard the scuffle taking place near the chart table.

"I couldn't believe what was going on and several of us stepped in to separate the two of them. The whole incident had been blown out of all proportion; it was such a trivial matter and left an uneasy atmosphere for the remainder of the leg. It was only after a few beers in the bar in Boston that the two could face the issue and finally make it up," Humphrey recalled.

Was There Life After The Race? – With time on their hands, the crew's minds began to turn to life after the race and conversations were focused on what to do next, where to go, what job to do, how to pay off the debts and how to readjust to 'normal' life.

In Cape Town, many of the crews had taken the initial step towards finding a job on their return to the UK, preparing CVs and following up contacts that they had made along the way.

"A great deal of soul searching was done aboard our yacht on Leg 5," said Jocelyn Walters, crew member on *Nuclear Electric*. Crews were discussing the prospect of returning home, what they would do next, how to further their careers and how to deal with the financial issues.

Record Breaking News – As the fleet headed north, news arrived that Olivier de Kersauson had broken Peter Blake's circumnavigation record, established on *ENZA*, by 2 days 10 hrs and 9 mins. Olivier had been sailing *Sport-Elec* and completed his circumnavigation in 71.5 days, 14 hrs and 10 mins. Although his average speed had been slower, he had sailed 1,500 miles shorter distance than Blake.

The news was of particular interest to the fleet as Olivier had joined them in one of their chatshows over the radio while passing in the opposite direction down in the Southern Ocean. At that time Olivier had been keen to know the position of icebergs sighted by the yachts.

Crossing The Equator – As the fleet headed up to the Equator, preparation began for the traditional first timer goopings, or Neptune's Feast. *Commercial Union,* the most northerly yacht in the fleet, was the first yacht to cross and carry out the ceremony. At this stage, *Commercial Union* was still *Group 4's* closest contender.

The Critical Matter Of Route Selection – Skipper Richard Merriweather commented, "Our strategy is to get through the Doldrums first, to pick up the north east trade winds on the other side before the others out to the west. We know we are likely to lose the breeze first but hope that we are far enough west to have enough breeze to keep moving. This is very demanding sailing - always trying to respond to the wind shifts and be on the right gybe often has us gybing four or five times a watch."

Motorola had by now almost reached the coast of Brazil and jokes abounded that Mark Lodge was going back to Rio to complete some unfinished business. He was due to get married on his arrival in Boston so rumour had it he was starting his stag party early!

Heading so far west, he was losing miles to the fleet and was some 176 miles behind the leaders. *Group 4* knew, however, that once *Motorola* started to head north it was going to bring itself right up the fleet very quickly.

"We wanted to go further west and cross the Doldrums but knowing *Motorola* could head north and cash in at any time, we knew we should start heading north ourselves," said Mike Golding.

The point at which the yachts crossed the Doldrums was the single most important decision of the leg.

On board *Toshiba Wave Warrior,* the crew was monitoring the movement of the Inter-Tropical Convergence Zone to identify the narrowest point to cross. The ITCZ is the area of high pressure known as the Doldrums that moves north and south. By plotting its co-ordinates daily it is possible to assess the most advantageous point to make a crossing.

However, *Toshiba Wave Warrior* was not able to reach the most favourable position to cross and subsequently suffered as she went through the Doldrums. The crew were disappointed with their performance. They were in 11th position, they had lost faith in their strategy and were generally fed up with the frustrating conditions. One crew member even told skipper Simon Walker that he felt he had wasted three years of his life!

A rallying cry was needed to boost spirits. They were, after all, in 2nd place overall and should have felt exceptionally good about that.

"I called all the crew up on deck and we discussed the situation we were in and I explained exactly what was going on. We looked at the fleet ahead of us and set ourselves new targets to beat those yachts one by one and slowly but surely we got ourselves back into 5th position," commented skipper Simon Walker.

"We are all in the gutter but some of us are looking at the stars."
Oscar Wilde

Nearly all the yachts suffered the effects of the Doldrums, though those to the west suffered less than those to the east. On *Nuclear Electric* a crew member reported, "The braver cabin mates are prepared to risk waves coming through an open hatch in exchange for fresh air to sweep away the fetid odour of sweaty T-shirts and unwashed bodies."

Soon after crossing the Doldrums, the fleet began to cross its outward track, a joyous moment for all the crews as it meant they had then completed their world circumnavigation.

Motorola's strategy soon began to pay off. It headed north and moved from 12th to 3rd position within three days, taking 103 miles out of the *Group 4* lead, recording the longest daily run of the leg.

A week out from Boston, the crews on board the more easterly yachts were tearing their hair out as the Bermuda high pressure system passed across them, leaving them becalmed for days. Tempers were frayed and crews were in despair as they watched themselves fall behind as yachts who were further back suddenly found wind and started to storm ahead.

Skipper of *Save The Children*, Andy Hindley, was exasperated after being becalmed for 60 hours. "We have lost 250 miles to the leaders, watched the yacht in 4th place overall come from 150 miles behind to be 200 miles in front and have had our other nearest rival sail up to us from 95 miles astern and then sail round us within sight while we sat still. I am totally running out of explanations for the poor crew."

The dispirited crew tried to seek some comfort by telephoning home. Portishead Radio became very busy connecting the crew to partners and families via the yacht's ship to shore link.

"I could tell the crew were bored when they volunteered to wash the deck or asked for the next job on the maintenance list," added Andy Hindley.

On *Global Teamwork*, Merfyn Owen warned, "One more week of this and it will be difficult to keep driving at 100%. At least when other yachts are in sight it does give an added impetus."

Concert crew member John Keating reported, "Twenty four hours of complete frustration. Helming for one hour 40 minutes yesterday, I managed to coax the yacht just one mile closer to Boston."

Other Things To Do Than Sail The Boat – With sleep less of a priority and the pace of life so much slower, entertainment aboard was much sought after on this leg. The twice daily radio chatshows became a medium for releasing the boredom, with each duty yacht coming up with something to spice up the days. Joke and anagram competitions abounded, while quizzes flew between yachts on the Inmarsat computer system.

On board *Group 4* the yacht mascot went missing. Floppy Bunny had been spotted up the mast and later in the vang but when his lederhosen were found swinging from the end of the boom, the crew presumed him drowned. *Global Teamwork* responded to the mayday call and rescued FB. It was not long however before *Group 4* received the first of a series of ransom demands. Correspondence of a poetic nature then continued across the satellites for the remainder of the leg until the mascot was eventually returned safe and well in Boston.

Nuclear Electric crew members were far more interested in the FA Cup Final than rabbits and prose. They taped the aerial of a personal radio to the yacht's radar dome and tuned into Radio Five Live's coverage of the match. "It was as clear as a bell," laughed crew member Pete Calvin.

Leaving the Southern Hemisphere behind, the crews said a fond farewell to the Southern Cross, a constellation of stars that had been with them for many months. Spotting new constellations in the Northern Hemisphere became a nightwatch pastime.

Keeping a look-out for suspicious ships was occupying the minds of the crew aboard *Ocean Rover* after a rather unnerving experience in the Atlantic. As they raced along, a ship came into view, but rather than continue on its course, it began to circle them, proceeding to go around them four times, each time getting a little closer. With piracy quite commonplace off the South American coast, it was not surprising that skipper Paul Bennett was a little concerned.

After many attempts he eventually managed to establish

contact with the ship's Polish captain on the SSB radio and discovered they were just curious as to what this yacht was doing out in the middle of the Atlantic. Paul was reminded of Chay's story of an earlier single-handed circumnavigation when he had encountered a Russian fish factory ship deep in the Southern Ocean near the ice pack. "Where was your last port of call?" signalled the surprised Russian Captain. "Southampton," signalled Chay. "And where are you heading?" asked the Russian. "Southampton," replied Chay. The Russian steamed off in disbelief, his comments to his crew members on the bridge unrecorded!

Time & Tide was more worried about the illumination of the sky one night as they entered the notorious Bermuda Triangle. In line with Cape Canaveral, the crew members were later to realise that what they had seen was the launch of a space shuttle which had left an amazing golden plume in the sky.

The Elements Have Different Forms – Even in light conditions the importance of safety can never be over emphasised as Alex Sizer on *Group 4* admits, having gone over the side of the yacht one calm night. She recalled, "We were sailing along at night in 15 knots of breeze with a flat sea. It was warm and I was wearing just shorts and a top. Thoughts of a life jacket and harness, after three weeks in calm seas, were far from my mind.

I was down on the leeward side of the yacht, changing the spinnaker sheet and guy but I must have got the wrong side of the guy because, before I knew it, the rope tightened and lifted me over the stanchions, catapulting me into the air.

I was terrified and tried to grab whatever I could. Luckily, I managed to get hold of the sheet but it started to slacken and I could feel myself slipping down towards the water. I thrashed my arms out above me and managed to grab hold of the boom preventer. By this time two of my watch had grabbed me and were hauling me back in. As it happened, not even my feet got wet!"

170

The fleet's main companions in its hours of woe were the hundreds of pink Portuguese Man O'War jellyfish which hoisted their own little sails and managed to sail right by. Dolphins and whales were not in abundance on this leg, although a huge humped-back whale was reported to have gone under *Group 4* and surfaced the other side.

It was not surprising that there was very little wildlife in the area known as the Sargasso Sea. Beside the proliferation of thick weed for which the sea is known, the sea was awash with all sorts of rubbish - a drawer from a chest, an old milk crate, a plastic garden chair and numerous worn ropes and mooring buoys.

Aboard *Time & Tide* the humour continued, despite its position at the back of the fleet. "There isn't a single person on board who wouldn't give their right arm (well we could trade a couple of spare legs) for just one small Southern Ocean blow. Our course is so random I'm waiting for a traffic cop to nip out from behind a swell, pull us over and charge us with sailing without due care and attention through a high pressure zone," joked skipper James Hatfield.

Nuclear Electric crew members expressed frustration at the situation: "The World's Toughest Yacht Race has become far too sedate, and some of us are wishing for a full Southern Ocean gale to spice things up a bit."

More Typical Conditions Return – It was not long before the fleet's wishes came true. Just five days out from Boston, the fleet was to experience its first real blow of the leg - a frightening reminder of the Southern Ocean.

After 31 days of warm weather and downwind sailing in shorts and T-shirts, it was suddenly time to return to the three layer thermals and don the old faithful foulies as a North Atlantic gale swept across their path. With head winds, big seas and 45 knots of wind the crews were once again dressed in full battle gear, busily changing and packing headsails, reefing and unreefing and watching some fantastic lightening storms. This was just what they

171

had all been waiting for - action - and, for the leggers especially, some real sailing.

Just three days before arriving into Boston, *Save The Children* was called to assist in an air/sea search for a stricken vessel with six people aboard which was in its vicinity. A distress signal had been picked up by RCC Norfolk and relayed to yachts in the area. *Save The Children* immediately altered course and headed towards the last recorded position of the yacht. Thankfully, the yacht was spotted by a seaplane and all aboard were safe and well. Their distress signalling equipment had gone off unbeknown to the skipper and crew. *Save The Children* was released to return to her course towards Boston.

The fleet arrived in Boston much earlier than the race organisers had envisaged, putting everyone in a panic. As *Group 4* sailed towards the finish line 34 days after leaving Cape Town and five days ahead of schedule, the race committee boat was seen hurriedly laying the outer limit mark of the line.

Motorola entered the harbour, some 16 hours later. With just two to three knots of wind, the crew was worried about going aground. A repeat performance of Sydney was something they were keen to avoid. Just in case, the crew prepared the anchor but this time they finished without incident in the early hours of the morning in 2nd place.

The crew of *Motorola* was overjoyed and the skipper Mark Lodge commented, "We are delighted with the outcome and are now in 3rd position overall." With his bride-to-be standing on the dockside to welcome him in, Mark was ecstatic.

And There Is A Happy Side To Racing – The news of Chay Blyth's knighthood for services to sailing reached the fleet just after their arrival in Boston. The crews were extremely proud of their sailing hero but Sir Chay took it lightly and was seen during the evening of the announcement dressed in scruffy jeans and denim shirt carrying brown paper bags

172

out of a local superstore.

Eleven days after the finish Mark Lodge was married in the pagoda beside the pontoon, with *Motorola* moored just outside. Sir Chay gave Mark's bride, Michelle, away. She looked stunning, dressed in a long, straight silk dress bought while visiting Mark at the stopover in Australia.

The skippers went on to a post-wedding dinner and later met up with the crews who were invited to join the happy couple for a real 'knees up' in an Irish pub that night. The place was packed and the party continued into the early hours of the morning.

WHAT MADE THE DIFFERENCE

The contrast between this leg and the previous leg across the Southern Ocean could not have been greater. In the much lighter conditions the race became highly tactical; for the crews the biggest problem now was boredom, not survival.

Thinking

Information Search and Concept Formulation – The use of private routers to help in tactical planning before the leg was now becoming much more widespread. This was the first leg that *3Com* used a router but unfortunately the early loss of all three spinnakers meant that the impact of the router's advice was lost. As an indication of the sort of Information Search and thought process that went behind route selection, Simon Walker's notes are reproduced below. This is an example of a complex decision making process.

"Deciding The Route

Initial Facts
- Time behind *Group 4* at start (1st place) – 22 hrs
- Time ahead of *Save The Children* (3rd place) – 33 hrs
- Difference in boat speed between top yachts in similar conditions – less than 1%.
- Leg 5 has big variables, e.g. the Doldrums, high pressure systems

Conclusion – Could afford to take big risk, as most likely way to catch *Group 4*. In fact this is our last real chance to do so.

Research Done Prior To Start – Routing charts – historical data of wind speed and direction over last 100 years. Very much indicates mean values. Indicates a westerly course favourable.

Extensive research was conducted on sources of historical data, and real time weather patterns available on the Internet. A specialist weather router in the US was consulted. A specialist weather router in Australia was also consulted and commissioned to run analysis of recent data.

Research on Doldrums crossing point based on data for last six years for 30 days of May indicates that crossing equator at 17.5 degrees west, the true wind is 10.1 knots. Crossing at 22.5 degrees west, the true wind is 11.6 knots. So on average the westerly course is better, but on closer inspection the averages consisted of less variable conditions in the west with greater variability in the east ie sometimes not much at all but at other times up to 16 knots.

This is the sort of calculated risk we are looking for, being reasonably confident that *Group 4* will sail the west route, as it was on average better, if not a little further.

Hindsight – *(wonderful stuff) we should have considered the far west option, but we dismissed it early on due to excessive distance sailed. Well done, Motorola.*

What Happened And Real Time Information Gained – Sailed up the line, ie the shortest distance to Boston, as this would take us to the easterly crossing point. *Group 4* covered us, shaping a similar course. *Motorola* went west, took early loss close to centre of south Atlantic high - real time data and prognosis from radio fax from Cape Town confirmed that this would happen. *Group 4* broke away as expected to the west.

First Problem – Although west did look unfavourable early on as it was close to centre of

175

Atlantic high, it then became favourable both in wind speed and direction. This enabled the westerly yachts to maintain their position in the race even though they sailed further, and in some cases to gain – *Group 4*.

Hindsight – *Perhaps a little closer monitoring of the western yachts and the western weather, we could have foreseen this. We did in fact attempt to sail west but the wind angle was unfavourable. Ironically those to the west had a better angle and so could sail further that way. This was a frustrating period!*

The Doldrums – We arrived at the Doldrums in a lacklustre 6th place, and being the most northerly yacht, slowed first. *Group 4* was 100 miles ahead. We monitored the Inter-Tropical Convergence Zone (ITCZ), the centre of the Doldrums, twice daily, for approximately a week beforehand. The data was from Meteo France (text) and Brazilian Navy (fax).

The line up looked good (ie at the point of crossing, the Doldrums were at their northern extreme) so we could sail quickly north in a good breeze, and hopefully they would drift south, combining our speed with the speed of the movement south, to facilitate a fast crossing).

We slowed as we entered the Doldrums, dropping at one point to 11th place. We calculated that we in fact **gained** 60 miles on *Group 4*, in our Doldrums crossing, but unfortunately this was not enough. *Save The Children* crossed at a similar pace and so stayed ahead.

Hindsight – *Our initial strategy for the Doldrums was sound, but perhaps more attention should have been given to the period before then.*

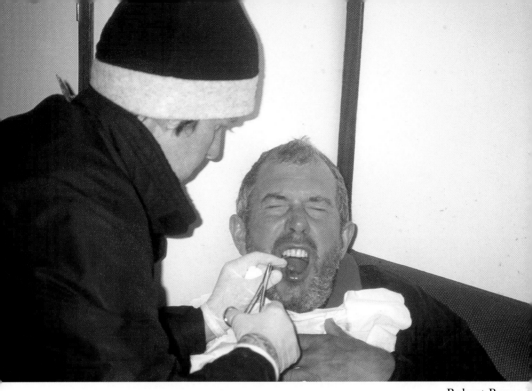

...ational Health Service stitching repairs.

...itching repairs on board *Ocean Rover.*

Robert Bruce

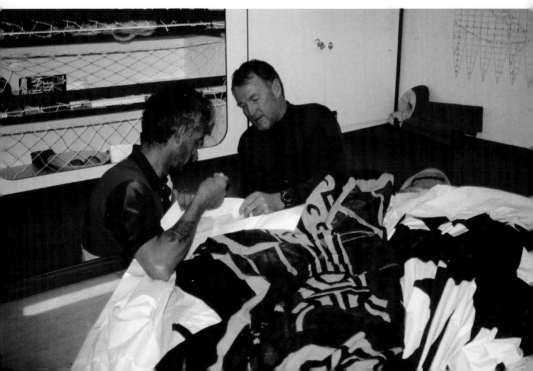

Clive Maso

Bird's eye view of the fleet at The Waterfront, Cape Town.

Archbishop Desmond Tutu blesses the fleet before it departs South Africa.

Stephen Mund

Stephen Munday

rewell Table Mountain, a majestic sight fades away.

he crew of *3Com* working together to achieve optimum boat speed as
ey head for Boston.

Mark Pepper

Mark Pepp

Commercial Union spinnaker team at work in the Doldrums.

Guess who blew the spinnaker?

Humphrey Walte

ncert sailing into the sunset.

Stephen Mun

A collision waiting to happen as the breeze picks up and the spinnakers fill.

And they are off at the start of the homeward leg – a short 3,000 mile sprint across the Atlantic.

Stephen Mun

Mark Pepper

ey crossed the latitudes and changed attitudes. The triumphant crew
Time & Tide arrives home safely into Southampton.

Mark Pepp

Group 4 returns victorious to Ocean Village, Southampton – champion of
the leg and the overall race.

And Finally ....

West proved best again as the north Atlantic high was oriented to the west, the better trade winds being between the centre of the high and the Doldrums. This we knew, but we hoped to have gained a lead sufficient to drift across in front of *Group 4* and take a westerly course.

The game plan was now to sail as efficiently as we could to the finish, to mitigate our early loss and to recover ground lost to our nearest rivals, *Save The Children*, in our gamble with *Group 4*.

This we did by careful short and medium term planning using the many US weatherfaxes available and a combination of hard work and determination.

To finish in 3rd place, and increase our lead on 3rd place to 42 hours was some consolation to the big loss to *Group 4*.

I still think it was worth a shot!"

Whereas Simon eventually decided not to take the western route for the reasons identified, Mark Lodge on *Motorola* elected to take an even more westerly route because, in his own words, "We had much more to win if the gamble came off than we had to lose if it didn't." Mike Golding was in exactly the opposite position as *Group 4* was now well in the lead overall and he was not prepared to gamble that away. He therefore adopted a more conservative strategy which attempted to balance his instinctive inclination to sail to the west, while covering the rest of the fleet which took a more central route. At one stage he sailed for four days on an unfavoured gybe in an attempt to get the rest of the fleet to follow him to the west, but ultimately to no effect. However he remained in control, covering the fleet.

Group 4 eventually won the leg because *Motorola* sailed too far west, losing ground, before heading north. Mike Golding did admit that he had wanted to go further west and that Mark Lodge had had the right strategy. Simon Walker's notes confirm that with hindsight he would have preferred to do likewise. Several other yachts managed to select very fast tracks up to the Doldrums – *Commercial Union, Save The Children* and *Concert* in particular. Sadly, all suffered the fate so graphically described by Andy Hindley as they watched all of their efforts destroyed by other yachts lucky enough to avoid the windless holes that they were stuck in.

Developmental

Empathy – In the light winds experienced for much of the leg, boredom set in and tempers flared. The mutual support and empathy that had been so much a feature of the fight for survival in the Southern Ocean started to disappear. The heat, the frustration, the resentment that this was 'a leg too far' (in the previous race the Cape Town leg had been straight to Southampton) all tested inter-personal relationships to the limit. Skippers suddenly found themselves counselling as much as skippering and, not surprisingly, some proved better at it than others. Tom O'Connor on *Pause To Remember* used his military experience of the problems of keeping soldiers motivated at times of inaction to the full. Referring back to his boom breakage in the previous leg he commented, "In a strange way, leading people in a crisis is almost easier than leading them when, for good reason, there is virtually nothing for them to do. You have to be so much more creative." A common observation was that people who were busy tended to motivate themselves; people who were not, needed empathetic handling. The parallel with project management is obvious when not all of the people can be busy all of the time. The leader has to fight the temptation to always be where the action is and accept that sometimes those who are inactive need even greater leadership.

Teamwork – For a lot of the time on this leg teamwork appeared not to be necessary as only the helm was really involved. Sail changes were few and far between. However,

Chay Blyth's advice of "Trim, Trim, Trim", was relevant in the light airs and discipline in the crew, particularly self discipline, became even more important.

Andy Hindley freely admitted that his crew hated most of the leg due to the apparent lack of challenge; similarly, a crew member on *Concert* admitted, "We are bored and . . . we are not sailing the yacht very well."

James Hatfield adopted a novel approach to counter the onset of boredom and the need for self discipline - he gave up smoking. "I realised in the Doldrums that there wasn't very much I could achieve with the yacht so I decided to achieve something else and gave up smoking." This act of self discipline seemed to be the answer for him.

A problem that continued to go unresolved on some yachts was that of interwatch rivalry. "Watch changes were the most difficult parts of the day," said one crew member. "With bickering and sniping between watches as to who had, and had not, done what, it became unbearable." One skipper freely admitted that he had allowed 'healthy' rivalry to go too far, to the point that it was 'unhealthy'. This will always be a problem for leaders to manage sensitively as competition can be a double-edged sword. James Hatfield once gave a bottle of champagne to a watch that had done particularly well; the other watch never forgave him.

Achieving

Influence – This was the leg when the skippers really did have time to manage their crews instead of spending the majority of their time on deck directing the sailing. When *Save The Children* was becalmed, Andy Hindley had his management and leadership skills tested to the limit as he coaxed his disgruntled crew through the problem. Richard Merriweather had a similar problem and it was here that the hours of relationship building throughout the race paid off. "Every crew member responded to problems in a different way and by now I could almost predict how people would react. I had to use my influence to manage each individual differently while retaining the cohesion of the crew and not appearing to favour one individual more than the other. Thank goodness in the Doldrums I had time to address the issue properly."

The skippers had been introduced to the John Adair leadership model (see Figure 1) during their training. It summarises the difficult decision facing any leader of balancing their time between task, team and individual issues.

Leadership Model

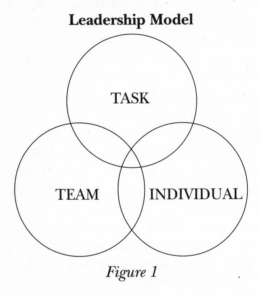

Figure 1

Figure 1 shows that all leaders have to carefully allocate their valuable time. It is a complex and inter-related balance between the demands of contributing to the overall TASK, managing and organising the TEAM, and getting the best out of the INDIVIDUALS. With a team the size of a Challenge yacht crew, the skippers should have been spending much more time on Team and Individual issues than on sailing the yacht; they had 13 crew members to do that.

On this leg, the management of the crew, and the different personalities within it, took up the majority of the skipper's time. In the Southern Ocean, through necessity, the difficult task of sailing the yacht had produced a completely different balance.

180

CAPE TOWN – BOSTON

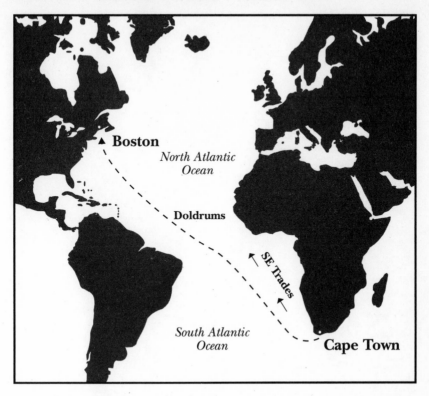

LEG 5 RESULTS

Position		Arrival Time (GMT)		Leg Time D H M S	Overall Position
1	Group 4	07 Jun	13:18:46	34 01 48 46	1
2	Motorola	08 Jun	05:42:16	34 18 12 16	3
3	Toshiba Wave Warrior	08 Jun	19:20:14	35 07 50 14	2
4	Courtaulds International	09 Jun	00:01:05	35 12 31 05	11
5	Concert	09 Jun	07:04:27	35 19 34 27	13
6	Save The Children	09 Jun	09:02:54	36 00 37 54 P	4
7	Commercial Union	09 Jun	16:28:38	36 04 58 38	5
8	Nuclear Electric	09 Jun	19:58:59	36 07 08 59 R	7
9	Global Teamwork	09 Jun	18:45:58	36 07 15 58	6
10	Pause To Remember	10 Jun	00:37:07	36 13 07 07	10
11	Heath Insured II	10 Jun	05:59:43	36 17 59 43 R	12
12	Ocean Rover	10 Jun	11:27:35	36 23 57 35	9
13	3Com	11 Jun	03:27:39	37 15 57 39	8
14	Time & Tide	11 Jun	23:20:58	38 15 50 58 P	14

P   Penalty   R   Redress

181

CHAPTER NINE

"This is not the end. This is not even the beginning of the end.
But it is perhaps the end of the beginning."
Winston Churchill

"The most overwhelming feeling I've ever experienced
was when I caught the first sight of the South Coast of
England. I knew then that it was all coming to an end.
They were mixed feelings but very strong emotions as
we passed The Needles and sailed down Southampton
Water – I kept thinking, 'This is it,' and asking myself,
'Do I want it to end?'"

Brian Beaumont, *Concert*.

BOSTON TO SOUTHAMPTON

Leg 6

The Last Port Of Call – The crews hugged each other as
they stood on the pontoon at Boston Harbour surrounded
by partners, families and friends. The final leg was about to
begin. This was the last time that they would be saying
"good luck" and "safe sailing" to one another.

It was an emotional moment for everyone and the
atmosphere was strikingly different from start days in other
ports of call. Instead of the enthusiastic backslapping and
calls of "see you in the next stopover for a few beers", the
crews stood together quietly sharing their last moments as a
group before they returned home to families and friends.

They knew that their dream was nearly over. They also
knew the special friendships that had been forged, the

incredibly strong team bonds that had been built, the close-knit 'fleet family' that had emerged, were all so unique that it would be impossible to find or even try to replicate them ever again. The Challenge was coming to an end and, in three weeks, this once in a lifetime adventure would be over.

Once on the other side of the Atlantic the crews knew they would have to face reality and return to normality. Partners and children would be waiting to resume family life, job searches would have to start and some would have to return to jobs they had left on hold. Businesses would need resurrecting, mortgages would need to be paid. Some would have to rely on relatives and friends to put them up before they could afford to rent or buy property again. Debts that many had left behind would need to be paid-off and others would return to pick up the pieces of a relationship that had just survived the course of time.

The race was an unknown event when the yachts arrived into Boston, but within a week of them being in harbour the place was buzzing with interested locals and business people. With BT's amazing publicity machine in action, radio interviews, TV coverage and press reports heightened the awareness of the race; the applications for Challenge 2000 began to roll in. Chay Blyth was in his element and the crews were having a ball. It was an exciting time and a success story for all to witness.

The stopover in Boston had been wild – a final time for the crews to really let their hair down, before the worries and stress of real life crept back into their lives.

The Re-start – On the start day, the frenetic activity usually displayed aboard each yacht was less evident. Crews were relaxed as it was, after all, just a short 3,000 mile sprint across the Atlantic. They were more concerned with saying their last goodbyes to fellow crew members than fiddling in the usual fashion.

As the official ceremony began, the crews moved back to their yachts and lined up on the foredeck ready to listen to

184

the addresses from the Mayor of Boston and the Governor of the State of Massachusetts who, in true American style, declared the day to be "BT Global Challenge Day".

It was blisteringly hot with temperatures already into the 90s. Boston Harbour, in the centre of the business district, was flanked by business and residential apartments and the prestigious Boston Harbour Hotel. The heat was building within this bowl and the crews were keen to get out onto the water and catch a little of the light breeze.

The start line had been laid close inshore to allow locals, families, sponsors and the familiar royal supporter, HRH Prince Michael of Kent, to watch the race start with ease. As it was, a plethora of boats of all sizes formed a farewell party out on the water.

Milling around before the start, the yachts jostled with the spectator boats who waved and shouted as the crews busied themselves on deck. This was going to be the first spinnaker start that the fleet had had. Much preparation and thought was therefore required in ensuring that the tactics for the start were clear and that crews knew exactly when to hoist the huge sail.

The gun sounded and *Global Teamwork* shot across the line in first position, closely followed by *Concert* and *Courtaulds International.* All the yachts were tightly bunched, vying for positions as they sailed away. The promotional kites looked magnificent and the sponsors were pleased.

In light shifting winds, the yachts were gybing back and forth coming so close it looked like many of them were touching. *Commercial Union, Group 4* and *Concert* were all closely packed. As the wind changed direction, *Group 4* started to gybe, coming very close to *Commercial Union* before the wind changed direction again and it returned to its former course.

All the skippers were keen to get a good start and do well on this final sprint home. Every one of the crews wanted to sail up The Solent in first place to receive the expected media and supporter welcome and to be the local

185

heroes. Each sponsor wanted it to be its yacht, its skipper, its crew. The resulting publicity and media coverage would be phenomenal – the top spot on all the news bulletins.

Getting out of the harbour took almost an hour. The spectator boats followed. The supporters were enjoying the summer's day, the jazz band, and the drinks that were flowing freely. The crews meanwhile were sweltering in the heat, gulping down soft drinks and water.

By the first evening, *Save The Children* had taken the lead. This was a great start for Andy Hindley and his crew who knew that this leg was important to their overall race result. They had lost third position overall to *Motorola* on the leg up to Boston and now needed to make up three hours to regain it. *Ocean Rover* also had its own personal battle. It was lying just four minutes behind *3Com*.

The Route East – This was still very much a race. Overall positions could still be improved. The battle for the final placing was underway.

The yachts headed south towards the imaginary waypoint, some 800 miles offshore. Chay Blyth had inserted this to keep the fleet south of the icebergs. They remained very close for several days and endured the terrible North Atlantic fog that rolled in each night around the George Bank and sometimes did not lift throughout the day. This was the foggiest month of the year and winds were also unusually light.

The three main considerations leaving the Eastern Seaboard of the States were the Labrador Current, Gulf Stream and Atlantic Drift. The effects of these could be immense and the yachts that had done their homework and best used the information would doubtless benefit the most.

Group 4 knew that both *Motorola* and *Concert* had used the same local meteorologist as themselves, and were watching to see how each skipper used the information and to what effect.

With all the yachts in such close range it was possible to

see the effects of current on yacht performance. *Nuclear Electric, Heath Insured II, 3Com* and *Group 4* were all close together one morning when suddenly, for no apparent reason, *Nuclear Electric* shot off ahead. The boost from the current was amazing. *Nuclear Electric* pulled away from *Heath Insured II* with ease and left *Group 4* standing. Shortly afterwards *3Com* picked up the same spurt and careered along beside them.

"It was truly incredible," commented Andrea Bacon on *Group 4*. "One minute *Nuclear Electric* was alongside us and the next it was two yachts' lengths ahead. We just saw them go, as if they had started their motor. Minutes later we witnessed *3Com* being pushed sideways by the current. She was under spinnaker and leaning right over. We could see the bottom of the yacht, she looked out of control and was very nearly pushed into the side of *Nuclear Electric*, broadside on."

Within just a few days of the start, two protests had been raised; one against *Global Teamwork*, the other against *Group 4* – both for the same reason, unused sails lying on deck. In a downwind situation this was hardly a weight advantage, in fact quite the opposite. Statements were sent to the international jury and the two yachts awaited the verdict. Given the closeness of the racing, any time penalty for either yacht could have made the difference of a place or two within the leg. As it happened, both protests were waived as the jury was not satisfied with the evidence that either yacht had infringed the ballast moving rule to enhance performance.

On day four *3Com* took the lead, the first occasion on which they had led the fleet throughout the entire race. The crew members were ecstatic as they headed towards the waypoint, but progress was slow as all the yachts became becalmed.

The Wind Dies – "Our elation at being at the front of the fleet is tempered by the complete lack of wind. During the night, the lightweight spinnaker hung limply in the damp

187

air like recently washed linen on the line. Nevertheless we are enjoying our position at the front and are fighting to hold it," reported the crew on *3Com*.

The creaking boom and the empty sails brought back memories of the days in the Doldrums. The crews were frustrated, they wanted to get home. This was supposed to be a short hop across the pond and they wanted it to be quick. After all, they did have a party awaiting them in Southampton.

Pause To Remember reported back to race headquarters that according to its Global Positioning Satellite system (GPS) it would be five weeks late for the BT Global Challenge Party which had been arranged for the return of the fleet on Friday 18 July.

The light winds and night-time fog continued for days. It was frustrating and demoralising for all the crews.

Nuclear Electric reported, "Sailing has become a painful, tedious and a mind numbing business, relieved only by the company of other yachts (eight in sight), which provide a constant yardstick against which to measure our performance."

On Friday 4 July American crew member Bill Shuff aboard *Group 4* was commemorating the Boston Tea Party, ceremoniously throwing a couple of tea bags over the side of the yacht.

On day seven a breeze brought *Group 4* into the lead, knocking *3Com* back by just a mile.

Tropical Storm Ana – A tropical depression, called Ana, was reported to be coming in behind the fleet with estimated wind speeds of 40 knots. Later the depression was reported to be an extra tropical one, but what did that mean? Was it to be more fruity than a tropical one?!

At that point the fleet really did not care. They were all so desperate for wind that they would have warmly welcomed any amount. As it happened, the depression was not as fruity as they had anticipated. Ana dissipated and by the time it reached the fleet it was just 25 knots.

However, it was enough to change the angle of the yachts and make life below decks more challenging thereby raising the spirits of the fleet.

"The mood aboard *Courtaulds International* is still very cheerful despite the weather. The leggers have welcomed the opportunity to experience the flavour of the Southern Ocean, having heard of nothing else from the core crew," said one.

John Keating aboard *Concert* reported, "Last night, for the first time this leg, I had to use the leecloth on my bunk, things are definitely looking up."

Group 4's lead was to be short-lived as the following day *3Com* regained its position and rounded Waypoint Alpha in first place.

The yachts that headed furthest south were doing well. *Toshiba Wave Warrior's* strategy at the start of the leg had been to do just that. However, when the breeze looked unstable *Toshiba Wave Warrior* lost its nerve, stayed on a bad gybe too long and lost miles to the fleet. "*3Com* was exactly where I would like to have been," reflected skipper Simon Walker.

While *3Com* decided to continue on a easterly course, *Group 4* and *Toshiba Wave Warrior* rounded the waypoint and headed north. This was to prove more favourable with currents assisting in their progress.

The winds continued and the fleet kept moving. *Courtaulds International* reported, "... a heavy swell, more wind and, more importantly, up to 10 knots of speed. We are now running down wind with the swell, not against it."

The swell however brought disaster for *Nuclear Electric*. A sudden lurch of the yacht caused a shock load which tore its spinnaker. Some 150ft of stitching was required and they had to revert to a smaller sail, suffering a consequent loss of speed. It had been lying in 3rd place at the time but soon dropped back to 7th. It was a blow from which *Nuclear Electric* was not to recover.

Fog Bound – As the yachts sailed north, the fog returned. *Save The Children* reported, "Last night the fog came in, it was thicker than before, mainly because we are heading north now and the warm air currents are condensing on the cold sea surface. It is so thick that we can barely make out the pirate picture on our spinnaker and even the wind hawk at the top of the mast is obscured by the dense mist."

With visibility so poor, the thought of coming up against an iceberg was at the forefront of most of the crews' minds. Thoughts and conversations were echoing the possible danger and the fact that the sinking of the *Titanic* had occurred in a position not too far from the fleet itself. The radar was being watched intently.

As a crew member on *Commercial Union* reported, "We are currently experiencing dense fog off the Grand Bank in iceberg territory. A very eerie situation that reminds us of our time in the Southern Ocean."

Meanwhile, *Group 4* reported some strange instrument readings which they could only put down to the atmospheric conditions. The currents were assisting the northerly yachts and *Group 4* was soon back in the lead.

The crew members on *Courtaulds International* were more concerned with their stomachs than the fog. Running low on food due to their slow progress, they threw their fishing lines over the side and caught a tuna large enough to feed 14 for two days.

Wildlife – This leg was proving to be the 'wildlife leg'. Never before had the fleet seen so much activity around the yachts: dolphins, whales, turtles, sunfish, tuna, petrels and shearwaters. There were several sightings every day and pods of dolphins would swim alongside the yachts and in the bow wave for hours.

Shearwaters were a common sighting. They were heading north along the Eastern Seaboard, around Newfoundland and up into the Arctic Circle before heading down through Scandinavia and across to Ireland for the summer months. Breeding takes place on just two particular islands in the world – Tristan da Cunha and Inaccessible where three million pairs breed.

Time & Tide reported having to swerve off course to avoid a whale which seemed content to lie just below the waterline directly in the yacht's path. Given that whales never sleep, this one must have been day dreaming, enjoying a mid ocean rest.

Pause To Remember was concerned with what was overhead. They were buzzed by the American Coastal Patrol and spoke with them on the ship's radio. *Heath Insured II* had radio contact with the *QEII*. The crew members were depressed when they were told that the liner would be back in Southampton the following morning. *Heath Insured II* still had five days to go!

On board *3Com*, legger Carol Pilkington was celebrating her 13th wedding anniversary. She stuck a special message in a jam jar and hoped that her husband, a core crew member on *Heath Insured II* behind, would find it bobbing in the water.

Heading For Home – With 1,000 miles to go to the finish, the yachts were still jostling for position. Five yachts were sailing in sight of one another and the pressure was really on. *Nuclear Electric* and *Heath Insured II* both succumbed to the pressure, one blowing the genoa and the other the heavyweight spinnaker. The sail repair teams on both yachts were set to work.

Among the fleet, the crew members were getting excited about the prospect of their first sight of England. A crew member on *Concert* reported, "It'll be wild when we see land for the first time and sail the few hundred miles up the Channel, clocking off the familiar landmarks: Bishop's Rock, Lands End, Lizard Point, Start Point, Portland Bill, The Needles... they'll be big moments, charged with excitement and emotion, and the miles will disappear. All of a sudden we'll be rounding the corner and heading up Southampton Water – the end of an incredible year."

Meanwhile Mike Golding, skipper of *Group 4*, was hoping to see land and get home without having to undertake the motherwatch duties. He had promised his crew in Boston that if they could get 25 miles ahead of their nearest rival, he would go below and cook and clean.

A battle with *Toshiba Wave Warrior* ensued, but the crew members of *Group 4* were determined to get their skipper into the galley. They worked with new vigour and energy and kept *Toshiba Wave Warrior* at bay. Mike duly went below, cooked the dinner and started cleaning the heads.

The yachts were moving into the Western Approaches of the English Channel and, given the closeness of the fleet, it was going to be an interesting finish. *Group 4* passed the Eddystone Rock and edged its way towards Plymouth in thick fog. Fog had hampered the race at the start of the leg and was doing the same at the finish.

This was familiar territory and *Concert* nostalgically reported they were now using their old faithful English Channel chart. "It even shows our plots from the Fastnet Qualifying Sail last June," said crew member John Keating.

Toshiba Wave Warrior was now 23 miles behind *Group 4*. It was busily repairing its race spinnaker in case the wind dropped on the approach up The Solent. After 14 hours, the sail repair team was nearing the end of the task. This was hopefully going to be their last repair of the race. After a day of frustrations, the fog cleared and the first sight of land cheered on the *Group 4* crew.

Chairman and Chief Executive of Group 4, Philip Sørensen was also delighted. He had been waiting rather impatiently to get a helicopter out to greet his crew. Six hours later Philip Sørensen was on board the ferry *Wight Scene* jostling among the emotional families and friends cheering *Group 4* across the finish line.

Heroes' Welcome – Dozens of spectator boats surged along beside them, while back in Ocean Village crowds lined the dock. It was 1.00am on Wednesday 16 July but nobody seemed to care – it was a moment to savour.

As the *Group 4* crew celebrated its victory, *Toshiba Wave Warrior* slipped across the line. Just one and a half hours behind the winners, Simon Walker and his crew were welcomed by the same huge crowd and by the *Group 4* crew. The celebrations continued when, less than two hours later, *Concert* came alongside the pontoon. The three crews were overwhelmed, it was a magnificent end to their voyage round the world. They had made it safely all the way and everyone felt very proud.

Meanwhile, further down the English Channel, a number of battles were still being fought. *Commercial Union* had made miles on *Save The Children* who had blown her heavy spinnaker. Now only three miles separated the two. *3Com* had overtaken *Nuclear Electric* moving into 6th place, while *Global Teamwork* had achieved the longest daily run of the leg, some 247 miles, which had brought her up into 8th position.

Further back, *Courtaulds International* and *Motorola* were lying neck and neck with *Time & Tide* bringing up the rear.

At 2.30pm on Wednesday afternoon, *Save The Children* and *Commercial Union* crossed the finish line separated by only 96 seconds.

Andy Hindley arrived on the pontoon to the sound of the crowds singing "Happy Birthday". A day late maybe, but his crew had postponed celebrations in case he lost concentration in the closing stages of the battle with *Commercial Union*. He did not and not only had they finished 4th in the leg, but they had managed to make up the time on *Motorola* and were 3rd overall.

Commercial Union was overjoyed to be back and received a warm welcome from ex-crew member Sean Blowers, of TV show *London's Burning*.

Out by The Needles, *Nuclear Electric*, *Global Teamwork* and *Ocean Rover* were fighting for position. *Global Teamwork* had continued to make good progress and was now ahead of *Ocean Rover.*

Not far behind *Heath Insured II, 3Com* and *Courtaulds International* were also battling it out and, as *Heath Insured II* passed Hurst Castle, it crossed the bow of *3Com* and began a luffing match all the way up The Solent. The two yachts were racing so close together they could talk across to each other.

The pressure was really on and, as the race continued up Southampton Water, the spectator boats were buzzing with excitement. *Heath Insured II* managed to keep up the pace and crossed the line three and a half minutes ahead of *3Com,* with *Courtaulds International* terrifyingly close behind. As the noise of the cannon resounded across the water, skipper Boris Webber let go of the wheel raising his hands in victory. However he had not finished. That was *3Com's* gun – his was three seconds later!

All in all eight yachts finished within an hour and four minutes. It was an amazing sight seeing them round the corner into Ocean Village, one after another. The crews were decked out in their best attire and the crew of *Ocean Rover* arrived sitting on their boom wearing Viking helmets.

There was hardly time to welcome one yacht home before the next was coming alongside. The atmosphere was electric. Balloons drifted up into the evening sky as fireworks rained down above the heads of the spectators. Tears rolled down the faces of families, friends and crews, all totally overcome with the emotion of the moment.

Time & Tide – Just one yacht remained to come in; *Time & Tide* was due early the following morning.

"Relatives, partners, sponsors and friends, met at 5.00am beside Calshot Spit lighthouse, Ocean Village," said Rosie Mackie, from The Centre *for* High Performance Development. "The atmosphere was filled with excitement. Sue Preston Davis, from the Time & Tide Trust, was kept busy on the telephone tracking the yacht's position. We stood chatting, waiting to hear when we could go. We finally boarded the ferry and set off to welcome home the incoming heroes. Within an hour the captain announced the first sighting of, 'A tiny red spot visible off the starboard bow.' *Time & Tide* was coming home. The emotion on the boat was visible. The early morning black coffee, essential for most of us, having been up all night, was gradually replaced by bottles of champagne brought on board in carrier bags.

The distance between the ferry and the yacht diminished. James and his crew were making about 8 knots and we were steaming towards them at 10 knots. Our on board disco kid could wait no longer. With full volume the boat vibrated to the sound of Tina Turner's 'Simply the Best.' The first few bars of *Time & Tide's* theme song were enough for the passengers. Everyone on board sang at the top of their voices. This was the start of a tribute to unique people on board the disabled yacht. Sarah Rowe, the skipper's girlfriend, borrowed a friend's binoculars and caught her first glimpse of the man who had skippered the first-ever disabled boat round the world, the wrong way.

After an hour of shadowing the yacht James announced that he was coming alongside for our first reunion with this amazing crew. After much emotion and laughter, James bore away towards the finishing line and to the making of history. The Royal Marines were standing by at Southampton's Ocean Terminal. Sue Preston Davis was frantically filling plastic mugs with champagne with one hand whilst wiping away the emotional tears that follow a three year project with the other.

The gun was fired. *Time & Tide* – the yacht, its skipper and its disabled crew, had circumnavigated the world the wrong way in 'The World's Toughest Yacht Race.' The welcome into Southampton was awesome. In pouring rain hundreds of spectators, all The Challenge skippers and crews cheered the crew home.

These were remarkable people respected by everyone but particularly the skippers and crew of the rest of the fleet. Only the other Challenge crews could really appreciate what the crew of *Time & Tide* had been through and even they found it hard to imagine how they coped when the going got tough.

Mixed Emotions – The sixth and final leg of the BT Global Challenge caused a mix of emotions. The crews were inevitably thinking about home and the future and contemplating the end of the race throughout the course of the 18 day Atlantic crossing. Following are a selection of thoughts and feelings that the crews expressed as they neared home.

"I was looking forward to going home, not that I'd had enough but I felt 10 months was a long time to be away. I thought the last leg was going to be a quick crossing, just two weeks. But after the first week without any wind I felt really frustrated. It seemed so unfair.

The most overwhelming feeling I've ever experienced was when I caught first sight of the South Coast of England. I knew then that it was all coming to an end. They were mixed feelings but very strong emotions as we passed The Needles and sailed down Southampton Water. I kept thinking 'this is it' and asking myself 'did I want it to end?'

Crossing the finishing line, however, was a truly wonderful feeling – genuine happiness throughout the whole crew. Strangely, I found it toughest coming ashore. I just didn't know what to say to my family and friends and I kept looking around for other crews."

Brian Beaumont, *Concert*

"A question which kept repeating itself inside my head, over and over again, was how would I ever find anything to fix my adrenalin addiction or match the euphoric feelings that this race had brought about.

The feelings of accomplishment, self satisfaction and camaraderie were unique. Although I knew that the memories would stay with me forever, I also knew that I would never feel or experience anything as strong and as meaningful again.

I was very aware that the race was something truly special and would take a lot of getting over."

Andrea Bacon, *Group 4*

"I was looking forward to getting back, settling down and becoming a total family again with Carol, the children and grandparents. We intend to go off, as a family, in two to three years time and circumnavigate the world in our own boat but right now it is important to me to settle down.

My wife was doing the last leg on *3Com* and this added a new dimension to the race. When the six-hourly position polls came out my first interest was her yacht. It was great to see them in the lead but I must admit I felt a little sad as I'd have liked to have been up there myself. We talked on the radio but found it very difficult. There are always people around listening, you can't be emotional and of course we couldn't talk about what we'd been doing or even the weather!

The finish was incredible. We crossed the bow of *3Com* just three miles off Hurst Castle and came up The Solent in a close luffing match, never more than 100ft apart. We were so close we could talk to one another and we battled it out right to the line, eventually crossing just three and a half minutes ahead of them.

The children and grandparents were on the support vessels, waving furiously. It was a tremendous moment."

Andy Pilkington, *Heath Insured II*

"I remember saying to myself one evening, just 2,000 miles from home, 'It is coming to an end and you've really got to make the most of it'. I was feeling content, although we weren't quite at the front of the fleet. We'd left Boston still desperate to win one leg and prove we could do it. It would have been wonderful if we could have returned to Southampton first.

All in all I loved the experience. *Toshiba Wave Warrior* was a very friendly yacht but what you had to realise in the situation we were in, was that tolerance was a virtue. I became much more tolerant and learned that the little things in life take you far. It was a case of really putting into practice what you knew, like saying 'Sorry'. 'Please' and 'Thank you' also went a long way, even in 40 knots of wind."

Ben Pearson, *Toshiba Wave Warrior*

"Leg six was the end of a great adventure. I felt we had been on the go for a long time but I wasn't looking forward to coming back. I wanted it to continue. It would have been nice to have gone home for a few days, seen everyone and then continued on our way.

Crossing the line was our 'Big Day' – we'd done it and we were triumphant. My biggest fear had always been that I might be injured and unable to finish the race but I came through relatively unscathed.

I know now that I really want to continue sailing. I love it."

Nigel Smith, *Time & Tide*

"I couldn't wait to get home. I got married just two months before the race and I had a wife waiting and a marriage I was really looking forward to getting started.

Not that I hadn't enjoyed The Challenge, but I felt that after having put so much into it, I wanted to get on with the next project, something new, something different.

Yachting photography has been my lifetime ambition and I'd achieved all I wanted from the race in that respect. My next project is to hold a photographic exhibition in London.

Two personal lessons I take away from the race are firstly being tolerant of other people and secondly the importance of setting long-term goals. I'm so glad that I set myself a goal before leaving so I knew what I had to move on to when the race finally ended."

Philippe Falle, *3Com*

"As we headed across the Atlantic my thoughts were focused on life without The Challenge. I knew it would not be easy.

The Challenge for me had not been about the sailing itself but the people. The bond formed between a group of 14 individuals was amazing.

This was really brought home to me by my absence on Leg 2. Having to leave the yacht was traumatic in itself, but more so because of what I was leaving behind, rather than the pain I was in.

Sir Chay talked about his 'little family' and that is exactly how it felt. The Challenge initiates such feelings. In the work place, few management teams I have ever worked with have shown such an attitude.

On this race there was no room for individuals and it has been a valuable exercise to participate in. For certain, I will miss the people and the spirit that such like-minded personalities generate."

Rhian Jenkins, *Global Teamwork*

"This last leg was so different from the rest. A short burst across the Atlantic and I would be home after 10 months away. I was looking forward to seeing my family and friends again, especially my two daughters, Ellie and Lydia.

Looking back on the race, I was disappointed with our performance. We had expected and deserved better with all our hard work. This had not shown through in our final 8th position. Nevertheless, we did manage to squeeze ahead of *3Com*, beating them by 10 minutes overall. Nail biting when you think it took us 30,000 miles to do it!

We spent much of the last leg talking about what we had achieved, where we had gone wrong and what our plans for the future were. Most had jobs to go back to but, for a few of us, the future was not so certain. I spent many hours thinking about how best to give my career a kick start and in what direction. I repeatedly asked myself several questions – 'Had the race and my experiences changed me?' 'If so, for better or for worse?' 'Would I find it easy to settle down again to 'routine' life?'

I was optimistic but only time would tell. In the meantime, I was itching to get back. I had a list of action points in my diary and I couldn't wait to get started on them.

I was coming to the end of an amazing chapter in my life and it was time to move on!"

Robert Bruce, *Ocean Rover*

"On *Pause To Remember* we seemed to spend the last two legs of the race trying desperately to remember and capture those moments that epitomised the race. I wanted to try and relive them in my mind. Not only the actions but the emotions as well. This proved almost impossible. Sometimes in certain conditions, either when we were becalmed or being hammered by gale force winds, a few of those events came to life again. Then as soon as the sun came out and the seas flattened, the memories faded into the dark recesses of my mind.

All I seemed to be left with were the extremities of the trip, the starts and finishes. The bulk of the race seemed to have merged into one blur where it became increasingly difficult to pick out those events that really mattered, or seemed to matter at the time.

It does seem that the only way to recapture the race is to go back."

Matt Reeves, *Pause To Remember*

WHAT MADE THE DIFFERENCE

This leg was another relatively short sprint with the wind behind the fleet – an unusual experience for a fleet now hardened to beating into wind. Yet again a small group of yachts elected to adopt a different strategy from the majority of the fleet and managed to take the top places. Possibly the most interesting behavioural aspect of this, the last leg, were the various thoughts of crew members coming to the end of this huge adventure, reflecting on what had ultimately made the difference between success and failure.

Thinking

Information Search – The three main considerations on leaving the Eastern Seaboard of the United States were the Labrador Current, The Gulf Stream and the Atlantic Drift. By now a familiar pattern of Information Search had emerged between the yachts. Some went to enormous lengths and some waited to be given the weather information on the day of the start. Yet again, not surprisingly, homework paid off.

Merfyn Owen had made a private visit to Boston the year before to research local conditions at the start. He was elated when he justifiably crossed the start line first.

Concept Formation – Mid-leg *Group 4* and *Toshiba Wave Warrior* broke from the pack and headed north and then east. Yet again this 'go it alone' strategy was to prove successful as both yachts encountered more favourable currents that assisted them towards their ultimate destination. They came 1st and 2nd with only an hour and a half between them.

Developmental

Developing People – As this was to be their final leg, many of the crew members pondered what had happened and what might have been in the previous 10 months. Some crews were disappointed with their yacht's overall performance as they felt that the crew's true potential had never been realised. This frustration was inversely linked to the amount of time that had been spent debriefing individual and collective performance and in developing the crew.

The extremes were remarkable. At one end of the spectrum, yachts were still trying to improve their performance almost up to the finishing line. At the other end, at least one yacht did not hold a single end-of-leg debrief throughout the race. The end-of-leg celebration was followed by the crew's dispersal for some well earned rest and the subject of performance was never raised again until the day of the start of the next leg.

There did not seem to be the same correlation with the amount of cross-training that was carried out. The *Group 4* crew was a team of highly focused specialists – each crew member had a clearly defined individual role from the outset and retained that function to the end. Crew members admitted a tinge of regret that they had not acquired a broader base of skills but the satisfaction of being an integral part of a superb sailing machine coupled with that of winning five of the six legs, and ultimately the race, more than compensated.

On *Time & Tide,* James Hatfield elected to have a core crew of eight of his more able-bodied crew members do the sailing while the balance were asked to provide a below deck support function. This apparent selection of first and second class crew members caused enormous resentment albeit that James would argue that his primary interest lay in getting the best performance from the yacht and in crew safety.

The bulk of the yachts fell into the middle ground with more cross-training and personal development occurring in those yachts which suffered the least number of crew changes during the voyage. *Toshiba Wave Warrior* in 2nd place adopted a totally different policy to the leader *Group 4*. On *Toshiba Wave Warrior*, each crew member was trained in several functions and moved freely between them. On *Motorola*, Mark Lodge admitted that he was training to the end. On *3Com*, there had always been an understanding that crew members could move from role to role as they wished, provided that they had learned the essentials from a fellow crew member.

The overall conclusion seems to be that individuals are more willing to sacrifice personal development for the good of the team if that team is winning. If the team is doing badly, then individuals expect changes to be made, and for a review of the things that are going badly. They do not expect simply to have more of the same. To finish low down in the rankings having rationalised that the crew did its best is one thing; to feel frustrated at knowing that the crew never realised its potential is another.

Empathy And Teamwork – One of the lasting legacies of the race is the increase in personal tolerance among the crew members. Indeed on this last leg, the high level of empathy was the factor that some crew members said they would miss the most. The close personal bonds, mutual respect, and genuine affection had reached a level for most that was unique in their experience of working teams. "I knew that I would never feel or experience anything as strong and as meaningful again," said Andrea Bacon on *Group 4*. She was probably echoing the sentiments of many others.

For those crews who had managed to develop such a high level of team work, the power of their teams transcended all else. By this last leg, there was a feeling that there was virtually nothing that these crews could not take on. The level of mutual support was such that the skippers knew that for much of the time their presence was redundant; Mike Golding's disappearance below deck to do the cooking and cleaning of the heads was a visible recognition of the competence of his team. The development of a group of individuals who had hardly known one another a year before to the level of teamwork exhibited on the last leg should provide an inspiration to project teams everywhere. The value of the application of the Team Building Blocks identified in Chapter 3 was validated by the overall placing of the yachts at the end. It would be an over simplification to say that the 'best' teams won, but it would be fair to say that the more focused and cohesive crews did significantly better than those who were not.

BOSTON – SOUTHAMPTON

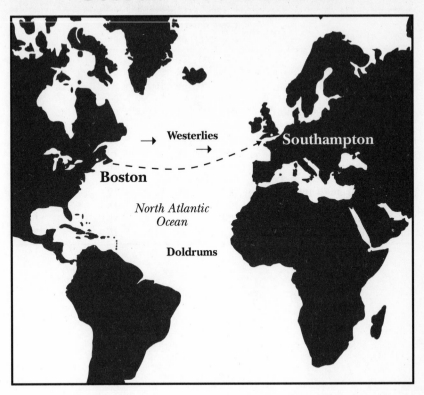

LEG 6 RESULTS

Position		Arrival Time (GMT)		Leg Time D H M S				Overall Position
1	Group 4	16 Jul	01:06:58	16	07	36	58	1
2	Toshiba Wave Warrior	16 Jul	02:39:46	16	09	09	46	2
3	Concert	16 Jul	04:07:41	16	10	37	41	13
4	Save The Children	16 Jul	14:32:23	16	21	02	23	3
5	Commercial Union	16 Jul	14:33:59	16	21	03	59	5
6	Nuclear Electric	16 Jul	18:11:21	17	00	41	21	7
7	Global Teamwork	16 Jul	18:29:17	17	00	59	17	6
8	Ocean Rover	16 Jul	18:54:29	17	01	24	29	8
9	Heath Insured II	16 Jul	19:06:06	17	01	36	06	12
10	3Com	16 Jul	19:09:55	17	01	39	55	9
11	Courtaulds International	16 Jul	19:09:58	17	01	39	58	11
12	Motorola	16 Jul	19:13:24	17	01	43	24	4
13	Pause To Remember	16 Jul	19:15:27	17	01	45	27	10
14	Time & Tide	17 Jul	08:34:49	17	11	04	49	14

FINAL RESULTS

Pos	Yacht	Combined Times							
		D	H	M	S	D	H	M	S
01	Group 4	161	05	25	18				
02	Toshiba Wave Warrior	163	11	14	34	+ 02	05	49	16
03	Save The Children	165	20	50	46	+ 04	15	25	28
04	Motorola	165	22	40	54	+ 04	17	15	36
05	Commercial Union	167	08	01	32	+ 06	02	36	14
06	Global Teamwork	169	20	27	56	+ 08	15	02	38
07	Nuclear Electric	171	01	29	10	+ 09	20	03	52
08	Ocean Rover	171	11	46	34	+ 10	06	21	16
09	3Com	171	11	57	30	+ 10	06	32	12
10	Pause To Remember	172	19	13	28	+ 11	13	48	10
11	Courtaulds International	173	19	26	12	+ 12	14	00	54
12	Heath Insured II	174	10	03	47	+ 13	04	38	29
13	Concert	174	21	36	29	+ 13	16	11	11
14	Time & Tide	176	18	09	55	+ 15	12	44	37

CHAPTER TEN

"To win is great, but not to know why you've won is unforgivable."
Mike Golding, Skipper *Group 4*

A recognition of man's ability to overcome the apparently insurmountable will always be a lasting legacy of the race. One crew member remarked, "In watching my fellow crew members perform acts of extraordinary effort and courage day after day, I realised that we are all capable of doing at least twice what we imagined. The instinct for survival forced us to exceed our self imposed boundaries of personal performance. History is littered with examples of ordinary people doing extraordinary things but the real challenge is how to find the motivational drivers that prompt such efforts; survival is only one of many."

LESSONS LEARNED

When Simon Walker was interviewed after the race as to what he had learned from the experience he replied, "How many days have you got?" His response was echoed time and time again by the other skippers and crew members who admitted that, as a concentrated learning experience, the race was without equal.

The BT Global Challenge is a unique case study in human endeavour. There are few events that combine so many elements in such a complex and dynamic environment. The crews had to cope with conditions impossible to replicate in training. Those skippers who had sailed in the previous race found it almost impossible to describe what it was really like to sail the 'wrong way' round the world and to prepare the new crews for the adventure they were about to experience.

Every single participant faced an unprecedented level of risk, extreme personal danger, discomfort, a weather pattern and environment that went from extreme heat and tranquillity to bitter cold and a ferocity that few will ever experience. There was little chance for extended sleep. Clothes were continually wet. The yacht was perpetually bucking up and down like a roller coaster and most of the time it was heeled over at 35 degrees.

With a complement of 14 men and women on each yacht, from different backgrounds, with different personalities and with different interests thrown together for a duration of 10 months, the race was clearly more about surviving these elements and one's crew mates, than about sailing.

There are few opportunities in the modern world to study human behaviour at such an intense level over such an extended period of time. While all of the crews learned many lessons on human behaviour and found out things about themselves, there seemed to be a clear pattern of those factors that made the greatest difference both in a positive and a negative way.

So what can we learn from this unique case study that could give guidance to leaders faced with the challenges of producing superior team performance in a complex and dynamic environment.

The Lessons – The main lessons learned from this race fit into four categories:-
   i   The importance of **a clear, unambiguous strategic intent;**
   ii The importance of **the use of High Performance Behaviours;**
   iii The importance of **five essential management skills;**
   iv The importance of **five personal behaviours.**

i. Set a clear, unambiguous, strategic intent

It is quite clear that human beings can achieve almost anything provided there is a vision which excites and motivates them, they can identify with it and take ownership.

Extraordinary Ability – "Before the end of this decade, we shall put a man on the moon and bring him safely back to earth," stated John F Kennedy in 1963 when the American space programme was riddled with failure and the Russians had leapt ahead in the space race. By 1969 this goal had been achieved.

Chay Blyth similarly had a dream. He wished to open up yachting – to him an elitist sport – to the average person and pledged to send 10 yachts round the world, manned by ordinary men and women with little or no sailing experience. By 1993, he had achieved his goal.

In both cases these bold dreams – thought outrageous at the time – proved to be an overwhelming success.

Both Kennedy and Chay Blyth set a clear vision, a strategic intent that was unambiguous and had definite success criteria.

A team of psychologists from Harvard visited Cape Canaveral at the height of the American space programme. They visited the gent's toilets where a janitor was mopping the floor. On being asked what his job was, the janitor replied, "I am helping to put a man on the moon."

For the participants in the BT Global Challenge, the commitment to their goal of sailing round the world was equally powerful. They were driven by a clear strategic intent – to sail round the world and come safely back to Southampton. The enormity of the task was rarely considered and the possibility of failure was unthinkable.

Once Chay Blyth had painted the vision, people were queuing up to participate. The majority of decisions were made without any rational thought. "It sparked my imagination – I just wanted to take part," was a common cry. There was no marketing plan, no corporate strategy, no financial plan. Just gut feeling. There were also those who felt they wanted to improve their own abilities, to develop their skills and mould their characters.

A sculptor was commissioned to carve a war memorial for the 50th anniversary of the D Day landings symbolising the British Tommy running up the beaches of Normandy. Faced with a featureless block of granite, he was asked how he would produce his sculpture and replied, "I will chip off all the bits that don't look like a soldier."

There was not one participant in the race who did not return looking "like a soldier".

The yachts which performed the best had a clear strategic intent which was discussed, shared and believed by the crew. "To be in the top three on every leg," was one stated intent. The yachts that merely stated that they were going out to win totally lacked credibility.

Mike Golding never actually said to his crew that they were going to win. His intent was to be consistent. "Be consistent and you *could* win the race," he said.

Clearly, before any team or organisation can perform to outstanding levels, it needs a strategic intent which must become the life blood of those who are involved. A vision for the future is not merely built on the current state of the organisation, or its past record. To increase sales by 10% or increase market share by 1%, compared to the previous year, is to set a target, not to dream for the future.

"High performing organisations paint a picture of what *could* be possible with only a slight regard for the resources and perceived restrictions. They cast their minds towards the end result and work backwards, rather than taking the present state of the organisation and working forward. They burst the walls of conventional thinking and inspire people to be possibility thinkers and to achieve the impossible," said Humphrey Walters of MaST International.

ii. The Use of High Performance Behaviours

While a clear strategic intent provided the bed-rock for high performance during the race, the difference between the yachts performing to an adequate level and those performing to a high level was in the continued use of High Performance Behaviours.

"The great thing about doing no preparation is that failure comes as a complete surprise."
Montgomery

Information Search – The key to winning any race is preparation. During The Challenge race, preparation took many forms from conditioning the crew to live together and ensuring the yachts could cope with the conditions ahead, to compiling the meteorological data bank for use during the voyage and obtaining local knowledge relevant to each stopover. Whatever the form, the yachts and skippers who *prepared most* ultimately *finished highest.* But preparation was itself a state of mind, in some cases a passion. Mike Golding had a passion to win that some skippers did not even pretend to have. Some crews had a passion to win that others did not. Ultimately success depended not on luck, skill, or even experience, but on behaviour, day in day out for 10 long months. That did not mean however that for Simon Walker and *Toshiba Wave Warrior* coming 2nd was a shattered dream. Rather that they walked off the pontoon in Ocean Village at the end of the race with no excuses, complaints or regrets – just the knowledge that they had been totally focused and dedicated, and had learned a great deal from the experience. They had given it their best shot. For other crews, there will always be an element of "if only" and an acceptance that if they were to do the race again they would focus on their attitude and commitment.

The first stage in preparation lies in the behaviour

called Information Search. The amount of data readily available that is relevant to sailing a yacht faster is almost mind blowing. During the voyage every sail change, every course change, and every plot produced more and more information. The challenge is how to collate, analyse and learn so that the process of Information Search becomes an ethos. What else drove skippers weak with exhaustion to retire to their bunks to read pilot books and routine notes? What else drove crew members to constantly seek knowledge that would improve their contribution to the yacht?

The final benefit derived from Information Search is that knowledge dispels fear of the unknown. The adage that "ignorance is bliss" becomes dangerous when reality is so much worse than ever expected that it creates an emotional low from which the spirit makes a slow recovery. Information Search can provide the knowledge that limits the unexpected.

Concept Formation – Armed with the right information, concept and strategy formation can begin. The level of technical skill among the skippers was so uniformly high that it was difficult for one yacht to simply out-sail the other; the skippers had to out-think one another. Sometime before the race Mike Golding decided on a strategy that would allow him to take best advantage of weather systems while covering the rest of the fleet at the same time. He summarised this strategy in his small personal notebook and, even at the end of the race, he would not divulge exactly what that strategy had been. The consistency of his results throughout the race led to his crew being criticised for being "too professional". Mike Golding viewed this description of "too professional" as one of praise rather than as the intended criticism.

Conceptual Flexibility – A further benefit of Information Search is that it allows those with mental self-discipline to develop several alternative concepts before any decision is taken. Equally it allows concepts to be held in reserve should circumstances change wildly. The Challenge was in many ways the ultimate complex and dynamic environment, and often major decisions had to be taken very quickly. However, such was the enormity of these decisions that a cursory look at the alternatives would not have done justice to the ultimate decision. Fatigue inevitably affects both the speed and the depth of decision-making. Some skippers even produced decision-making check lists to ensure that they had covered all of the angles when they were tired and cold. It is the attitude that produces such an approach that is so important.

Developing People – If the key to racing is preparation, that preparation lay in part in the skipper's ability to develop the raw material he had been given in the form of 13 amateur crew volunteers. One of the key decisions at the point at which the crews were first announced was whether to focus on sailing skills or team dynamics. The final result suggests that the crew that had evolved a structure for living together before going on to acquire their sailing skills as a **team**, were cohesive. The crews that learned their sailing skills as a **group of individuals** tended to stay that way. The lesson is here for project team managers faced with a multi-talented disparate group of individuals: get the team dynamics right and the skills will take care of themselves. Conversely, if the team dynamics are not right, a great deal of talent can be squandered.

The experience of the race proved that crew members had the potential to develop both collectively and individually throughout the race. Sadly the development of some crews started to tail off after Rio, simply because the development of people was not part of their culture. This resulted in frustration from these crew volunteers who felt that their growth as a sailor finished at the end of the first leg. The waste of potential and the consequent dissatisfaction affected several crews badly.

Empathy – This was the area in which most skippers would admit they were challenged most. It is always difficult for a professional to understand the apparent fumbling incompetence of a beginner. It is also difficult for a highly competitive achiever to understand the aversion to risk of those less driven than himself. The greatest strength of all of the crews lay in their diversity but this placed great demands on a skipper who was not naturally empathetic and who could simply not understand the different motivational needs of his crew members. Several skippers, however, consciously worked on their empathy level to great effect – proving that empathy is a skill rather than an in-bred talent. Boris Webber admitted that his whole approach to his crew changed both collectively and individually as a result of his becoming more empathetic. The yacht's performance changed dramatically as a result, the crew was much happier and Boris enjoyed his command so much more; the ultimate 'win-win' situation. However, it was not only the empathy level of the skipper that had an effect, those crews who actively strove to be empathetic with one another also had fewer losses and performed better. They admitted that on occasions such an approach demanded both restraint and self-discipline but that their desire to win made both worthwhile for the improved performance that resulted.

Teamwork – Such was the weight and complexity of a Challenge yacht that it was literally impossible to sail it competitively without an element of teamwork. The performance differential lay in to what extent teamwork was developed. Watching the fumbling start at Southampton in September 1996 and the supremely competent finish at Southampton in July 1997 showed the extent to which the crews had improved. However one area of constant disquiet throughout the voyage was aimed at some crew members refusal to become totally committed team players. Some skippers got round the problem by

214

allocating singular roles such as helming, or winch operation to such 'loners'. Others had to recognise that having paid £18,750 for their berth, individual crew members were difficult to discipline.

There is little doubt that the more successful a yacht became, the greater the level of 'buy in' from the individual crew members. Everyone wants to be an integral part of a winning team. Sadly, some try and disassociate themselves from less successful teams. James Hatfield was saddened that a frequent comment on *Time & Tide* was, "I hope that we won't be last into Southampton." Few ever said, "What can I do to prevent us being last into Southampton?"

Building Confidence – Throughout the race, individual crew members produced levels of performance or showed individual acts of heroism that far exceeded their own, as well as everyone else's, expectations. In many cases the path to such an outstanding level of performance lay in developing the self confidence of the individual concerned. In one instance a skipper was washed overboard and the whole watch immediately executed a well rehearsed recovery drill and had him back on board in seconds; in another, a skipper came on deck to see the whole watch frozen in terror at the sight of a crew member being dragged along behind the yacht. The skipper himself had to recover the unfortunate individual. The first crew had the confidence to act in an emergency, the second one did not.

Confidence grew throughout the race from a combination of coaching and encouragement. There was a difference of opinion between the skippers as to the extent to which their crew members needed recognition. Not surprisingly, those crew members who received recognition performed best. This improved level of performance heightened the self confidence of the individual who then earned further recognition; another win-win cycle. However, no one individual could be good at everything and one area in which the skippers had to focus their

215

leadership skills was in ensuring that individual talents were used to best effect, thus building the confidence of the individual concerned. The overall level of confidence of the crew of *Concert* rose markedly after it had overcome its dismasting. The crew had proved to itself that it could overcome any adversity and self confidence grew.

Some skippers admitted that they had to be particularly careful that the inevitable banter and 'crack' in the crew did not erode the self confidence of the more sensitive crew members. Building confidence is a skill that requires sensitivity to the dangers of creating reckless over-confidence, while recognising the need to build up the overall confidence level to take on the unexpected.

Influence – The ideal situation was one in which every member of a crew was persuaded by the merits of a particular course of action. With this 'buy in' behind him, the skipper could be confident that the crew would tackle the task with full commitment. However the motivational driver for each crew member was different, as was the response to different lines of argument.

Inspiration is also about influence; several crews were inspired by the obvious heroism of their skippers in conditions of extreme danger. The influence that such acts had on the overall level of confidence in the crews has already been documented, but a skipper's ability to persuade and influence was perhaps one of the least measurable behaviours and yet one which had considerable effect on crew commitment and morale.

Presentation – A well conducted, confident and practised crew brief from the skipper inspired more confidence in a crew than any other act. Surprisingly, several skippers chose not to take the opportunity afforded by such a performance as often as they might. The basic skills of effective presentation are probably one of the easier skill sets to acquire but many a brilliant strategy has fallen on deaf ears through poor presentation. Preparation, empathy and confidence are required ingredients for a presentation.

Proactivity – It was Chay Blyth himself who offered the advice before the race that one of the key attributes of a good crew volunteer was the ability to anticipate. Those skippers who evolved sound procedures for compiling a meteorological data bank were themselves in a better position to anticipate bad weather. Those crew members who elected to cross-train one another during the voyage in order to reduce the effects of sudden injury were being proactive. Those skippers who strengthened their rigging prior to a storm were also being proactive. Proactivity did have a part to play and was yet another result of attitude –"Are we controlling the race, or is the race controlling us?"

Continuous Improvement – "If we gained a mile, the weather must have improved, if we lost one we had sailed badly," said Mike Golding.

For some crews, the drive for continuous improvement went from the start line to the finish line. Every sail change, every course change, every watch change provided an opportunity for debrief and review. On some yachts this process went on hour by hour, day by day for the whole voyage. After the first few days it simply became a way of life. Some crews finished the race with very different drills from the ones they had been taught before the race; they had evolved their own drills through continuous improvement, and were convinced that they were better. Was it the fact that the drills were better, or that the crew believed that they were better, that produced the improved performance? Other yachts virtually ignored the opportunity for review and, on at least one yacht, there was not a single debrief on a sail change from the beginning of the race to the end. That particular yacht did not do very well and its crew members were not satisfied with their own performance.

The yachts who dedicated time to training during the stop-overs, rather than resting on their laurels, also gained from this discipline.

iii. The Five Essential Management Skills

It soon became clear that the skipper's credibility depended on the level of personal standards that he displayed. He was either accepted or viewed cynically by the crew depending on whether he 'walked the talk.' In some cases a very dictatorial style worked because the skipper kept extremely high standards. In other cases where the skipper tried to be 'one of the boys' and a perpetual 'good news merchant' his credibility faltered over the months and he lost that vital level of respect.

In such a hostile environment with emotions such as apprehension, fear, depression, uncertainty, boredom and fatigue to contend with, the skipper's role was not an easy one. Coping with the 'task' in an extremely complex and brutal external environment, as well as organising the team and caring for the individual was altogether a daunting prospect.

Clear Job Allocation – It was obvious that on some of the yachts jobs had not been clearly allocated. Some skippers felt that this would happen naturally, and that it was important that everyone should be able to do everything. This led to a great deal of uncertainty as well as sloppy work.

In the high performing yachts, crew members had specific functions which they were expected to perform. Inevitably as these functions were mastered there was a tendency for boredom to creep in. Those skippers who succeeded in giving the crew members added responsibility or even a change of work function kept their workforce motivated.

It would be unthinkable in an organisation reliant on teamwork not to have clear job allocations, or an understanding as to how to co-ordinate with the next person. A working knowledge is important, but it is essential that people know exactly where they personally fit into the

218

overall strategy. Only then can they concentrate on making their part of the chain as efficient and successful as possible.

Providing Information – The more dynamic and complex the environment at sea, the more information the team needed. On some of the yachts, information was seldom shared and this often led to gossip and questioning. The skippers who performed well spent a lot of time in informal and formal briefings, keeping the crew informed of what was happening, why they had taken certain decisions and what they felt they may have to do in the future. They even spent time explaining why they had changed their minds and what the new decision was going to be. In several cases the decisions taken meant a high risk for the crews and the downsides were carefully explained. This created a terrific atmosphere of involvement, and in several cases, when the gamble paid-off, gave the skippers tremendous credibility. When it went wrong there was rarely any blame attributed because the crew had taken part in the decision making.

In any high risk, fast moving environment, it is the sharing of information that creates a motivated team dedicated to winning and high performance. Uncertainty breeds discontent and cynicism.

Delegation – Most of the high performing skippers delegated very well and trusted their crew. They created confidence by rarely interfering.

Delegation is always at the top of any leadership list but it is seldom successfully implemented. It is important to give people responsibility, to make them accept that responsibility and to leave them with it. People often have more talent and capability than they are given credit for.

Avoidance Of Blame – There was seldom a blame culture on the yachts. The phrase 'leave it on the wave behind' was one that was adhered to in some cases. Learning from mistakes was essential but the next wave was the one that could create the next problem so forward thinking and concentration were vital.

In many organisations, post mortems take up management time and often motivation drops. People tend to ask not what was right or wrong, but whose fault it was. In a blame culture people seldom perform to a high level for fear of failure. They play safe and concentrate on mediocre performance. By the time the blame has been apportioned the next 'five waves' have swamped the organisation.

Quick Resolution Of Inter-Personal Problems – There were several inter-personal problems between crew members, some of which were allowed to fester. In a number of cases, the skipper took it upon himself to ensure that he found out what the problem was and sorted it out. Some skippers were clearly unused to managing such a large team and were either unaware of potential problems or shied away from conflict. This caused bad feeling. It seemed appropriate in some cases to allocate shared jobs to people who were wary of each other and this often gave new understanding and respect for each other. If a problem was left to fester too long, it became much more difficult to correct.

iv. The Importance of Certain Personal Behaviours

Given the intense nature of the race, it is clear that the starting point of a harmonious and high performing crew was for each member to accept his or her personal responsibility.

Keeping Fit – Personal fitness was vital in order to sail a Challenge yacht round the world. The Southern Ocean legs were extremely arduous and required a degree of stamina that most of the crews had seldom faced before. In today's demanding work place, those with both mental and physical stamina are able to cope and come out on top. No longer is it a world of long lunches and short working days. There is an increasing demand for higher productivity from each person with far longer working days which can only be sustained through fitness.

> *"Physical fitness is to mental fitness what water is to life."*
> **Vince Lombardi**

Some of the crew members were less fit than they should have been and it affected their whole stamina chain as well as their own personal ability to cope mentally with many days at sea.

Being On Time – Lateness on the race was unacceptable. Mike Golding told his crew, "You're only late if you want to be." It was arguably the factor that caused the most aggravation on each yacht. It was very easy to gain a reputation for bad time-keeping but difficult to lose it. Lateness signified a lack of reliability. In an environment where dependence on others was crucial, anything that was going to erode this trust caused uncertainty and resentment.

People are seldom on time at work. Meetings rarely start promptly, phone calls are seldom returned on time, appointments are rarely started or completed on time, the service engineer rarely arrives when he says he will. It seems acceptable to have a great excuse. The oceans do not wait or accept any excuses – nor do successful people.

> *"Having someone say that they can set their watch by me is one of the greatest compliments they can pay me."*
> **Humphrey J Walters**

Apologising Early – In a complex, ever-changing environment actions have to be swift and based on the situation at the time. Mistakes can easily be made and wrong decisions taken. With the hostility and brutal power that the yachts faced, it was inevitable that a crew member would do something wrong that could put the crew and the yacht in jeopardy. The best policy was to apologise early before the issue led to a whispering campaign. Some people feel apologising is an indication of weakness. The reverse is true since those who admit they have made mistakes gain respect.

Avoiding Gossip – During the race there was always plenty of scope for gossip. Where decisions had to be made and people had to work in close proximity, especially in the early stages of working with each other, gossip was inevitable. It was usually directed towards the leadership or management. People enjoy finding another's Achilles heel. There was no doubt that where gossip was at its highest, performance was at its lowest. It was essential to try and nip it in the bud wherever possible. Many yachts adopted a policy of "talk directly to the relevant person, or shut up." Skippers had to keep their ears to the ground and hunt out gossip before it affected the atmosphere on the yacht.

At work, people gossip endlessly, largely because they have time on their hands or the strategic intent of their organisation is unclear or not exciting enough. It is a truly unhealthy and dangerous behaviour.

"Nothing flatters a person more than knowing that you feel them worth flattering."
Anonymous

Saying 'Thank You' – It was essential that everyone on board the yachts worked together to propel 42 tons of steel through the water as fast and safely as possible. Everyone went to work to helm, change sails, cook or clean. It proved very important to thank people quietly for a job well done. Simple courtesies, often forgotten in everyday life, made a tremendous difference to the motivation of the crew and the atmosphere of camaraderie. It was rare if the cooks of the day were not thanked individually by everyone for each meal – however simple – or if the sail change crew was not

222

thanked by the management for a job well done. Gratitude helped in creating an environment of willingness and an everlasting bond between the crews.

In many organisations doing the job is taken for granted. "That's what you get paid for." However, thanking people when they are doing something right can have a lasting effect.

The race was a demonstration of human endeavour. The highs and lows, the successes and failures and the achievement of a global circumnavigation could be related back to the skills and behaviours of 14 crew members, each on a 67ft yacht. The successes and failures of businesses today in a complex and dynamic environment are largely determined by the skills and behaviours of their employees. The lessons learned from this amazing Challenge can be related directly back to the office environment. They will undoubtedly be related forwards to the Challenge 2000.

HIGH PERFORMANCE CHECK LIST

i   Have a clear strategic intent

ii   Develop High Performance Behaviours

iii   Motivate the individuals within the team

iv   Provide clear job specification and success criteria

v   Concentrate on essential management skills

vi   Set high personal standards

vii   Regularly review the above

CHAPTER ELEVEN

*"Those who do not learn from the past are
condemned to repeat it."*
Eddie Obeng

The departure of the yachts from Southampton
captured the public imagination. National television,
radio and press covered the event and generated huge
interest. Whereas the standard BT contact rate on the
Internet was 10,000 hits per day, the race generated
50 times that amount at the start and maintained the
level at 350,000–400,000 hits per day during Leg 1.

MANAGING THE BT RACE
SPONSORSHIP

Creating The Mindset Of Success
And Delivering

The Extra Mile – Imagine it is a cold Monday morning and
you have enjoyed a weekend in the country. Suddenly you
are asked to take over running a round the world yacht race
and make the event a commercial success.

Such was the brief given to the BT Global Marketing
Communications Team.

"I am an urban animal," John Luff, Head of Global
Marketing Communications stated. "I hate boats and in fact
I don't even have one in my bath. Why on earth did BT
become involved in a yacht race, and why me?"

Perhaps John was exactly the right choice. He had
financed his university studies largely by being a stand-up

comedian in his spare time. "Normally I wrote the jokes," smiled John ruefully. "I've never performed to someone else's script, and I seldom find other people's material very funny."

The BT Global Challenge turned out to be a huge commercial success for BT and the other sponsors. They received 35 million hits to their worldwide web pages on the Internet; they involved schools; they influenced governments; they captivated and impressed audiences in many countries round the world and gained interest in areas far removed from the route that the yachts sailed. Most importantly they gained unprecedented publicity out of all proportion to the cost of their sponsorship.

Saving The Cavalry – For the Marketing Team this was not an easy project and did not start with a positive "Gung ho" cavalry charge, with all guns blazing. In fact they almost felt as though they were riding over the horizon to save the cavalry. The deal with The Challenge Business had been finalised and signed. There was no escape and it was their job to run with the event and get the show on-the-road.

Like many visionary ideas the BT Global Challenge seemed to start with an absence of rational thinking. Thankfully, once the initial shock had been overcome John Luff realised, as had the senior executives of BT who had made the original sponsorship decision, that the event was not about yachting. The Challenge focused on the whole BT ethos, "Let's talk". Given the right creative thinking, coupled with an implementation team who were experienced and efficient, here was a tremendous opportunity to excite people, talk to them and build relationships.

The BT executives had not lost their marbles – quite the reverse. They had grabbed an idea and raced ahead of traditional thinking so often associated with the downfall of mundane organisations trying hard to differentiate themselves in the market, without the courage to think 'outside the box'.

So how did one of the largest organisations in the UK manage to capitalise on this event, generate enthusiasm and sustain a high level of performance for such a long time? To take a project which was way beyond anything BT had ever done outside the UK, make it work and change the minds of a sceptical internal audience was no mean feat.

From Sceptical Beginnings....

BT is not a sports sponsorship company. The company had often been bombarded with ideas ranging from running a Formula One racing car team to sponsoring cricket. It had a clear policy of supporting and putting money into events that ploughed some of the money back into the community. It felt that the very people who buy its products and services should benefit from BT's success. The second criteria was that it should be UK based.

The BT Global Challenge fell short on both accounts – or so it appeared! It was seen as a 'sports event' and was a global enterprise with very little involvement in the UK once the yachts had left Southampton.

To add further weight to the argument of the sceptics, the original Global Marketing brief really had three parts:-

i. To raise awareness of BT by making the brand and logo known round the world;
ii. To provide an opportunity for corporate hospitality;
iii. To get press coverage.

So why utilise a yacht race? Surely TV or newspaper advertising or the normal trade shows were obvious alternatives? Using these traditional routes to get a message across however, would mean that BT would be seen as the same as all its competitors. Why should people want to talk to BT when they had other potential suppliers that looked exactly the same? Where was the differentiation and excitement? Where was the charisma, dynamism and creativity?

227

These three elements transformed the mindset of a fairly traditional successful organisation, to one of calculated risk-taking with all the implications that this ethos brings with it along the way.

Changing The Mindset – The project team had to convert the sceptics, and achieve 'buy in' throughout the organisation. It took a lot of courage, but it worked.

The team concluded that it really was a case of, "Let's talk to people differently from everyone else."

Two major decisions had influenced the way people acted and thought at BT.

Until the early 1990's, BT had been an organisation little known outside the UK. In fact more people overseas thought BT stood for the American company, Bankers Trust, than they did British Telecom. It was realised that in order to make any impact on the ever-increasing global telecommunications market, and cope with the speed of growth in this sector, BT would have to form alliances.

To try and go it alone would require huge amounts of money, an understanding of local politics throughout the world and the nuances of local culture. BT had to find a short cut, and find it fast. Forming alliances was the chosen route. Like all strategic decisions, the key to success was the ability to work with other people and form bonds. It was not about deals, it was more about harnessing talent and working with others from different organisations. This was the first important change in the mindset of BT.

The second major change in thinking involved Telecom '95 – the trade show in Geneva – which was attended by all the major players in the telecommunications industry. At these shows, organisations would create a 'Disney World' of products, supported by the usual 'logo overload', brochure glut and flowing hospitality. John Luff and his team decided to break the mould and try something different.

"We realised that we had to create a 'talking

environment' with no distractions. We knew that people wanted to chat about their problems rather than press buttons. In fact, some of the technology which we traditionally showed, was so leading edge it frightened the socks off prospective customers."

John and his team held their breath and made a radical decision. They would build a stand in the form of a café with tables and chairs, and provide shade from trees with nooks and crannies where people could come, sit, talk and relax in a "talking atmosphere". There would not be a product in sight, no brochures and just enough branding to ensure people knew they were at a trade show, not in the Champs Elysée. They also ensured that the display was manned by bi-lingual team members capable of discussing global strategy with senior managers in their own language. They realised that customers and prospects just wanted to talk. They did not want to be blinded with technological gobbledygook. If they felt comfortable, then deal-making would follow.

Imagine trying to persuade a highly technical organisation such as BT, which had built its reputation on technical innovation and excellence, that the way to influence future customers was to give them a cup of coffee under a palm tree. No box of tricks, sci-fi displays or electronic wizardry – just trees and coffee!

"My board presentations were slightly comical," related John Luff. "'Why have you broken with tradition?' my colleagues asked. 'The tried and tested methods worked in the past, why take a risk with something different? Trees! – are you sure?' We could all have been sacked, and our nerve was sorely tested," added John, "but I had one trump card. These same people wanted me to run a yacht race – how bizarre."

Telecom '95 was an enormous success. The gamble had paid-off and people wanted to talk to BT. The penny had dropped that if BT could create a talking environment then relationships could be built which would lead to business. It seemed simple. BT's competitors had tried to create a similar environment, with the same objectives but had relied on the traditional product display route. BT's success was due to the desire to be different, and this they achieved spectacularly.

Let's 'Telecom '95' The BT Global Challenge!! – Suitably armed with these two objectives – to work with others in alliances and to be different – John Luff and his team realised that what appeared at first to be "just a yacht race" was, in fact, the largest global relationship marketing programme that had ever been attempted. All they had to do was apply the same creativity and courage to the BT Global Challenge as they used for Telecom '95 – establish a clear plan of action and create a talking atmosphere. 'The World's Toughest Yacht Race' could surely become 'The World's Biggest Relationship Marketing Programme' and create the same differentiation which BT had already used to its advantage.

The phrase was born 'We need to Telecom '95 the BT Global Challenge.'

The objectives changed dramatically when it was realised that the main focus of BT's activity should be directed landwards as opposed to looking at the yachts' activities on the ocean. They clearly defined the audiences they were trying to reach, and realised that they had become involved in a complex and dynamic operation that would require different treatments in the various parts of the world that the yachts were going to visit.

The Challenge Of Reaching The Correct Audience

BT was trying to reach a wide audience. Talking and influencing the governments of the particular countries was crucial if they were to gain acceptance and be able to do business. Suppliers, business partners, BT staff and stakeholders were also important. BT further extended its scope to include schools with a very effective campaign to get involvement from children through BT Educational Services.

Most of the yacht sponsors had applied the same

creativity but in most cases were using The Challenge for different reasons.

Group 4 sponsored a yacht in the BT Global Challenge as a means of endorsing the key principles on which its business had been built – integrity, reliability and skill. Those same qualities were essential for the success of a yacht and the team building and training elements were synonymous with the company's internal philosophy.

The Time & Tide Trust wanted to raise public awareness of its cause. Nuclear Electric, as the winning sponsor of the British Steel Challenge, saw the opportunity to build on the public relations success of the previous race. The project team were able to capitalise on lessons learned to make the BT Global Challenge an outstandingly successful sponsorship which met all their objectives.

Serco Group Plc, who sponsored the yacht *Save The Children*, was keen to give its employees ownership of a project with an outstanding charity, as well as bind employees together with a common interest. The Serco name hardly appeared on the yacht but the sponsorship was known by everyone within the company and generated tremendous interest.

Commercial Union raised worldwide awareness of its brand name and, at the same time, worked hard to involve its own staff. Commercial Union did this by recruiting, as a crew member, a well known actor, Sean Blowers, from the TV show *London's Burning*. They took advantage of his on-screen death, his renewed marriage vows in Rio de Janeiro and his subsequent injury to achieve publicity. The company also used extensive media relations to highlight its involvement, to focus on the energy, commitment and challenge of the race and to maintain human interest and publicity around the world. The results were spectacular. Massive media exposure as a result of celebrity involvement, national newspaper links, fund raising, corporate hospitality, multi-media coverage throughout the UK and on the Intranet, all contributed to a hugely successful internal and external awareness raising campaign.

Raising brand awareness was also very much a Rover goal. Its corporate aims were to exploit business to business links and work with major customers. In the same way that other sponsors used the media, Rover targeted its yacht, its crew and the visual message presented by the race, to provide coverage for its product. However, it was the global nature of the race which attracted Rover to invest in sponsorship. The company saw an opportunity for world-wide promotion of its broad range of products – Rover, Land Rover and MG.

Getting The Show On The Road

The first key decision that BT made was to establish a steering committee under the leadership of Phil London. He had a tight experienced team which included Alan Brough who led on strategy and content for the business-to-business events and Anne Goodman for project management. They established a working relationship which was to provide the strength and guidance needed in an environment as complex and unpredictable as the conditions the crews were battling with out at sea.

Phil London was well placed. He had led the Telecom '95 project with the same team. He could answer the motivational question as to why the different stakeholders were involved. He knew the varying goals of these stakeholders and was able to put a plan together for the project management of the race. This was in itself a huge project. The steering committee was formed which was broken up into parts both geographically – the ports of call for the race – and technically such as project management, PR, finance and relationship programmes. While Phil and Anne drove the day-to-day challenges in project managing the programme as the yachts travelled round the world, Alan Brough concentrated on the tasks of planning the business-to-business events for each stopover.

As the yachts raced round Cape Horn, the first events were being set up in Sydney. At the same time, the Cape Town events were being planned and implemented. Therefore to incorporate the lessons learned from Sydney to Cape Town, the processes had to have flexibility – and they did. The controls which Phil London had in place were rigid. His budget could be amended but only after significant negotiation and the time-frame in which the marketing was being done was strictly governed by the race.

Alan and his colleague, Beverley Robinson, developed a programme of business events in each port of call. They realised that to attract the required audience they needed to create something more substantial – more business focused – than just a yacht race.

The first was the Global Information Exchange (GIE) through which they were able to invite managers whose job was to look after the communications within their own organisations, and present to them the latest thinking in telecommunications. The second was the Global Executive Forum (GEF) which had similar objectives but was aimed at Chief Executives. Finally there was the BT Global Challenge Showcase which presented a range of solutions from BT and other sponsors in an almost 'exhibition type' environment, and which clearly demonstrated that BT was at the leading edge.

Added to these clearly focused business gatherings, there were a number of social events, including the reception held at Government House in Wellington, the various prize-giving events and discreet dinner parties involving dignitaries such as HRH Prince Michael of Kent.

These events were extremely successful. In all cases BT's policy of using the imagination and curiosity the yachts generated, coupled with high quality well organised business events, created exactly the right atmosphere for talking to customers and prospects. In New Zealand, for instance, BT managed to build relationships with 25 out of 30 key influencers they had targeted.

Success Screaming At Success

The departure of the yachts from Southampton captured the public imagination. National television, radio and press covered the event and generated huge interest. Whereas the standard BT contact rate on the Internet was 10,000 hits per day, the race generated 50 times that amount at the start and maintained the level at 350,000–400,000 hits per day during Leg 1. Furthermore, up to 80% of these contacts were from outside the UK. BT installed additional fax lines so that up to 32 simultaneous calls could be taken. Even the Project Director was taken by surprise as 100% of the interest in the race was positive.

Through media interest, the project team generated the equivalent of £36 million of advertising and had over 10,000 media features. There were 236 hours of broadcasting on television and radio – equivalent to almost six working weeks – and a huge quantity of printed material.

As *Time & Tide* tore up The Solent for the finishing line on 17 July the success of the BT Global Challenge was clear for all to see. Whatever the order of finishing, whatever the time taken and whatever the investment, the world was a smaller one which was immeasurably more aware of BT, the yacht sponsors, disabilities and even of the UK. The real skill would now be in learning the lessons and transferring the message forward by four years to the millennium and the next race.

WHAT MADE THE DIFFERENCE

This chapter has examined how BT managed the race sponsorship project rather than how the yachts sailed round the world. The planning which the BT Project Office carried out and the way they successfully organised this massive global relationship marketing programme are worthy of examination. In the same way that skippers and crews who adopted High Performance Behaviours performed significantly better than those who did not, project performance was enhanced by their use.

Thinking

Information Search – BT had been involved in the British Steel Challenge, providing the race communication medium. The value of this knowledge became apparent after the start of the BT Global Challenge, allowing BT to spread the word of the business opportunities created by technology.

Concept Formation – In deciding to sponsor The Challenge, BT senior executives had devised a marketing concept that far exceeded the boundaries of their previous strategic marketing thinking. The ability to think 'outside the box' had been demonstrated by BT's radical stand design at Telecom '95, but The Challenge concept went even further in terms of truly global ambitions. A small core of lateral and creative thinkers were backed, in resource and commitment, by BT's senior executives. The lesson is that you have to put together a team with a proven track record in conceptual thinking and put the full weight of corporate resource behind them. Once committed, there can be no going back.

BT senior executives realised the potential of the BT Global Challenge. Despite the fact there were five other long distance yacht races taking place during the course of the race, they identified this one as different. The difference was the other races were professional, crewed by professional sailors. The BT Global Challenge was a yacht race for amateurs and was a tribute to human endeavour.

Conceptual Flexibility – Once the decision to sponsor the race had been made, a number of different potential approaches were identified by John Luff and his team.

They certainly looked beyond the yacht race, were able to identify the opportunities and they made things happen.

The project team had to be extremely flexible on what they offered and to whom, in the different ports of call. What worked in Rio de Janeiro would not necessarily work in Wellington. The team had to be prepared to change the format at very short notice. The key was to produce what was right for the audience not what the project team thought they should provide.

Developmental

Empathy – It was clear to BT executives that the success of Telecom '95 was partially a result of giving customers what they wanted. During the BT Global Challenge they could put technology into a business context and show the benefits and implications to the audience of the BT Global Challenge Showcase.

Teamwork – In today's world of increasing choice, the difference between products and customers' needs, is difficult to assess. All too often, suppliers offer too many sophisticated products and not enough personal advice and guidance. The successful organisations are those that are able to build relationships with the customer and instil trust and respect. BT learned the wisdom of relationship marketing and capitalised on it during the course of the race.

Building Confidence – The company had learned from Telecom '95 that they could show themselves to be more than a mere PTT. The BT Global Challenge, and in particular the BT Global Challenge Showcase, built on this. The generally held belief that BT was Bankers Trust was dispelled. The Global Executive Forum was brought into the BT Global Challenge Showcase which allowed senior players in BT to meet their customers and build their confidence in BT's global communications network.

Presentation – The BT Global Challenge Showcase was undoubtedly the ultimate presentation of BT's strengths. It was a suitable vehicle to demonstrate new ideas to both the technological audience made up from the Global Information Exchange and the Global Executive Forum which was run in parallel at the BT Global Challenge Showcase.

Influence – The BT Global Challenge also allowed the world to see that BT was a truly global organisation rather than solely a British company.

CHAPTER TWELVE

REFLECTIONS

"There were many motives for ordinary people to volunteer to take part in the BT Global Challenge. However, what was abundantly clear was the spirit of camaraderie that existed between all the participants. It was an interesting experience for many, to be spending so much time with such a diverse group of people, from all walks of life.

Conversations between people were often far deeper and more open than was normal. Diaries were written with far more passion and feeling. Indeed, it was often the first time a lot of the volunteers had ever written down their thoughts in such an organised way. Barriers came down much more quickly and crew members were soon at ease with each other, despite being on competing yachts.

Perhaps the most interesting part of the whole adventure, was the range of emotions that people experienced and saw in others. Enormous elation on arrival and deep depression among some, due to the constant battering taken in the Southern Ocean. Everyone experienced mood swings, and there was no place to hide.

For many it was a chance to see how they could cope with themselves and with their crew mates. A lot of people were surprised at their own ability to endure the discomfort, the cold, the wet and the brutal conditions, and still come out smiling.

One thing for certain, there are few people – if any – who wouldn't endorse The Challenge, and if asked by a hesitant voice would reply:-

"Do not hesitate to take part. You will never regret it and I wouldn't have missed it for the world."

There are not many occasions in life where a group of people will react so positively.

For me, it was a privilege to be among so many adventurous spirits. Beware the organisation that can harness so much positive energy on dry land, in ordinary life. Now that would be something.

The following pages set out a collection of contributions from crew members and skippers which capture some of the feelings and emotions experienced during the voyage.

They mean a great deal to the authors. I hope they will mean something to you."

Humphrey Walters, Ocean Rover

Although there were many motives for participating, most people applied to take part through a spirit of adventure, rather than for any rational reason.

"The decision to take part in the BT Global Challenge was one of the few I have ever made without a moment's consideration. This opportunity would fulfil a lifetime's ambition – to circumnavigate the globe – and give me the chance to break away from a career that was leaving me unfulfilled.

For four years the training and preparation governed the running of my life, and for the last 10 months the race has been my life. It has been 10 months of lifetime firsts and all my expectations and dreams have been satisfied.

It is now difficult to believe I have been away for almost a year – little has changed back home apart from the government! I have changed though. I am confident in my ability to overcome almost any problem – I am ready for anything. I feel fired with an endless energy that I discovered while in the Southern Ocean.

Shortly after rounding Cape Horn, I wrote '... somehow another threshold, self-imposed by years of habit, is exceeded and I manage to raise my game once more and do what needs to be done. We have reserves way beyond those we normally draw upon and it follows that we have potential previously untapped. This is a lesson which should not be forgotten when we get back.' It seems I haven't forgotten.

'Would I do it again ?' A question asked so often.

It is very easy to remember the amazing experiences – experiences which have been enjoyed by so few; the camaraderie of a team taking on the world, the awesome power and magnificence of the oceans, and the sighting of icebergs and of land after weeks at sea. It is equally easy to forget the hours of back-breaking work, the boredom induced by an unchanging routine and the periods of adrenalin-charged fear.

In the relative luxury of home, it is difficult to recall the awful diet of freeze-dried food, the sleep deprivation, the lack of personal space and the months spent away from family and friends. It is almost impossible to objectively consider the question while on terra firma.

I recall giving it due consideration at sea and deciding emphatically '**no**'! I will probably stick to that, but I would not have missed the first time round for all the tea in China!

Will Stephens, *Global Teamwork*

"I look back on the race with a huge amount of satisfaction. It has been everything I hoped and expected and more, much more. Our performance as a crew has been incredibly rewarding, beyond our wildest dreams.

Personally I feel that I know myself better; my strengths and weaknesses, my character, my hopes and ambitions. I have learned the importance of living life and making the most of every moment. I know that in the future I will put my heart and soul into everything I do – my job, hobbies and private life. I realise now that the more you put into something, the more you get out.

241

I also realise how much influence I have over others and the necessity to harness and direct that power in a positive direction. Equally, I appreciate the need to undertake the responsibilities that accompany such a position. I have gained so much more confidence in myself and in what I can achieve. I feel that anything is possible if you have the right mind-set and I am looking forward to the future with relish.

I have made friends for life within our crew, on other yachts and in ports of call. I have memories that will live with me forever, good and bad. What an immense overall experience – quite unique – I feel privileged."

Grahame Gibson, *Group 4*

"As skipper of *Toshiba Wave Warrior*, I had certain expectations of my crew and of the race. I have to say that many of my hopes were vastly exceeded, while other issues I had suspected could be a problem, never arose.

I genuinely enjoyed the experience. I welcomed being part of a team, and I became and remain good friends with all my crew. This I had not expected and it goes some way in compensating for not winning the race.

I knew from very early on in the campaign that we had a very good chance of winning, considerably better than most. We did do well and there is a sense of achievement.

Personally, I learned the need to implement management systems early on. I was good with the fun stuff, such as weather research, yacht preparation records, and victualling but I forgot the basics, such as accounting. This meant we had a bit of sorting out to do later on!!

People management was essential and motivation particularly important not only when things got tough but also when times were quiet. The lessons were simple, they were normal everyday life experiences, but in difficult situations.

Simon Walker, Skipper *Toshiba Wave Warrior*

"It was with naïve enthusiasm that we left Southampton on board *Nuclear Electric* as favourites to win. We arrived in Rio in 10th place after learning the meaning of the words 'frustration' and 'disappointment'.

Nuclear Electric finished the race in 7th position overall – we had our strengths, but made some mistakes. It was a fantastic adventure. We crossed the most ferocious and inhospitable oceans of the world. I will not be going back to the Southern Ocean, my inner-self tells me it is for icebergs and albatross, not for me.

The race demanded incredible amounts of mental and physical perseverance, but we did it – I now know I can do anything, if I have to. All it takes is determination and commitment.

'Would I do it again ?' – **no**. 'Would I encourage others to do it?' – **most definitely yes**.

As Chay Blyth says, 'The Challenge is an opportunity for ordinary people to do something extraordinary.' I am not sure my friends would agree I am ordinary! I hope the last year changed me in a positive way. I don't know yet – maybe those close to me can see a change.

For me, the achievement started in July 1993, having never been on a boat, and ended in July 1997, having successfully raced round the world. I have exploded a life-long myth – the myth that adventure is for others.

As a Training Manager in real life, I will be able to use the experience focusing on leadership, teamwork and performance – that is the current challenge."

Jocelyn Walters, *Nuclear Electric*

"The race was everything I thought it would be and more. I loved it and would happily do it again. And the crew exceeded my expectations, the sum of the parts really added up and they formed a great team.

I was naturally disappointed about finishing 6th overall. I felt we were capable of 3rd or 4th position but we had our share of bad luck; we broke equipment and we made mistakes.

For me personally, the Southern Ocean was the most enjoyable part. I felt a real sense of achievement and I got the biggest buzz from seeing the crew on a high.

I have learned just how essential it is to have the right management skills. Before the race I was aware of the basics but had no idea just how important they were."

Mervyn Owen, Skipper *Global Teamwork*

For the crews, the vastness of the oceans made an enormous impression. The few who had sailed before undertaking The Challenge had only ever crossed The Channel on a day crossing or taken part in coastal sailing. Very few crew had been out of sight of land.

The start of the race provided a rude awakening for the majority of the crew.

The Start – We're Bound For Rio

We're off and bound for Rio
With our hearts all full of hope,
But a force eight off The Needles,
Doesn't leave a lot of scope.

Breakers at the Bridge's Buoy,
All foam and spume and spray.
The start of the Global Challenge,
Just had to be today.

The motion is appalling,
The slamming hard to bear
Eyes bright from the tension.
And just a touch of fear.

Our faces pale and sometimes green
(It's not the prettiest sight you've seen)
We're all looking much the same.
And there's many a tasty breakfast
Returned the way it came.

But this is just for starters,
Our trials are yet to come.
We'll face much bigger seas than this,
Before this race is done.

So brace up all my hearties,
(Take a rain-check on the parties)
This first page of our story,
Writ large –
'No guts no glory.'

Alan Rudge, Global Teamwork

For the first time in their lives, crews were to spend days at sea with no other yacht or ship in sight. Only visits from dolphins and birds provided any sign of life, other than their crew mates on the yacht.

The living environment of the yacht was tiny and cramped. The ocean scenery vast and never-ending.

Ocean Space

Ocean space,
Moving, sighing,
Sky's dome
Gilding, glinting,
Tinting waves with gilt.
Sun's supremacy
Beating, heating,
Dominant with dripping sweat.
Frustrations fester,
Joking, jibing,
Silencing the restless urge.
Sea and sunshine,
Wind and water,
Lifting, dripping,
Ocean space.

Helen Bentley, Nuclear Electric

The first leg to Rio de Janeiro was also a chance for the crews to become an efficient team. It was seen as a continuation of the training sessions that all the crews had been put through in the build-up to the race. Not everyone was at ease with equipment and the relatively complicated procedures required to sail an ocean racing yacht.

Yachting Terms – Perchance To Dream?

I often sit on board and dream
of yachting terms that I have seen
spinnakers, dobbers, jammers, cleats
ludicrous items around my feet.
It never ceases to amaze,
How muddled up I get – and phased,
by listening to my colleagues talk,
sounds like Polish as they work,
around the deck with measured ease,
with these items – "more outhaul please."
Blow me sideways which one's that?
green and white, red, yellow or black?
When that's sorted out at last,
they want the cunningham nipped up fast.
Back to panic – can I hide?!
Behind the mast or perhaps surprise,
I know which jammer to release,
which rope to pull and winch with ease.
159 has shown the crew,
he knows his luff from leach and clew
and when the final praises come,
he triumphs in the eyes of some,
but others feel he is inept
worry not for I have slept!

Humphrey Walters, *Ocean Rover*

The next hurdle for the Challenge fleet was the infamous Cape Horn and entry into the Southern Ocean. Not one of the crew knew what to expect. A handful of the skippers had been round before, but they were reluctant to tell the crews anything, either because they felt it best the crews did not know the truth, or they found it impossible to describe the conditions. Everyone was apprehensive and they knew that the relatively easy first leg was not really what The Challenge was about. There was no going back.

Southern Ocean Night Watch

As I sit in the cockpit,
Waves crash down the deck
They are cold, they are icy
And get down my neck

The night it is dark,
There's no moon and no star
The wind is howling
And is heard from afar

There's only the two of us,
The helm and I
We know this is dangerous
And think we could die

But there's no going back
So onward we go
With storm after storm
The yacht's going slow.

Andrea Bacon, Group 4

"It had always been my goal to finish the race in the top five, so having achieved 4th position overall I feel reasonably happy. Having been a crew volunteer on the last race I had experienced the Southern Ocean before and really didn't wish to go back unless I felt I had a chance to do well. What was the point of going through it all again? The Southern Ocean is about surviving and protecting the yacht. The race can be lost in the Southern Ocean, but it is won in the Atlantic.

My crew formed a tight unit and had a very good attitude towards racing. As one of The Challenge Training Skippers, I had the advantage of knowing most of them. However, they knew me as a familiar figure in a training role and it was difficult, at first, for them to see me as a 'real' skipper in racing mode.

My past experiences as a crew volunteer helped me appreciate what the crew were feeling and going through during the course of the race. They respected that and when I asked them to undertake a sail change in freezing conditions they knew I had previously done exactly what I was now asking of them.

Having taken on the challenge of running a campaign, leading a team, managing and organising a sponsorship, I now feel sure I could do much more. These experiences, coupled with sailing in the Southern Ocean, make everything else seem achievable now. My sailing experience has been gained over a relatively short period, I had never sailed before the British Steel Challenge, and I believe I have been reasonably successful. I now know I can learn quickly and feel I do have something to give. That gives me great confidence in taking on new projects and moving into new areas, such as business."

Mark Lodge, Skipper *Motorola*

Never Again

Can I take you by the hand
And share with you a test,
Of mind and matter hard to find
In any other place.

One hears of winds and massive waves
When sitting by the fire,
It's not until you see and brave,
This ocean's terrible ire.

The Southern Ocean at its height,
An awesome place to be,
With power and violence, cynical might,
She frightens the likes of me.

Imagine if you will the charm,
Of soaking clothes and boots,
Of bunk that's seldom ever warm,
And sleeping bag wet through.

I don my foulie gear on fast,
It's time to go on deck,
To helm the boat into the night,
In 60 knots of wind.

I wave to you to crawl my way,
To help me drive the boat,
To sit awash with freezing spray,
A feeling so remote.

At last our time on deck has run,
The other watch to cope,
Their eyes are sunk, no sense of fun,
Just fear, fatigue and hope.

That soon our yacht will get a rest,
From this pounding so severe,
We wonder how she stands the test,
Or has the heart to bear.

And with this lull we get a time,
To smile, to laugh, to joke,
To reassure we're doing fine,
We'll make it, proud but broke.
Think of yourself when nice and warm,
How might you have begun,
To cope and smile and carry on,
Ten thousand miles from home.

Humphrey Walters, *Ocean Rover*

Christmas was spent at sea, deep in the Southern Ocean. Almost all the yachts had made a terrific effort to celebrate as traditional a Christmas as possible. It was a chance to have some fun after five weeks at sea.

For all the crews it was a Christmas they will never forget and for once the wind gods were kind. It was a relatively peaceful day. It was not long, however, before the next storm arrived – Boxing Day – and brought the crews back to reality. It was fun, while it lasted.

An Awful Christmas Ode – Dec '96

Christmas is coming, we should be getting fat,
But all we've got are Frusli Bars
– And orange ones at that !
The water's now in short supply,
The matches are all gone.
We're rationing the wine gums,
And sharing half a scone.
The pub's 2,000 miles away,
There's no TV to see.
Oh, what a Merry Christmas Day
This promises to be !

250

We have to sleep in four hour bursts
And walk along the walls,
Cold showers on deck are commonplace
When the skipper "sail change" calls.
When helming, we're too high, too low
Watch rivalry is banned.
There's miles and miles of empty sea
No distant sight of land.
We're out of Santa's reindeer range,
The postman's never here.
Oh, what we'd give for fish and chips
And a pint of English beer !

Helen Bentley, *Nuclear Electric*

Christmas at Sea

The crew are getting ready, the advent cards are set
It's nearly time for Christmas day, what present will
  we get?
We've put our red gloves out to dry, all hanging in
  a row
And left the lights on in the way, the entrance clear
  to show.

When Santa comes we hope he knows we've all been
  good and kind
And always help each other and been often pure
  of mind.
So as he flies to other lands and crosses o'er the sea
We hope he makes a rescue stop for the GT crew and me.

The landing could be tricky though, the pitching,
  rolling decks,
It would be a disaster if Santa's sleigh was wrecked.
So hopefully an albatross will act as guide for him
To make approach, prepare to land and alter the
  main trim.

Thus when we wake on Christmas morn, all eager for
our treat,
Each one of us will find our gloves and then take up
    a seat,
Unwrap our present, oohs and aahs and more for us
    to eat
Perhaps we'll get some warm socks too, to warm our
    chilly feet.

Then lunchtime comes, we'll sit down, well maybe
    three or four
The skipper always listening out and standing by
    the door.
We've piles of food and maybe drink and crackers full
    of fun,
And all around the gentle sea reflected by the sun.

It will be odd to celebrate this family time of year
So far away from those we love and cherish, oh so dear.
But on this yacht we have our friends with whom
    to celebrate,
And without doubt this Christmas will be really,
    really great.

                    Gordon Cunningham, *Global Teamwork*

The second Southern Ocean leg was said to be the worst,
but no-one knew what 'the worst' meant. The fleet's last sight
of land was the rocky outline of Tasmania. It was not long
after, that the first of a series of ferocious storms hit the fleet.
This was the worst weather the yachts had encountered and
it took a terrific physical and mental toll on all the crews.

Tasmania

Dark navy coastline, rocky stacks,
Stark rising headland, hills that beckon
Tempting landfall, welcome haven,

252

Fourteen yachts will slip right past.
Foregoing green and stable pleasures
Heading South to inclement weathers,
Decks that lurch and waves to chill us
With fearsome winds to head our track.
The Southern Ocean knows no limits
Tests our nerve, resolve to win.
We dread its temper, know its anger
Hate its moods but love its splendour.
Enter in? We know we will,
It's homeward bound, sweet bitter pill!

Helen Bentley, Nuclear Electric

"My reasons for doing the race, like many of the crew, were complex. I wanted to travel but didn't want to do so aimlessly. I wanted to take a year off and to meet new people, but most of all I wanted to win.

In reality, the race was a far greater experience than I had anticipated. The Doldrums, far from being lifeless and empty were dramatically beautiful, the sunsets off Tierra del Fuego made it like nowhere else. Leg 2 though, our first trip into the Southern Ocean disappointed me. I wanted to see worse conditions than I had ever seen, much worse. In fact we saw no more than 55 knots of wind, like January in the English Channel. Our second dip into the far south delivered everything I had hoped for and more. I stopped wishing for worse weather quite early on.

We returned to Southampton in 3rd place which I am proud of. We didn't win but there are things I would do differently, if I could do it again. I have learnt about winning, although I feel the race was more than that! It was an opportunity to learn about myself and the limits to which I can push myself both mentally and physically."

Ian Wolter, Save The Children

Southern Ocean

Snarling, crashing, cynical, rough,
Cold that bites the core.
Winds that churn the massive waves,
Surely there's no more!

Foredeck nightmare, freezing fingers,
Time to change the sails.
Courage tested to the limit,
Strength that never fails.

Falling off the steepest waves,
Helmsman tries his best.
Peaks so steep they tower above you,
Close your eyes and feel the rest.

Decks awash with freezing water,
Clothes that never dry.
How much longer in this ocean?
Sometimes makes you cry.

Waiting for the weather fax,
Isobars so tight.
Can't believe there's further turmoil,
Another day to fight!

Slowly we are on our way,
To happier days ahead.
Coast of Africa beckons us,
A miracle we're not dead.

Southern Ocean, thank you Ma'am,
Not a place to go.
Unabated power and violence,
Few have seen it so!

What a tribute to my colleagues,
The banter never failed.
Courage of a group of people,
Envy of the world.

Thinking back in days to come,
Of such a terrible test.
Do not forget what you have done,
Pride within your breast!

Humphrey Walters, Ocean Rover

The crews only companions down in the Southern Ocean where the albatross. They would hover alongside the yachts, their head turned towards the yacht and their beady eye staring at the crews. The sight of the albatross provided a form of comfort – there was life in these hostile waters.

The Albatross – My Friend

When you have seen
the wind and the rain,
and the towering waves with the spray;
you're never surprised
to be totally deprived
of wildlife that's gone far away.

Amazed to be told
there's one who is bold
and prospers and lives every day;
majestic and proud,
with a wingspan so broad
and she travels for miles far away.

A friend do I crave
who seems able to brave
my concern for this terrifying place;
to watch them so able

whilst gliding so stable
brings a confident smile to my face.

They circle so low,
skimming waves to and fro
their wingtips just touching the foam;
with effortless flight
whilst we hold on tight
they watch so we don't feel alone.
They only forsake
our yachts in their wake,
when the waves and the winds hit storm force;
but soon they return
whispering " now it's your turn
a short lull will arrive in due course."

I hear of the dangers
which sickens and angers
that anyone harms such a friend;
of tuna fish lines
with hooks that entwine,
and causes a terrible end.

They must have a right
to carry on flight
untroubled by man's careless way;
but how do you fight
for the albatross' right
when countries and greed hold their sway?

When you have seen
the wind and the rain
and the towering waves with the spray;
I will always savour
and consider an honour
to have seen life the albatross way.

                    Humphrey Walters, *Ocean Rover*

As the crews arrived in Cape Town there was continual talk about the conditions and how terrible the crews had found them. Needless to say, once on dry land, the experience became one of pride and never regret. There was a whisper among some crew that they would like to go back and try the Southern Ocean again. Bravado perhaps or was it madness? We will never know.

Southern Ocean

Southern Oceans are grey, Southern Oceans are black
Everyone says that "I'm not going back"
But somewhere deep down, a bright ember glows,
Which given time's healing will certainly grow.
It's all about courage and facing the test
And knowing, despite all, you still came off best.
Now it's behind you, the fire burns within,
It's part of your make up, you didn't give in.
Whatever life's challenge, whatever the stakes
You can rest assured now, you've got what it takes.

Alan Rudge, Global Teamwork

"What can I say about the race itself? It's a long way round the world, and beating to windward in the Southern Ocean is not the most pleasant way of spending your day. The passage of time dulls the memory of the battering, cold, damp, and chronic fatigue. The outstanding memories of the good things persist – albatross wheeling and soaring thousands of miles from land, humpbacks jumping, icebergs at sunset, southern lights spanning the sky in great shimmering curtains, seeing the hills of Africa on the horizon as we pulled north, out of the Southern Ocean. The list seems endless. It's a beautiful world, and we are extremely privileged to have seen such things."

Stewart Briggs, Toshiba Wave Warrior

"The Challenge of a Lifetime? Perhaps! I don't think any of us will ever know. But no-one can take away the achievement. For me I have never looked at it as a 'Challenge of a Lifetime' – I did not want to build it up into something it may not have been, nor spend the rest of my life looking back at 1996/7. I will simply move on to other challenges. But to anyone who ever asks : 'Was it worth doing?', I will always say 'Yes without a doubt'. Having had time to reflect and, given the opportunity, I would do it again. And now being back in normal life, I am beginning to miss it – the emotions, the passion, the camaraderie, and the simplicity of purpose."

Mark Baptist, Motorola

The Last Watch

Watches, watches, changing watches
Always seems the call at night,
Just asleep and gently dreaming
Comes the rouser into sight.

Watches, watches, changing watches
Into gear and back to wheel,
Then it's forward to the foredeck
Dreaming of that last warm meal.

Watches, watches, changing watches
Soon the time for bed draws near,
Down below the next watch stirring
Watches, watches, make sleep dear.

Gordon Cunningham, Global Teamwork

"When Sir Chay Blyth spoke the words 'I've just signed your contract, you are in the race', I had no idea that 67ft of steel and 13 strangers would completely overtake my cosy way of life.

Being a race, not just a sail round the world, I expected and found the training prior to the team announcements to be disciplined, thorough and loads of fun. The Challenge promised to suit my craving for competition and my need to continually test myself. I also wanted to taste the fruits of sweet success.

What I didn't fully appreciate until the end of the first leg was that in reality my fellow crew all had different expectations, different tolerances and different degrees of hunger to win.

On reflection, even though my thirst to win was never quenched, I saw what a struggle it was for 14 completely different personalities and characters to live together for weeks at a time, even when mother nature was at her kindest. In fact it was during the good weather that friction was at its highest.

Over the duration of the race, I learned a great deal about sailing, but I also learned a great deal about leadership, management and human nature, all of which I hope to put to good use in my future career.

My one regret – the potential on our yacht was never fully harnessed. Had it been channelled in the right direction I know in my heart we could have done better."

Lyn Guy, *Ocean Rover*

During the leg from Cape Town to Boston the crews had time on their hands to reflect on what a great adventure the race had been and realised that soon it would be over.

Privilege

Life's a real mystery
So what is it all for?
We struggle to earn a living
To prevent us becoming poor.
But then what are life's riches?
Most of us have got it wrong,
It's not about money in your pocket
Or where you live or feel you belong.

Take for example a BT ocean racer,
And the sacrifices they have made.

259

It's not about the accolade,
Or the monies they have paid.
For they have seen natures rising
And the setting of the sun
A crew of fourteen people
All working together as one.

The humpback whales, the flying fish
The icebergs and the sharks
The mountainous seas and the Southern Cross
And the nights that are so dark.
But mostly the moon that lights the way
And the stars so utterly breathtaking
The feeling of being privileged
To be part of this journey we're making.

This world of ours is a precious place
And one that needs preserving
Our human nature is one of greed
And few of us are that deserving
What we have experienced first-hand
Is a cut above the rest
Where else can you see such wonderful things
And still put your character to the test?

Rhian Jenkins, Global Teamwork

Leaving Boston was a very emotional time for all the crews. After three years of preparation and 10 months of racing, they knew their dream was about to end. Across the Atlantic reality awaited.

Sad Goodbyes – Boston

Reality dawns as we say our goodbyes
We feel ourselves tremble with tears in our eyes
For this is the last farewell we will share
As we set off for England and all we have there.

Relationships end here, there's no place beyond
It's time to return to those whom we're fond
Friendships however we must retain
As we know all others think we're insane.

What happens next we don't really know
Except we'll be feeling terribly low
The adrenalin buzz will sadly be missed
As will the stopovers where we got **!"
There's one final party for us to share
So we leave Boston keen to get there
Let's get back to England and meet all our folks
And enjoy all the music, the beer and the jokes.

Andrea Bacon, Group 4

As the fleet set out across the Atlantic the fog engulfed them for several days, reducing visibility to just 50 yards and producing an eerie silence.

Fog – An Eerie Night Sailing

The fog it has engulfed us
It's cold, it's wet, it's grey
We're trucking along at 8 knots
And all we can do is pray.

It's my turn now on iceberg watch
But there's nothing I can do
We all know that the radar
Doesn't pick up bergs, it's true.

So we're living on a knife edge
Wondering what to do
We can only hope that light will come
And we'll be safely through.

Andrea Bacon, Group 4

"I undertook The Challenge in order to turn my life upside down; to get out of the rut I felt I was in; to have a great adventure and to change the direction of my life. I had never sailed before and, as a late recruit, my first ever sail was just five months before the off.

I knew that The Challenge wasn't going to be easy. I'd heard the tales of the Southern Ocean; the intense cold; huge waves; being pushed to physical and mental limits, but I was also excited about the prospect of seeing nature at its best – dolphins, icebergs, whales, sunsets and starry skies.

The Challenge became all I thought it would be and far, far more. The Southern Ocean was just like it had been described, but in a bizarre way I relished every new challenge it brought – be it a sail change in pitch blackness with 50 knots of wind and waves crashing down the deck or the simple task of trying to clean my teeth while the boat was pitching about in a storm.

I savoured every moment of personal success, however small.

My only regret is the result that *Heath Insured II* achieved. This will always be a huge disappointment to me, despite the achievement of actually racing the 'wrong way' round the world.

It was a great privilege to take part in The Challenge and I wouldn't have swapped the experience for anything."

Dave Bracher, *Heath Insured II*

Nearing The End Of The Race

A lump in my throat, a tear in my eye
I'm feeling down, when I should be high
It's the end of the race and I've goodbyes to say
Then it's time to move on and go my own way.

I will not forget this, tough though it's been
Memories will linger of all that I've seen
Conditions suffered, may well go untold
Some stories are just for me to behold

It's a lifetime experience and something quite rare
Friendships I've made I will value with care
So onwards we truck now, biding our time
Hoping to be the first through the line.

Andrea Bacon, Group 4

"I soon began to ask myself why I wanted to do the race. My conclusion was simple; to see if I could and if so how well I could do it. I suspected that I could complete the race but had no idea what was involved in sailing a yacht, let alone racing one round the world. I had practically no sailing experience apart from brief and very wet attempts at windsurfing. My goal was hence quite clear; to complete the race making a full contribution as a member of the team.

For *Courtaulds International,* the race was a roller-coaster of fortune and misfortune. Had my level of achievement been measured simply on finishing position, I would have already guaranteed self-inflicted dissatisfaction by the end of a disastrous first leg. It had become clear that everyone's motives were different. For some, to win was the only reason for taking part. Others simply wanted to get round, however long it took. As for me, I was able to take pleasure from the fact that I had not become disillusioned by our poor showing and that my enthusiasm and enjoyment grew as the race progressed. I came to realise that you must be single-minded in your determination to do your best and enjoy the experience, whatever happens!

So what about now? How do I feel now the race is over? In a word, 'satisfied'. Yes, I desperately wanted to finish higher up the fleet, but I did go the distance. As to whether I made a valuable contribution in doing so is best judged by others, but I know I did my best. I have also learned a huge amount about sailing, people and indeed myself.

The big question now is; what next? The 'call of the sea' gets into your soul and I am certain it will never leave me.

The only thing missing from the race was sharing the many, many special moments with Sharon, my wife. The end of the race and The Challenge for me will be when that has happened and she knows first-hand what the last 10 months have really meant to me."

David O'Ryan, *Courtaulds International*

"It was the emotion of it all, as much as anything that struck me. Whether someone felt good or felt down had much more to do with the other crew members than the conditions or the way of life.

Every aspect of family life was apparent – enlarged, exaggerated. There were numerous times that I heard in someone's voice the frustrations that there was not 14 people like themselves on board, to winch as hard as they did, to respond as quick as they could, to think exactly like they did. But you had to respect other people's abilities and inabilities and treat them with consideration.

I don't believe that we showed enough kindness, real kindness, when things were tough. We didn't go out of our way to help, to pamper, to think outside of ourselves.

I know how it is to feel under-valued and how things can wear you down. I know how it feels to be supported, to be trusted, to be valued. It feels good."

Jan Humphries, *Pause To Remember*

"Yes, there have been some unhappy moments but on the whole I have got everything I expected from the race, and more. If I were to do the race again I am sure there are many things I would do differently, but then hindsight is a wonderful thing.

Home now, but I am back on *3Com* for corporate hospitality. I love the yacht and I don't want to leave. September will see me back at work, but only in body. I know I will continue an involvement with future Challenge projects.

I am proud to have done it now it's all over, and I am looking forward to even greater challenges."

Malcolm Thornley, *3Com*

"Chay promised an adventure and that was exactly what I got. I signed up for three legs of The Challenge and was thrilled to be able to undertake the final two as well.

Some of the conditions were absolutely dreadful. In icy water we aqua-planed around the foredeck, the unlucky ones landing on cleats or other strategically placed yacht bits, the lucky ones landing on someone else. All soaked to the skin.

Even though the Sydney to Cape Town leg was horrendous, it was infinitely preferable to the weeks sitting in the sun with no wind on the Cape Town to Boston leg. I found the Southern Ocean beautiful and would love to see it again, perhaps Chay should sell day trips!

We had a fantastic reception at the end of every leg, with many skippers and crew turning out to welcome us in; one of the advantages of coming in late. I loved the stopovers. The yachts and crews took over the ports and we were surrounded by familiar, friendly faces. Back home, I still imagine seeing crew shirts in the crowds. I have made some great friends among my crew and throughout the fleet.

I don't think the race changed my character a great deal. I thought I'd be hard as nails when I got back , but I'm still soft as anything and my confidence level hasn't increased. I did become very aware of how people cope with different disabilities and learned how to appreciate the person beyond.

I do feel I've achieved something phenomenal though. We all have, and that is something I carry with me every day.

Carol Sear, *Time & Tide*

Last Sunday Of The Race

So this is it ..
Our last Sunday at sea
Whilst I am reflective
Some are full of glee

So this is it ....
The race end draws near
Southampton dock beckons
And I shed a tear
So this is it ...
The Challenge is done
Tough though it was
It's been such good fun

So this is it ...
Farewells to be said
Time to move on
Though my heart feels like lead.

Andrea Bacon, *Group 4*

Finally, on 16 and 17 July, the yachts arrived home in
Ocean Village, Southampton to the carnival atmosphere
that BT had intended. Suddenly, the spirit of adventure that
had driven the crews to cope with the journey and the
conditions was about to end. Whatever anyone says, every
one of the crew volunteers will have been affected by The
Challenge. They will be different in some way and the
question is, will they and their families be able to cope over
the next few months and years? Only time will tell.

"Arriving back in Southampton was for me a time of mixed
emotions. I knew it was time to come home and I was looking
forward to new challenges – a new job was an exciting prospect.
However, I was feeling sad about leaving the others.
Living so close to people you build up a different sort of

266

relationship, something that is unique and can't really be explained. We were a close crew and we will still see a lot of each other."

Richard Angell, Concert

Time & Tide

"A tiny red spot" was all he said
As the Captain reported a sighting ahead.
We looked and we looked and there she was
We were stopped in our tracks and had to pause.
For this was the yacht we'd watched from the start
In this awesome race she's taken a part
Respected by all, they'd achieved the extreme
They raced with the able and achieved their dream.

Not one able bodied was allowed on this yacht
They all had a strong disability they'd fought;
And now they were here to tell to the world
The story of challenge that they'd unfurled.

By sailing the latitudes
They'd changed the attitudes
Of people who seemed to fail to accept
That disabled people can be just as adept.

The disabled crew were all safely back
To raptuous applause they'd all learnt the knack
Of talking to camera, TV and crew
Before disembarking and feeling anew.

The rain poured down as they all came in
With fizz Chay let the fireworks begin
A wreath was proudly place aboard
We were all so proud of this crew's reward.

Rosie Mackie, Centre for High
Performance Development

"The BT Global Challenge is still the most amazing thing I have ever done in my life. It had so many exciting and different aspects from which to learn ... the training, raising the necessary funds to compete, the starts and arrivals into port, the racing and competitiveness, the highs and lows, the emotions and personalities of the people involved, the fantastic celebrations during the stopovers and our wonderful arrival home after 10 months.

The race certainly lived up to all my expectations and I felt very lucky to race into Southampton on a high. I have enormous admiration for our skipper Richard Merriweather, who encouraged and cajoled us into pushing ourselves past our own personal limitations. My one hope is that the lessons I learned about myself during the race stay with me for a very long time."

Margot Douglas, *Commercial Union*

An Adventurer Comes To Earth

This race, this adventure has gone by so fast.
Another milestone in my life, it has passed.
I'm getting older with each passing year.
I'll still get bolder, of that I've no fear.

But where am I going, what do I gain?
A nest of memories, of peaks attained.
From outside my life it appears so complete.
Outsiders talk with envy, with longing, sometimes with pique.

As one gets older, perhaps wiser too.
You see yourself not as others see you.
There are icons to avoid it has to be said.
A company car, a pension, yes I'd rather be dead.

But though life is for living, a joy to behold.
Every adventurer needs someone to hold.

To have and to cherish, to talk to and hear.
To share all the joys and all of the fears.

My life has been varied and still it will be.
I've now found a woman to share it with me.
I've put up barriers and minefields, back in the past.
Now I know that those days they can't last.

I'm ready to love and have it returned.
With someone with whom my passion has burned.
To share the long nights and dream on ahead.
Not solo, but shared and together instead.

Mervyn Owen, Skipper *Global Teamwork*

If I Had My Life To Live Over

If I had my life to live over –
I'd dare to make more mistakes next time.
I'd relax. I would limber up.
I would be sillier than I have been this trip.
I would take fewer things seriously.

I would take more chances.
I would climb more mountains and swim more rivers.
I would eat more ice cream and less beans.
I would perhaps have more actual troubles,
But I'd have fewer imaginary ones.

You see, I'm one of those people who
Lives sanely hour after hour, day after day.
Oh, I've had my moments and
If I had to do it over again, I'd have more of them.
In fact, I'd try to have nothing else.
Just moments, one after another,
Instead of living so many years ahead of each day.

I've been one of those persons
Who never goes anywhere without a
Thermometer, a hot water bottle,
A raincoat and a parachute.
If I had to do it again,
I would travel lighter than I have.
If I had my life to live over,
I would start barefoot earlier in the spring
And stay that way later in the fall.
I would go to more dances.
I would ride more merry-go-rounds.
I would pick more daisies.

Written by a 70 year old Texan lady and circulated
to the fleet by Elaine Adams, *Global Teamwork*

APPENDICES

APPENDIX I

THE CHALLENGE ONE DESIGN YACHT
SPECIFICATIONS

Rig	Bermudan Cutter
LOA	67ft (20.42m)
LWL	55ft (17.76m)
Beam	17ft 3m (5.26m)
Draught	9ft 6in (2.82m)
Top of mast from waterline	85ft 3in (25.98m)
Height of mast above deck	79ft 5in (24.20m)
Displacement	37 tons at half load
Ballast	12 tons

Sail Areas

Mainsail	926 sq ft (86 sq m)
Genoa	1,480 sq ft (137 sq m)
Spinnaker	3,780 sq ft (351 sq m)

Mast	Atlantic Spars
Sails	Hood Sailmakers Ltd
Winches	Harken
Deck Gear	Atlantic Spars & Lewmar
Rigging Screws & Terminals	Sta-Lok
Running Rigging	Liros Dyneema & Polyester ropes
Engine	130 hp Perkins
Generator	27 hp Perkins
Fuel	385 gallons
Water	242 gallons
Hull Construction	50B mild steel
Deck	316 stainless steel

Navigation & Communication Equipment

GPS	2 Magnavox
Radar	Raytheon R40XX
VHF	Skanti 3000
SSB	Skanti 8024
Computers	2 Toshiba Notebook
Inmarsat-C Telex	Thrane – Thrane

Designer	David Thomas
Drawings	Thanos Condylis (C & S Yacht Designs)
Builder	Devonport Management Ltd

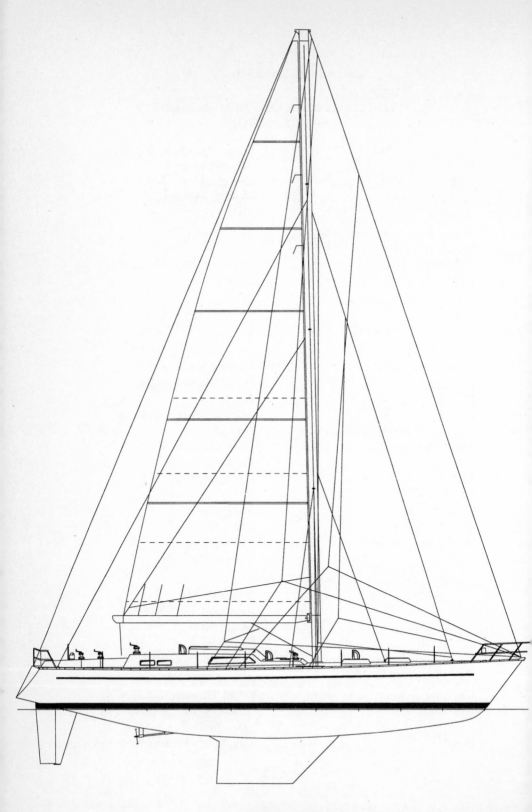

Challenge Yacht

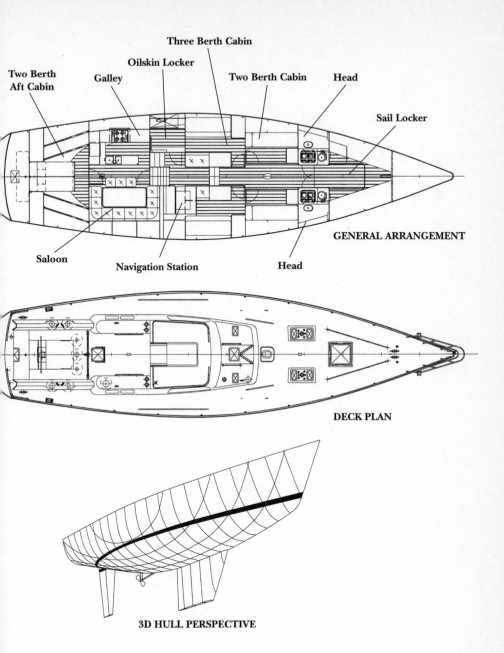

Two Berth Aft Cabin

Galley

Oilskin Locker

Three Berth Cabin

Two Berth Cabin

Head

Sail Locker

GENERAL ARRANGEMENT

Saloon

Navigation Station

Head

DECK PLAN

3D HULL PERSPECTIVE

thanos Condylis
C & S yacht designs

275

APPENDIX II

YACHT SPONSORS
AND SKIPPERS

Commercial Union Assurance – One of Europe's leading insurance companies offering a wide range of life assurance and general insurance policies. Commercial Union is the largest marine insurer in the world and has operations in over 50 countries through a network of wholly owned subsidiaries and associated companies.

Richard Merriweather – Aged 31, Richard previously skippered and managed the 90ft replica pilot schooner *Spirit of Scotland*, teaching young people to sail. He became skipper of *Commercial Union* in the British Steel Challenge, taking over in Rio de Janeiro after the departure of the previous skipper. A keen dingy sailor, Richard trialled for the Olympic Soling team before skippering *Commercial Union* in the BT Global Challenge.

Concert – Concert Communications Services is a joint venture between the communications empires of BT and MCI, two of the world's largest telecommunications companies. The alliance came in 1993 when BT invested $4.3bn to acquire 20% of MCI stock. Concert has a range of services for businesses worldwide and caters for the telecommunications needs of big multinationals.

Chris Tibbs – A professional skipper, aged 40, Chris completed two Whitbread Round The World Yacht Races before the BT Global Challenge. The first, on *Norsk Data* (ex-*Great Britain II*) in 1985/6 and the second in 1989/90 as first mate on *Liverpool Enterprise.* An accomplished racing sailor in small yachts, he has also managed a number of large yachts and taken part in regattas including Antigua Race Week, La Nioulargue and Cowes.

Courtaulds International – Courtaulds plc is an international chemical company with operations in 43 countries. The makers of International Paint, they are the world's leading manufacturer of marine and yacht paint. All 14 yachts in the BT Global Challenge fleet were coated with their products.

Boris Webber – Aged 33, Boris has been involved in professional yacht racing for many years. On completion of the BT Global Challenge he became the first South African to sail round the world, the wrong way. Previous races include South Africa to Uruguay, across the South Atlantic and Round Britain and Ireland, when he finished 1st in his class.

Global Teamwork – As reflected by the name, eight organisations combined to sponsor this yacht. The consortium comprised four computer equipment and service suppliers – Amdahl, Hewlett-Packard, Sun Microsystems and Tandem, three telecommunications networks equipment companies - GPT, Nortel and Ericsson and the database company Oracle.

Merfyn Owen – An ex-Merchant Navy engineering officer, Merfyn, aged 34, competed in the notorious Fastnet 1979 and sailed round Cape Horn in 1994. He is a naval architect and has designed and built a number of racing and cruising yachts including the Open 30 ULDB Maverick. He was responsible for the project management of *Thursday's Child* and *Hunter's Child* in the 1994/5 BOC Challenge.

Group 4 – Security organisation Group 4 Securitas (International) BV operates in over 35 countries worldwide, from the USA to the Ukraine. The company has over 40,000 employees and an annual turnover of more than £500 million. Except for the duration of the BT Global Challenge, they own *Group 4* and use her for promotion and training.

Mike Golding – Mike, aged 37, skippered the yacht *Group 4* in the British Steel Challenge 1992/3, finishing second. In 1994 he beat the world record for the fastest non-stop, single-handed westabout circumnavigation, which he undertook in the Challenge yacht, *Group 4* before sailing it to victory in the BT Global Challenge.

Heath Insured II – The Heath Group is an international insurance and reinsurance broker, operating from London. The group has offices round the world and employs nearly 3,000 people dealing in broking, as well as, financial services and risk management. The UK-based group ranks in the top brokers listed on the London market.

Adrian Donovan – An ex-officer in the Merchant Navy, Adrian had sailed over 120,000 miles before undertaking the BT Global Challenge and was one of the most experienced seaman in the race. Aged 39, his ocean racing experience includes a two-handed transatlantic race and a race from Antigua to the Azores. He was skipper of *Heath Insured* in the British Steel Challenge.

Motorola – Motorola is one of the world's leading providers of telecommunications, semi-conductors and electronic systems and components. Their equipment includes radio pagers, mobile phones, data communications, automotive, defence and space electronics and computers.

Mark Lodge – A crew member in the British Steel Challenge, Mark competed on board *Commercial Union*, quickly becoming first mate. At the end of the race, Mark, aged 32, started working for The Challenge, skippering yachts on charter. He became training skipper for the BT Global Challenge before being appointed skipper of *Motorola*.

Nuclear Electric – A subsidiary of British Energy plc, Nuclear Electric Ltd owns and operates the Sizewell B reactor and two gas-cooled reactors, providing about 14% of Britain's electricity needs. Co-sponosrs Magnox Electric plc operates six magnox stations and one hydroelectric plant and has 8% of the electricity market.

Richard Tudor – A Welshman from a keen sailing family, Richard, aged 37, has accumulated a great many offshore racing miles. A sailmaker by profession, he skippered *British Steel II* in the first Challenge race, winning the first leg and leading on the second when the yacht was dismasted. Richard undertook the Round Ireland race in 1994 and skippered *Pride of Cardiff* to first place in the 1995 Teacher's Round Britain Challenge.

Ocean Rover – The Rover Group, now part of the BMW organisation, produces a range of vehicles, from the Rover 800 to the Land Rover Defender, Discovery and Range Rover. Their three prestigious marques, Rover, MG and Land Rover, formed the distinctive livery of their yacht. Rover has 33,000 employees and exports its products to more than 100 countries.

Paul Bennet – An ex-naval engineer, Paul aged 39 has been a keen sailor since his schooldays. After 19 years in the Navy, Paul set up a sail training school in Gosport and also undertook a number of yacht deliveries across the Atlantic. He subsequently became a senior instructor at the British

Sailing Academy in Cowes and before undertaking the BT Global Challenge he skippered *Ocean Rover* on a Round Britain tour.

Pause To Remember – Funded by a syndicate of sub-sponsors, *Pause To Remember* was launched to help raise the profile of the Royal British Legion and their work. The yacht was named to promote the call for the nation to observe a two minutes silence on 11 November each year, remembering all those who have died for their country in wars.

Tom O'Connor – Irishman Tom O'Connor, aged 32, skippered open angling boats during his teens and began competing in dinghy racing championships at the age of 20. After joining the Irish Air Corps where he became a Captain, he continued to enhance his sailing skills, qualifying as the Irish Defence Forces' Chief Instructor. He was navigator of *Spirit of Ireland* during an attempt to break the Round Ireland record.

Save The Children – *Save The Children* was funded by Serco, an international task management contractor providing engineering and support services. The yacht was used to raise the profile of the charity which was set up 77 years ago to help children deprived by poverty, discrimination and political upheaval. The charity supports children in the UK and abroad.

Andy Hindley – Andy, aged 31, was one of the three crew members of the British Steel Challenge who went on to become a skipper in the BT Global Challenge. Having raced dinghies while at school and later yachts, Andy joined the Navy and was sponsored by the Ministry of Defence during his degree. After completing the first Challenge race, Andy became a training skipper notching up 60,000 miles on Challenge yachts.

3Com – The 3Com Corporation has been involved in the computer networking industry for 16 years. Today, they have 71 offices in 20 countries and over 32 million people use their networks. With global data networking at the heart of their business their products connect users throughout the network from the individual desktop computer to the World Wide Web.

Dave Tomkinson – The oldest skipper in the race, Dave, aged 43, has been a professional yacht skipper for the last 16 years and works as a sailing instructor. He has made several Atlantic crossings with full crews and two-handed and made many yacht deliveries, logging over 200,000 miles. Dave has a wealth of ocean passage-making knowledge and a broad experience of sailing craft from 100ft schooners to dinghies and trimarans.

Time & Tide – The Time & Tide Trust, together with a number of other businesses funded the yacht *Time & Tide*. The trust is a charity devoted to promoting sporting activities for disabled people. This was summed up by the *Time & Tide* yacht slogan: 'Racing The Latitudes To Change Attitudes'. Each of the crew members of *Time & Tide* had to overcome a disability or life-threatening illness in order to take part in The Challenge.

James Hatfield – Aside from skippering *Time & Tide*, James, aged 41, is a founder member of the charity. Born with a hole in the heart, James underwent eight open-heart operations. Determined to take up sailing, he built his own boat *British Heart* and undertook the first Mini Transat. In the 1980's James became the first person to sail single-handed round the world from the Pacific to the Atlantic via the Magellan Straits. The feat was undertaken, primarily, to raise money for research into heart conditions and raised £360,000. He was awarded an MBE and the title of Yachtsman of the Year in 1987.

Toshiba Wave Warrior – Toshiba Information Systems (UK) Ltd is the UK's market leader for portable PCs. They were suppliers of portable computers to the BT Global Challenge, with each yacht carrying two Toshiba Notebooks for navigation, weather forecasting and global communication purposes. Toshiba has a long record of sports sponsorship that take human endeavour to the limit and is sponsoring a yacht in the 1997/8 Whitbread Round the World Yacht Race.

Simon Walker – At the age of 29, Simon was the youngest skipper in the BT Global Challenge and like Mark Lodge and Andy Hindley, was a crew member in the British Steel Challenge. A computer engineer, Simon had previously undertaken seven transatlantic yacht deliveries. On his return from the first Challenge race, Simon skippered a Challenge yacht in the Arctic Circle. His racing experience includes the Fastnet Race and the 1995 Teacher's Round Britain Challenge; he was first mate aboard the winning yacht, skippered by Richard Tudor.

GLOSSARY OF NAUTICAL TERMS & EXPRESSIONS

Aft	Towards the back of a yacht
Backstay	A rigging wire connecting top of the mast to the stern of the yacht
Ballast	Weight placed to stabilise a yacht
Boom	Spar that runs along the bottom of the mainsail, fixed to the mast at one end
Bow	Front of a yacht
Broach	To swing broadside on to the sea
'Broadside On'	Yacht moving sideways
Buoy	A marker used for navigation, mooring or racing around
Chatshows	Twice daily radio link-up between the yachts to convey yacht position and exchange news
Cockpit	Aft working area of a yacht
Coffin Bunk	Small bunk almost completely walled in
Companionway Steps	Steps leading up onto deck from central passage
Deck Blocks	Fittings through which ropes are led
Dismast	To lose, through breakage, part or all of the mast
Doldrums	Also known as Inter-Tropical Convergence Zone (ITCZ) Area between the weather systems of the Northern and Southern hemispheres characterised by frustratingly light winds, major shifts in wind direction and sudden violent squalls

Duct Tape	Very strong, multi purpose sticky tape
Eddies	Swirling underwater currents
Equator	Line of latitude at 0 degrees – equal distance from both poles
Furious Fifties	Area between 50° and 60° latitude noted for very strong wind and huge seas
Forestay	Wire rigging that joins top of mast to the bow of the yacht
Galley	Kitchen
Genoa	A large headsail
Ghost Along	To move particularly slowly
GPS	Global Positioning System. Satellite navigation which gives yachts exact latitude and longitude position
'Grind The Winch'	To wind a winch to tension a rope
Guardrail	A safety rail along the side of the yacht
Guy	A rope used to adjust the position of a spinnaker pole
Gybe	To alter a yacht's direction by steering until the stern swings through the wind
Halyard	Rope for hoisting a sail or flag
Heads	Toilet/Basin/Shower
Headsails	Sails flown between the mast and the bow of the yacht
Helmsman / Helm	Person steering the yacht
Inmarsat-C	A digital store and forward messaging service, using satellites
Jammer	Fitting on the deck or mast that secures a rope
Kite	Another term for a spinnaker
Latitude	Angular distance north or south of Equator, measured from 0-90 degrees north or south

Lee	Sheltered from the wind – possibly by an island or land mass
Leecloth	Side cloth of a bunk for preventing occupant from falling out
Leeward	Downwind side of yacht
Longitude	Angular distance east or west of the Greenwich Meridian, measured from 0-180 degrees east or west
Luff	Front edge of a sail
Luffing	To turn the yacht into the wind
Luffing Match	Two yachts close racing – one forcing the other to turn into the wind, reducing boat speed and slowing the yacht
Mainsail / Main	Largest sail on a yacht which is secured to the mast and the boom
Mate	Person second in command, after the skipper
Motherwatch	The 'housekeeping' watch on board a yacht. Crew on motherwatch cook and clean
Neptune's Feast	Traditional mariners ritual carried out when a person crosses the Equator for the first time. Usually a messy affair when leftover food is poured over the individual to absolve them of their sins
Peeling	Changing from one spinnaker to another by hoisting the new one inside the one already flying
Position	The exact point on the earth's surface at which a yacht is located. This is determinded by the geographical co-ordinates of latitude and longitude

287

Port	Left-hand side of the yacht
Preventer	Rope used to secure the boom from swinging unexpectedly across the yacht.
Red Protest Flag	Code flag B. Flown when a yacht wishes to protest against the behaviour or actions of another yacht
Reefing	Reduces the area of the main sail by furling up the bottom of the sail
Roaring Forties	Area between 40° and 50° latitude noted for strong wind and huge seas
Rig / Rigging	Wires or ropes which support the mast
Saloon	Sitting / Dining area
Screaming Sixties	Area between 60° and 70° latitude noted for exceptionally strong wind and huge seas
Sheet	A rope
Sidetape	Webbing straps which hold up the leecloth of a bunk
Spar	Strong pole
Spike	A pointed tool used to quickly unlock a shackle
Spinnaker / Kite	Large, full-bellied sail that is flown out in front of the yacht, usually when the wind is right behind the yacht
Spinnaker Sheet Ease	To let out a little more of the rope holding the corner of the spinnaker
SSB Radio	Provides long range services – communication to shore and receipt of weather faxes

Stanchion	Pole supporting the safety wire running around the side of the yacht
Starboard	Right-hand side of the yacht
Stay	Rigging wire
Staysail	A small sail flown between the mast and the inner forestay
Stern	Back of a yacht
Squall	Sudden and frequent gusts of very strong wind, usually accompanied by rain
Swell	Wave motion caused by the effects of the wind
Tack	A manoeuvre to alter the direction of a yacht by steering until the bow swings across the wind. The sails also swing across the yacht until the wind fills them on the opposite side
Trade Wind	North East and South East winds in the Atlantic blowing continually towards the Equator. Named after the traditional trading ships which sailed a course using these winds to best advantage
Trim	To alter the set of the sails
Trimaran	A three-hulled yacht
'Under Motor'	To proceed using the engine
Vang	Spar which secures the boom down and forward
Watches	Teams within which the crew operated taking it in turns to work, sleep and eat
'Water At The Mark'	Racing term used when a yacht has right of way and requires more room as it is rounding a racing mark

Winch	A drum around which the sheets are turned to tension and ease out the sails
Wind Hawk / Vane	Instrument at the top of the mast which indicates the direction of the wind
Wind Shadow	A windless area or patch caused by the position of another yacht or landmass
Windward	Upwind side of yacht